JOHN SARGENT

BY
THE HON. EVAN CHARTERIS, K. C.

WITH REPRODUCTIONS FROM HIS
PAINTINGS AND DRAWINGS

CHARLES SCRIBNER'S SONS
NEW YORK
1927

JOHN S. SARGENT (CIRCA 1878).

Preface

IN the two years which have elapsed since the death of Sargent, his reputation has passed through and survived a critical period. It has endured the searching test of the Memorial Exhibition at Burlington House, when many of his least successful works were submitted to scrutiny. It has withstood in popular esteem the reaction which there was every reason to expect would follow the sensational sale of his drawings and studies at Christies. His popularity has, in fact, suffered no perceptible diminution to the present day. From this it might be augured that his fame, great as it is, will be maintained in the future. It is not the purpose of the present volume to affirm or question such an assumption. Time, assisted by those qualified for the task, can alone determine the place which he is entitled to occupy in the history of art. The present record of his life and work will, however, it is hoped, help to explain why he painted as he did, and show the influences to which his art was subject.

In the course of the text will be seen the names of the many people who have kindly supplied letters and information, and to whom my grateful thanks are due. Miss Sargent authorised me to make use of the documents found in Tite Street after her brother's death.

Mr. J. B. Manson, with the help of the list of paintings prepared by Mr. Thomas Fox in America, has compiled the catalogue of Sargent's works in oil, and this, it is believed, is now approximately complete.

I am also indebted to the National Gallery, Millbank, to Mr. Carter, Director of the Fenway Court Museum, Boston, to the Minneapolis Institute of Art, and to the Boston Art Museum, for leave to reproduce pictures in those galleries; and to Mr. Charles Carstairs of Messrs. Knoedler and Mr. Croal Thomson of Barbizon House for giving me access to the collections in their possession of photographs of Sargent pictures.

Mr. Charles Whibley has been good enough to read through the proofs.

Contents

List of Illustrations

Chapter I

JOHN SINGER SARGENT was born at the Casa Arretini in Florence, on January 12, 1856. The house stands on the Lung' Arno, within a stone's-throw of the Ponte Vecchio. Facing its windows, and on the other side of the river, there rises out of the waters of the Arno a row of houses whose walls here and there, tinted by age to the colour of amber, carry the tones of the river up to the russet roofs with which they are crowned. Above these, again, can be seen Bellosguardo, Monte Alle Croce, and away to the east the outpost foothills of the Apennines.

The father of John Sargent was FitzWilliam Sargent, who was born at Gloucester, Massachusetts, January 17, 1820. Fitz-William Sargent graduated in medicine at the University of Pennsylvania in 1843. From 1844 to 1854 he was surgeon of Wills Hospital, Philadelphia. Eminent in his profession, he published works on minor surgery, in their day textbooks in the medical schools of America, which he illustrated himself. He was, above all things, American. In his frequent writings on political topics, patriotism was the guiding influence; nor was this affected by his migration to Europe. On June 27, 1850, he married Mary Newbold, the only child of John Singer, of Philadelphia, and Mary, daughter of William and Mary Newbold, also of Philadelphia. Lineage and early indications of promise acquire significance when they culminate in a master talent.

The genealogy of John Sargent calls for more than a passing reference.

On the paternal side John Sargent's descent can be traced back to William Sargent, who was born in England, and appears in the town records of Gloucester, U. S., as the grantee of two acres of land in 1678. Nothing is known of his career. It can only be presumed that he was a mariner, as in 1693 he was taxed as owner of a sloop. It is known, however, that he married in Gloucester, on June 21, 1678, Mary, daughter of Peter Duncan and Mary Epes of Gloucester. The English ancestry of Mary Duncan has been traced with certainty. Her family originally came from Devonshire. There is a Peter Duncan who was instituted to the rectory of Lidford, Devon, in 1580. His son, Nathaniel Duncan, married in 1616 at the Parish Church of St. Mary Arches, Exeter, Elizabeth, daughter of Ignatius Jourdain. In 1630 Nathaniel Duncan, his wife and two sons, sailed for America. It is therefore to a Puritan stock that John Sargent traces his origin, to a family which, when the call came "for the church to fly to the wilderness," joined those devout and ardent spirits, who, with John Winthrop at their head, migrated to the colony of Massachusetts in order to practise with greater freedom the austerities of their religion.

The descendants of William Sargent and Mary Duncan, through their third son, Epes Sargent (born 1690), have shown themselves honourable and efficient citizens of the United States, never reaching to any outstanding eminence, but maintaining a certain ordered and reputable level of intellectual activity, and following their professions with success. They have figured in law and commerce, in medicine and literature, as artists, as soldiers in the War of Independence, and as captains in the Merchant Service. Included among these descendants of Epes Sargent, in addition to John Singer Sargent, the subject of this memoir, may be mentioned that prolific writer, Epes Sargent (1813–80), remembered as the author of "Life on the Ocean Wave," and Charles Sprague Sargent, born 1841, the distinguished authority on forestry and horticulture, who was drawn by John Sargent in 1919. All these descendants of Epes Sargent show a fine regard for obligations in private life and public service, and for duty as part of the very order and nature of existence. Strands of this Puritan thread, varying with environment and occasion, and adapted to new strains, enter into the web and woof of the family history.

On the side of his mother, Mary Newbold, his ancestry

can be traced to Caspar Singer, of the Moravian belief, who migrated from Alsace-Lorraine to America in 1730. The descendant in the sixth generation of this Caspar Singer, namely John Singer, the grandfather of the artist, married Mary Newbold, daughter of a family which had moved from Yorkshire to America in 1680. John Singer himself was a well-to-do merchant, successor to a prosperous business which he had inherited from his father. Thus the ancestry of John Sargent has been domiciled in America on the paternal side since 1630, and on his mother's side since 1730—the one originating in Devonshire, the other in Yorkshire. The mother of John Sargent was a woman of culture and an excellent musician. She also painted in water-colour. She was vivacious and restless in disposition, quickly acquiring ascendancy in any circle in which she was placed. In her family she was a dominating influence. She was one of the first to recognize the genius of her son, and in a large measure responsible for his dedication to art. As a girl she had travelled in Italy. The magic of that country never ceased to exercise its spell, and within four years of her marriage she persuaded her husband to give up his practice, and in 1854 to sail for Europe and take up their residence in Florence. Fitz-William Sargent had, by his practice in Philadelphia, made himself of independent means. His wife, Mary Newbold, was sufficiently well off to render the pursuit of his profession on financial grounds unnecessary.

Europe, in the words of Henry James,* had by this time been "made easy for" Americans. Just as in the seventeenth century the drift of movement had been from East to West, so now, two hundred years later, the tide had turned; and the drift, under conditions and directed by motives in no way comparable, it is true, had set from America to Europe. The new world, animated by the impulse to track culture to its sources and discover for itself the origins of artistic inspiration, had begun that steady pilgrimage which, not always with the same object in view, has continued to the present day. But by the middle of the nineteenth century "the precursors" had accomplished their work—

* Henry James: "William Wetmore Story."

not the work of settlers and backwoodsmen, as in the case of their forbears—but the sorting and registering of the first contacts and preliminary adjustments between a new civilization and an old. The traditions, the institutions and customs of Europe had been reported upon by numberless explorers, and its highly specialized complications had been tested and, if not mastered, at least successfully confronted. Migration to Europe was an established practice. Rome and Florence already bore abundant witness to the process of American infiltration. It was, therefore, as an already recognized type of pilgrim that the Sargent family arrived in the old world; though it was long before they were to find a last and settled home in Europe. The Continent, with its provocations to restlessness and its various appeals, tempted them for many years to constant movement: Florence, Rome, Nice, Switzerland, the watering-places of Germany, Spain, Paris, Pau, London and again Italy, were in turn visited by the family in their wanderings.

It would be of interest if we could estimate the effect of these nomadic habits on the fancy of a child and trace the results in his maturity. It would be an error to deny them some influence. Europe, passing as it were on a film, must have dwarfed the sentiment of early associations, and tended to slacken the hold of locality and even tradition. At any rate, it is possible to find in Sargent's art qualities certainly congruous with such an exceptionally restless childhood.

A letter written in 1863 or 1864 by FitzWilliam Sargent to his parents throws light on the upbringing of John Sargent, and the influence of Channing, Emerson, and ten years of wandering in Europe on a New Englander's view of the Scottish Cathechism.

> The boy (John) is very well; I can't say he is very fond of reading. Although he reads pretty well, he is more fond of play than of books. And herein, I must say, I think he shows good sense. I have just sent him after a book to read for a half-hour, to keep him in trim, so to speak, and after a while I shall trot him out for a walk on the hills. I think his muscles and bones are of more consequence to him, at his age, than his brains; I dare say the latter will take care of themselves. I keep

him well supplied with interesting books of natural history, of which he is very fond, containing well-drawn pictures of birds and animals, with a sufficient amount of text to interest him in their habits, etc. He is quite a close observer of animated nature, so much so that, by carefully comparing what he sees with what he reads in his books, he is enabled to distinguish the birds which he sees about where he happens to be. Thus, you see, I am enabled to cultivate his memory and his observing and discriminating faculties without his being bothered with the disagreeable notion that he is actually studying, which idea, to a child, must be a great nuisance. We keep them all (the children) supplied with nice little books of Bible stories, so that they are pretty well posted-up in their theology. I have not taught them the Catechism, as someone told me I should. I can't imagine anything more dull and doleful to a little child, than to be regularly taught the Cathechism. You may teach them who made them; you may give them a correct idea, so far as you can understand it yourself, and make them comprehend it, of God and of our Saviour, and of the sacrifice of Christ for sin and sinners; you may teach them the nature and meaning of Sin, and of our need of a Saviour; of Death and of Everlasting Life, etc. But I am sure it would bore me dreadfully to be obliged to learn the Cathechism, although I hope I know all that it contains pretty well. I remember that Mr. Boardman once asked me, at a Sunday school examination, "What is the chief end of man?" and I told him *Death*, at which he professed to feel some surprise, and I know my teacher, good Mr. McIntyre, (the little man who afterwards *seceded*), supposed I had made an extraordinary mistake. But the fault was not mine, but the stupid wording of the question; if I had been asked, what was the object of God in creating man, I had sense enough to have been able to give a correct reply. And so Emily and Johnny I believe, can give the substance of everything in the Cathechism important for them to know, as yet, or which they can, as yet, to any good degree comprehend, without inspiring them with a dislike to books in general by making them "go through" the Cathechism. I confess (and I hope you will not be hurt) that I am not able myself to give the exact replies to the questions of the Cathechism. To me it is the dreariest of all books.

In 1862 the family was at Nice at the Maison Virello, Rue Grimaldi. In a neighbouring house with an adjoining garden was living Rafael del Castillo, of Spanish descent, whose family had settled in Cuba and subsequently become naturalized Americans. Rafael's son Benjamin was of an age with John

Sargent, and from this date the two became close friends. He
also made friends in these early days with the sons of Admiral
Case, of the American Navy, and with Mr. and Mrs. Paget, and
their daughter Violet (Vernon Lee). With these and others
John Sargent and his sister Emily (born at Rome in 1857) were
constant associates.

Patriotic motives decided FitzWilliam Sargent to send his
son into the Navy. The arrival of United States ships of war
at Nice gave a chance of testing the boy's taste for the sea.
But it was found that he was much more interested in drawing
the ships than in acquiring knowledge about them.

The fire within him, burning to record and express, was
already at work. Every day was quickening his powers of observation and his precocious aptitude. In a letter written in
1865 to his friend, Ben del Castillo, while the family were vainly
seeking a climate that might restore the health of a sister, Mary
Winthrop (born at Nice, 1860), he shows the alertness of his
visual faculty.

PAU,
April 16, 1865.
DEAR BEN,
We got to Pau on Wednesday. We stayed at Toulouse a day,
and Mamma took Emily and me to the Museum, and we saw the horn
of Roland, and the pole and wheels of a Roman chariot, and many
pictures and statues. The next day we got to Bordeaux in the afternoon, where Mamma took Emily and me to the Cathedral, where
King Richard the 2nd of England was married to an Austrian princess.
The windows of the Cathedral were filled with beautiful stained glass;
one of the windows was round, and the glass was of a great many
colours. The cathedral is very old. Bordeaux is a fine old city.
The quai on which our hotel was is very wide, and the river has a great
lot of large ships in it and a great many steamers. We left so early the
next morning that I had not time to draw any of them; but they would
have been too difficult for me, I think. In crossing the Landes from
Cette to Toulouse, and between Bordeaux and Pau, we saw many
sheep, and the shepherds were sometimes walking on stilts, very high,
so that they may see further over the Landes while their sheep are
feeding. Near Cette we saw a lot of storks on the shore of the sea
which runs up into the country, and there was one very large lake with

several towns on its banks. The name of this lake is Etang, and I believe that one of the towns is called Aigues Mortes.

We came from Bordeaux to Pau by rail-way in about five hours. We had very cold rooms in the hotel, and the weather was very bad for a while; it snowed every day for more than a week, and sometimes it snowed very hard, but the snow melted directly. After that, the weather cleared up, and we had some very fine days, so that Minnie could go out in a carriage. We heard the birds sing in the trees, and two or three days we heard a Cuckoo whistle so prettily. We see the mountains covered with snow from our windows; they look so beautiful. Poor little Minnie is getting thinner every day. She does not care for anything any more. Emily and I bought her some beautiful Easter eggs but she would not look at them. She never talks nor smiles now. Good-bye dear Ben; write soon.

Yours affectionately,
JOHN S. SARGENT.

From Pau the family moved to Biarritz. From Biarritz he wrote again to Ben del Castillo. Here, again, appears his pre-occupation with the visible world, as if its primary purpose was to supply copy for his sketch-book. The thing actually seen, apart from any fancy that it might set in motion, counts for more than is to be expected in the outlook of a boy of nine.

BIARRITZ,
May 18th, 1865.

DEAR BEN,

Day before yesterday we went to San Sebastian where there is a fort on the top of a hill. Near the foot there are a great many English soldiers' graves; I have a little picture of one in my album. I also made a little picture of the Battery, and a good many ships. While I was sitting down drawing one of the tombstones, Mamma and Papa went up to the fort on the top of the hill, leaving Emily and me, because the hill was too steep for Emily to go up. While I was drawing something some of the workmen who were making a new road up to the fort, came and hid Emily and me under a rock, because they were just going to blast a rock half way up the hill. These English soldiers who are buried on this hill, were killed in an attack made in 1813 by the English army which came from Spain into France to conquer Napoleon. The brother of a lady whom we know in Pau commanded the troops who attacked the fort which was garrisoned by the French. The soldiers were buried just where they were killed.

St. Sebastian is a very clean little town. There are two very large churches there—one of them is a Cathedral. The houses are very tall and every window has a balcony. We staid two days at a hotel which has a view of the sea. One evening we saw some men packing codfish in baskets to Saragosa, every day they send a great many fish to different parts of Spain. We came to Biarritz at about half past 9, and we left St. Sebastian at almost seven o'clock. Just as we got into the omnibus it began to rain, but when we got to the station it rained very little. Fortunately when we got to Biarritz it did not rain much, so that we got home without getting wet. But when we got to the house the doors were all locked and Madame Lisalde had gone to bed and the nurse was asleep and so we had to knock a long time before we could get in.

> Your affectionate friend,
> JOHN SARGENT.

On June 22, still at Biarritz, he wrote again:

> BIARRITZ,
> *June 22nd*, 1865.

DEAR BEN,

    I am making a little collection of shells for you, but I do not think I will have many because we will go to Pau very soon. Papa sent me a very nice book on shells from London. There was no storm in the Bay of Biscay since Papa left us. To-day the sea was very rough but we do not feel uneasy about that, for we hope that he has landed safely at Boston, the Captain of the Asia said that they would be there to-day. Papa sent us a beautiful book with nice stories of domestic animals, such as dogs, horses, donkeys and cats called "Our dumb companions." It is full of nice pictures, and I am copying some of them for Papa. He also sent Emily a nice book about embroidery, and some books to Mamma.

    We are going to Pau on Saturday week and will stay only a few days, to get ready to go to the Eaux Bonnes. Mamma has promised to take us to see the Chateau there where Henry Quatre was born. I hope you will write to me soon.

> Your affectionate friend,
> JOHN S. SARGENT.

Later in the summer Mrs. Sargent and her children went to London to await the return of Mr. Sargent from America. In October they were in Paris, and another letter to his friend records the sights and events which had impressed him during his first visit to London.

PARIS,
Oct. 13th, 1865.

DEAR BEN,

I am sorry that you did not get the letters that we wrote to you last. We have often thought of writing to you since we knew that you had not received them, but we have been so busy sightseeing that we have not had time. We spent several weeks in London, and the things which interested me most there were the Zoological Gardens the Crystal Palace, the South Kensington Museum. At the Zoological Gardens we saw the Lions fed, and I rode on a camel's neck, and Emily and I rode on an elephant. I made several drawings of the animals there. At the Crystal Palace we saw models of some of the animals which lived upon the earth before man. I copied several of them: the Iguanodon, Labyrinthodon, Pterodactyle, Ickthyosaurus Megalosaurus and Mammoth. The Mammoth was sitting on his hind legs eating the leaves off a tree. At the South Kensington Museum we saw some very fine paintings of Landseer, the celebrated animal painter, and a very fine picture by Rosa Bonheur called the horse fair, but the most curious thing there was an oyster forming a pearl; the oyster was in spirits of wine. On our way to Paris we stopped at Sheerness to see the Great Eastern. We took a little row boat and a couple of sailors rowed us to her, about three miles. We went on board, and saw a great many pieces of the cable, and the first officer gave Mamma a piece of it. Yesterday we went to the hotel de Cluny, and saw very curious things; there were several cases filled with stone tools made before men knew how to work in iron; they were taken out of caves in different parts of France; there were lots of bones of different animals taken out of the same caves. We saw a very curious ship that looked as if it had been made of gold. It was full of men holding ropes in their hands, while others were ready to beat on drums. I believe it was presented to one of the Kings of France by an Emperor of China.

I am

Your affectionate friend

JOHN S. SARGENT.

P.S.—Give my love to your Father and Mother.

The letters are slight, but not without significance. There is no irrelevance or comment; he catches the essential trait of what has roused his interest, and records it with few words. It is no ordinary boy of nine who, on dismounting from the elephant at the Zoological Gardens, sets to work to "make several drawings of the animals there."

Chapter II

IN May, 1868, the family was in Spain visiting Madrid, Valencia, Cordoba, Seville and Cadiz. From Cadiz they sailed to Gibraltar and on the journey were caught in a storm. The vessel was in peril; Sargent, however, seems to have been as little disturbed by danger in his boyhood as he was in after years. In Spain the heat was great, the inns abominable. The fortress of Gibraltar impressed the boy more than the scenery and those Spanish galleries which later were to exercise such authority over his taste and art. In the summer they were in Switzerland, and at Mürren they met Mr. Joseph Farquharson, when the future Academicians began a friendship which lasted till the death of Sargent. Mr. Farquharson, some years senior to Sargent, impressed by the boy's talent, gave him his first lessons in drawing a head. Mürren was only one of many halting-places. Mrs. Sargent, with her insatiable love of travel, had succeeded in convincing everyone else concerned that it was more economical to be on the move than to remain stationary. This locomotive disposition, therefore, was not the expression of a family fidgety in habit, but had economy as well as enlightenment for its aim.

The winter of 1868–69 was spent in Rome, on the Trinità dei Monti, and here the momentous decision was made as to Sargent's future. Every day that passed had emphasized his affinity with art. In Rome a German-American landscape painter, Carl Welsch, long since forgotten, took an interest in the boy and noted his aptitude for drawing. He invited him to come and work in his studio, and Sargent used to spend the mornings in copying the water-colours of Welsch.

Those who frequented the society of the Sargents also recognized that the boy possessed a talent of no ordinary quality. The recognition became vocal; it was supported by his mother

STUDY OF TURKEYS.

and reluctantly admitted by his father. The idea of a naval career was first shelved, then irrevocably dismissed. It was agreed that in due course he should study seriously for the career of a painter.

Here there may be noted a superficial resemblance to the career of another distinguished American, James Whistler, who in his youth was destined for the profession of a soldier. Whistler, however, was actually entered as a pupil at the Military Academy of West Point, and it was only after three years that his inability to master the elements of chemistry, his habit of decorating his military exercises with the irrelevant fancies of his pencil, and his incapacity to bring his ideas of discipline into line with those of the authorities, led to his retirement. His breakdown in his *viva voce* examination in chemistry at least enabled him to say: "If Silicon had been a gas I should have been a Major-General." *

It is idle to speculate what would have occurred had Sargent been forced to pursue his naval career. Swinburne, writing of Jowett, Master of Balliol, expresses the belief that had the Master taken to hunting he would have been a hard rider to hounds. We may be equally confident that had Sargent been driven into the Navy, his force of character and sense of duty would have carried him to the top. Meanwhile his education was continued with such changes in his preceptors as were necessary to keep pace with the changes in habitation. Greek, Latin and mathematics, the conventional curriculum, were supplemented by music and foreign languages, in which he quickly began to excel.

In the spring of 1869 the family were as usual on the wing, visiting Naples and Sorrento. A letter from Sorrento gives an idea of their wanderings and what they saw.

SORRENTO,
May 23rd, 1869.

DEAR BEN,

I wrote a letter to you some days ago before we left Naples, but it has got mislaid and I cannot find it. We are staying at the Hotel Cocumella which was once a convent and at every door on the bricks

* E. R. and J. Pennell, "Life of James Whistler," p. 33.

there is Riposo, or Pace, or Silenzio. The day after we arrived at Naples, we went to the old town of Pozzuoli and Baiae and on the way there we went to the crater of the Solfatara a volcano near Pozzuoli. We also saw the caverns of the Cumaean Sybil, on the banks of the Lake Avernus. The Museum of Naples is very fine and more interesting than either the Capitol or Vatican at Rome, because all the bronzes and frescoes from Pompeii and Herculaneum are there.

We went to Pompeii a few days ago by railway only three quarters of an hour from Naples. It is very interesting, and you see the houses of Glaucus and the heroes of Bulwer's "Last days of Pompeii."

The houses are very well preserved and the walls of the rooms are generally covered with frescoes, but they have taken away the finest frescoes to the Museum of Naples. In the house of Diomed you see the cellar where Julia his daughter and a lot of women were suffocated, and we saw the oven where 81 loaves of bread were found, which have been taken to the museum, they are enough cooked by this time. You are not allowed to give anything to the guide who shows you about, and they sell photographs of Pompeii to you instead.

Day before yesterday we sailed for the Island of Capri 14 miles off. We went first to see the Blue Grotto the entrance of which is so small that you get into a little boat and lie down in the bottom of it. But when you are in, it is very large. The light all comes from the water, which is of a light blue and is reflected on the roof. From the Blue Grotto we went to the Villa of Tiberius, which is perched up on a peak about 1360 feet above the sea, and a little lower down is a place called the Salto di Tiberio, where Tiberius used to throw off his victims into the sea. It is 1335 feet high, and if you throw a large stone over it is almost 30 seconds before it falls into the sea. Then we saw the natural arch which is very fine.

After you left Rome, Ma gave me a large album of white Roman binding to stick photographs in, and I have stuck in about 60 of Rome and a great many of Naples. I have a good many old Greek and Roman poets, and I am trying to get the first Caesars. I will get some photographs of the Museum at Munich, where there are some very beautiful statues.

We will leave Sorrento on Monday, day after to-morrow, and we will be seven days in getting to Munich. The first night we will spend in Roma, the second at Ancona, third at Padua, the fourth Botzen, Innsbruck, Munich, and from Munich we will go to Carlsbad in Bohemia for waters for Papa.

Madame Darij told me to thank you for her, about your kind message as to the health of her quadrupeds, Diana and Adone, who are alive and kicking. Before we left Rome Mr. Darij gave me 28 coins and

WATER-COLOUR SKETCH (1869).

some intaglios and he gave Emily also some intaglios, but to Violet he gave two oil pictures, 23 coins and a lot of intaglios, one of which she has had set in a ring.

Mamma and Papa send their love to your father and mother, and hope they will write soon. Emily sends her love to you and your father and mother, and give mine too, and accept a great deal for yourself.

I remain your affectionate friend,

JOHN S. SARGENT.

P.S.—Address to Poste Restante, Carlsbad, Bohemia.

Sargent, now thirteen years old and specifically pledged to the profession of an artist, was busy in and out of season with his pencil—observing and noting before getting to work, crouching over his sketch, then lifting his head and holding up the drawing the better to criticize. The drawings were precocious, not in imagination, but as literal records of what was immediately before him. He drew whatever came to hand, never worrying to find special subjects, but just enjoying the sheer fun of translating on to paper the record of what he saw. He seems, as a boy, never to have drawn "out of his head." The usual fancies from history and mythology, which even the gravest artists in boyhood have turned to, do not appear to have engaged his attention. He was much more taken up with things there before his eyes, the shadow of an oleander on a wall, the attitude of a fellow-traveller in a railway carriage, the bronze figures round the tomb of Maximilian at Innsbruck, a country cart, a statue, or a corner of architecture—any detail, in fact, of the visible world.

The winter was spent by the family at Florence, 4, Via Solferino, and here Sargent followed his studies at a day-school kept by a Monsieur Domengé, a political refugee. This winter too he went to dancing classes. He told me that on one occasion the usual pianist was unable to attend, and the class was on the point of being dissolved when it was remembered that someone who played and might be willing to fill the vacancy lived on the floor above. Presently a handsome old lady dressed in black silk came into the room. He noted a certain faded elegance about her as she took her place at the piano. The lady was Jane Clairmont, now seventy-two years of age, the mistress of Byron, the mother of Allegra, who, after wandering over Europe as a governess, had finally settled in Florence, and was living on the proceeds of a legacy left her by Shelley. She died in 1879. For some time before her death there had been living as a lodger in her house in the Via Romana a certain Captain Silsbee, of the American Mercantile Marine. Captain Silsbee was a friend of the Sargents. He was a typical American skipper, dramatized by a buccaneering appearance and by a crop of piratical legends and tales of "moving accidents by flood and field," which, though guaranteed by his appearance, had no other support. One of his stories which gave great delight to Sargent as a boy was that of a fall, when in command of a steamer, into an oil tank, and of his being left so long to struggle in that medium before he was pulled out that his hair positively refused ever to curl again. As far as looks went he seemed the last man in the world one would expect to be interested in Shelley; nevertheless—perhaps he felt the darker side of his calling required some spiritual antidote—the fact was that the master passion of his life was Shelley and Shelley relics. Vernon Lee relates that he would "come and sit gloomily in an armchair, looking like some deep-sea monster on a Bernini fountain, staring at the carpet and quoting his favourite author with a trumpet-like twang quite without relevance to the conversation." A stranger would to his astonishment hear interjected into the discussion "O World, O Life, O Time," or one of the shorter lyrics, from a member of the party who had till then attracted attention only by his appearance and his silence. Silsbee had long known that Jane Clairmont had in her possession certain manuscripts of Shelley; and these he had made every effort to acquire. To strengthen his position he had dug himself in under the very walls of the fortress, and, as we have seen, taken up his residence in the same building as Jane Clairmont, in the Via Romana. It was even said that he never ventured far from the house lest the owner of the manuscripts should die during his absence. When, however, Jane Clairmont did die the Captain was in America. He rushed back at once to Florence to wrest from Jane's companion and niece the papers which he had failed to obtain in the old woman's lifetime. Then arose an unfortunate complication. The niece, mature in years and gifted with few of the graces which appeal to buccaneers, had long nourished a secret flame for the Captain. She declared her passion and proposed a bargain; the manuscripts should be the Captain's, but he must take her in marriage as a term of the deal. The Captain refused to pay the price; he left the Via Romana and the manuscripts and fled from Florence. This story was told to Henry James, and within a few weeks he produced "The Aspern Papers." The hero, it will be remembered, evades the offer in a state of the deepest embarrassment with the words, "It wouldn't do, it wouldn't do." In Sargent's narrative the American skipper showed no embarrassment and merely expressed profound annoyance at losing the manuscripts. In 1900 Sargent did a charcoal drawing of Silsbee, which now hangs in the Bodleian. Silsbee died in 1904.

The Sargents, after the usual summer wanderings, passed the winter of 1870 at Florence at 15, Via Magenta. The Anglo-American colony had considerably enlarged. Arthur Lemon the painter, Heath Wilson, the Oakleys, the Eyres and Bronsons and many others were there. The Sargents' house became a centre where the colony often gathered. Two of the Sargent children had died, Mary Newbold in 1853 and Mary Winthrop in 1865. John thus became the eldest child. A fifth child, Violet, who afterwards married Mr. Ormond, had been born in Florence in February, 1870. There were therefore now three children in the family, John, Emily and Violet.

Mrs. Sargent was now at liberty to press on with the artistic education of her son; the decision had been made. He was entered as a student from the life at the Academia delle Belle Arti, where he quickly asserted his superiority and gained the annual prize. During the spring-time, when not engaged in his classes, he would set out with his mother to sketch in the neighbourhood, in the Boboli Gardens, or in the Poderi of Fiesole, or among the valleys and slopes that curl and tumble from the mountains to the plain, or among the olives and cypresses at their feet. The inspiration of his mother, her directing energy and her own deftness in sketching were there to stimulate and abet him. She was prodigal of her sympathy and encouragement. One receives an impression of activity and thoroughness, of an animating spirit bent on enlarging the endowment she had so confidently detected in her son. It was not enough to have relegated the naval career to limbo, she had to justify the change of course for which she had been responsible and reconcile her husband to this dedication of his son to art.

Sargent was at this time tall for his thirteen years, slim of form, warm in colour, his hair dark, a look of alacrity and welcome in his eyes, a gait that was brisk and decided, and spirits that broke lightly into laughter. "A big-eyed, sentimental, charming boy, playing the mandoline very pleasantly." * He was already an indomitable worker, with a disposition mellow with kindliness and goodwill. If he was sometimes imposed on, and if his good nature sometimes seemed to warrant aggression, this could never be carried far. He had a hot temper, a reserve of pugnacity, which was not so deep down that it could not be roused. Two hectoring contemporaries in Florence found their attempts at bullying met with a response which effectually secured immunity henceforward for their intended victim. This militant spirit in Sargent was always capable of being roused under sufficient provocation and was finally to land him in difficulties of a legal kind in England.

* Mrs. Hugh Fraser, "A Diplomatist's Wife in Many Lands," i., p. 143.

Chapter III

THE Sargents spent the winter of 1871–72 in Dresden, the summer of 1872 in the usual to-and-fro among the resorts of Switzerland and the Tyrol. In the autumn they were back again in Florence in the Villino della Terre Via dei Serragli. Edward Clifford the artist was a visitor to Florence that winter, and like everyone who saw Sargent's work he realized that it held promise of an exceptional talent. It was already more or less understood that Sargent should study in Paris. Clifford opposed the idea and begged that he should come as a pupil to London. The vogue of respectability was just then at its height in England; Paris and respectability were regarded as inconsistent. The study of French art meant Montmartre and the Latin Quarter and if there was something sinister in the ordinary life of Paris, student life was the summit of all that was detrimental. To attempt an artistic education in that capital was to ride for a certain fall. This was the view of the kindly Edward Clifford, and he impressed it on the Sargents with the fervour of a prophet. He offered the security of his own studio as an alternative. He was eloquent over the sheltered advantages of an education in England. His appeal was sincere and tinged with the zeal of a puritanic faith. The so-called "wicked nineties" were still well below the horizon. The choice therefore lay between London with its solid repute and its artistic atmosphere, which, if in some respects uninspiring, was at any rate staid and securely academic, and Paris with its crying dangers but with its studios at the moment quick with experiment and new ideas. The choice for parents of that date and with New England traditions was no easy one to make. It cannot have been without misgiving that Mr. Sargent decided for Paris; a decision which, if we take into account his views, was proof of the liberality of his

17

judgment and his belief in his son. Never was foresight better
rewarded.

In the interval the Sargents pursued their usual wanderings,
and in February, 1874, the year which was to see Sargent established in Paris, they took apartments on the Grand Canal,
Venice. Two letters of this date, written to his cousin Mrs.
Austin, record some of his early estimations of old Masters, and
the difficulties which attended the study of art in Florence.
His admiration for Tintoretto never varied; to the end of his
days Tintoretto remained for him one of the supreme masters
of painting.

15, Via Magenta, Florence,
March 22nd, 1874.

Dear Mrs. Austin,

I thank you very much for your kind letter and for your kindness in taking the trouble to get me these photographs, which I have
always regretted not having bought while I was in Dresden.

According to your letter, I send back the two little ones, with a
thaler note, and beg you to get me three of the ten groschen size.
No. 78 is the Adoration which I particularly desired, but the other
one, No. 82, is almost as beautiful, so, if you please, I shall have them
both, and another picture also by Paul Veronese, *the finding of Moses*;
this is, if I remember rightly in the third large Italian room, on the
left and perhaps opposite the Correggios. You will know it by the
very fine figure of the princess, leaning on another woman. These
three at 10 gr will make a thaler exactly, unless the Thaler has changed
its value of 30 gr. since we were in Dresden.

I am sorry to hear that the magnificent Tintoretto has not been
photographed, for I remember it as being very fine, but I must content
myself with a little outline of the principal female figure in one of my
Dresden Sketchbooks.

Since seeing that picture, I have learned in Venice to admire Tintoretto immensely and to consider him perhaps second only to Michael
Angelo and Titian, whose beauties it was his aim to unite. If my
artistic cousin Mary would like to read about Tintoretto, and know
the opinion his contemporaries had of him, before his pictures had
blackened and faded, and before the great pictures on the ceiling of
San Rocco in Venice were used as sieves for rain water which was
collected in buckets on the floor, she may find in the royal library an
old Italian book entitled "Le Maraviglie dell' Arte, ovvero Vite degli
Illustri pittori Veneti e dello Stato" by Ridolfi. This book contains

detailed biographical sketches of Titian, Veronese and Tintoretto besides other Venetian painters, and expresses the then current belief that Tintoretto was rarely equalled and never surpassed by Paul Veronese. I hope Mary keeps up her drawing and frequents the "Sammlung der Gipsabgusse" where she will find no end of models in heads and statues. Thanking you again for your kindness I remain, with much love from all to all,

Your affect^{ate} cousin,

JOHN S. SARGENT.

15, VIA MAGENTA, FLORENCE,

April 25th, '74.

DEAR MRS. AUSTIN,

I have been waiting all this time to send this letter with one from Mama but she has been hindered by severe colds and getting ready to leave, and I will no longer postpone thanking you for the beautiful photos that you were so kind as to send me.

We are packing up in order to leave in the first week in May but the date of our departure is rendered rather uncertain by the provoking fact of my having sprained my ankle very severely two weeks ago on the stairs of the Academy; I am yet unable to use my right foot, and this prevents our leaving on the first of May as we had intended. Then our destination has been changed by reports of Cholera in Venice and of unique artistic training in Paris, so that we are bound for the latter place where we hope we may perhaps meet you. The Academy in Paris is probably better than the one here and we hear that the French artists undoubtedly the best now-a-days, are willing to take pupils in their studios. I do not think however, that I am sufficiently advanced to enter a studio now, and I will probably have to study another year at the Academy. We go to Paris now for a short time to make enquiries about this, which will decide whether we go to Paris or not for next winter. This unhappy Accademia delle Belle Arti in Florence is the most unsatisfactory institution imaginable, human ingenuity has never contrived anything so unsatisfactory. It was closed for two months from Christmas to March while the Professors and the Minister of Public Instruction deliberated a thorough reform in its organisation, and when reopened the only perceptible change was that we, the students from the cast, were left without a Master, while the former Professor vacillated and still vacillates between resigning and continuing his instructions. However, this has been of no more consequence to me since my sprained ankle keeps me at home where I have a very handsome Neapolitan model to draw and paint, who plays on the

Zampogna and tamburino and dances tarantellas for us when he is tired of sitting. I hope Mary perseveres in the Fine Arts and compels her model to dance when he is tired.

I am,

Yr. affect^ate cousin,

JOHN S. SARGENT.

In spite of cholera scares Venice was their first objective. Here they met Whistler, who, born in 1834, was now in his fortieth year. It was to prove a critical year in the history of Whistler's fame. He had before this made his headquarters in London, and in June he was to hold an exhibition of his works at 48, Pall Mall. His work, although accepted on more than one occasion by the Royal Academy, had each year tended to create a little more bewilderment amongst the critics, who, beginning with guarded benediction, were now in 1874 emerging into a state of declared and open disapproval. The picture of his mother had been in the first instance rejected by the Committee of the Royal Academy in 1872, and subsequently accepted only in consequence of a threat of resignation by Sir William Boxall, a member of the Council. Not only, therefore, was he ill at ease with established Academic opinion, and at war with the critics, but he had already mystified and estranged the public. He was now contemplating a further challenge to the art world of London, by an exhibition of his collected works destined to be aggravated by his adopting a nomenclature for his pictures borrowed from the vocabulary of music. The device was intended to emphasize the significance of individual pictures. Thus the famous portrait of Miss Alexander had as an explanatory title *Harmony in Grey and Green*, while other pictures were described as *Symphonies*, *Arrangements*, *Variations*, or in the case of the picture of *Cremorne at Night*, the subject of Ruskin's hysterical attack, as *Nocturnes*. It was a novel departure, by no means likely to make converts or temper the hostility he had aroused. In any case, Whistler stood apart from the main current of English painting. His work was as remote from the minute accuracy of the Pre-Raphaelites as it was from the pictorial anecdotes then in fashion on the walls of the Academy.

To the older generation, in the words of Millais, he was "a great power of mischief among younger men." Conciliation in any form was not one of the gentle arts which his genius was at any time ready to practise. He was essentially a fighter. The battle he was waging in London had certain resemblances to the struggle going on in Paris. But whereas in London he was single-handed, in Paris the innovators could count on numbers.

Whistler was enthusiastic over his young compatriot's water-colours and drawings. Thus began distinctly friendly relations between them which lasted till the elder artist's death in 1903. Later, when Sargent was as yet little heard of in England, Whistler was one of the earliest to direct attention to his work. In 1894 Sargent, a consistent admirer of Whistler's painting, together with St. Gaudens, tried to get him to decorate one of the large panels on the stairs of the Boston Library. Whistler described this as an act of "rare and noble camaraderie."* The project hung fire. He got as far as making notes for the design, which he told Mr. Pennell was to be a peacock ten feet high; but the scheme never matured. Sargent used to say that Whistler's use of paint was so exquisite that if a piece of canvas were cut out of one of his pictures one would find that it was in itself a thing of beauty by the very texture and substance into which it had been transformed by his brush. It has more than once been said that the two painters were far from friendly to one another. This is contrary to the fact. Temperamentally it is true, they differed profoundly. There was in Whistler an overt antagonism to opinions and accomplishments with which he was not in sympathy that to Sargent was incomprehensible. Nor was his appreciation of Sargent's maturer work by any means enthusiastic. Yet, unlike as the two men were in most respects, their relations were uniformly friendly, and no one enjoyed Whistler's devastating wit more than Sargent.

To someone who brought a commission to Whistler and with consummate folly insisted that the suggested picture should be a "serious work," he retorted that "he could not break with

* E. R. and J. Pennell, "The Whistler Journal," p. 34.

the tradition of a lifetime." That was a vindication that entirely delighted Sargent. It was the sort of rebuke that anyone who tampered so clumsily with an artist's susceptibilities thoroughly deserved. But Sargent had not got Whistler's ruthlessness. He could never have replied to the student who said his trouble was to paint what he saw. "Your trouble will begin when you see what you paint."

The summer of 1874 was spent by the Sargent family at Benzeval. In August they moved to Paris and took up their residence at 52, Rue Abbatrice. It was the official beginning of Sargent's career as a painter. He at once started work at the École des Beaux Arts, which was then presided over by M. Yvon. From the following it will be seen that he was very soon faced with an examination, and that the prospect filled him with all the normal perturbations and misgivings.

52, RUE ABBATRICE,
Oct. 4th, 1874.

MY DEAR BEN,

Caro il mio ben. I am in the midst of my exam and very busy consequently I can only write a few lines to thank you for your kind and interesting letter.

The exam is the Concours de Place for the life school of M. Yvon and it seems unreasonably long difficult and terrible. It began on the 26th of September and two weeks are still to come. The épreuves de Perspective et d'Anatomie are over; I wish I might say as much for the Dessin d'Ornement which is in store for us tomorrow morning. But the supreme moment is one of twelve hours wherein we must make a finished drawing of the human form divine.

Heaven only knows whether I shall get through; also Heaven alone could bring such a miracle to pass; therefore let us implore its aid and do our best. After this Concours my regular winter work will commence at the Atelier.

Has this summer been pleasant to you ? I have never passed a more delightful one. We have been as you know in the habit of spending our summer in the land of rocks and cheeses as Violet calls it, and the sea shore has been such a pleasant change that I have no doubt we will return to Normandy or Brittany next year.

We look forward with much pleasure to your flying visit next Xmas. Please take pains to inject your eye with belladonna that we may judge if your description is as accurate as it is amusing.

CAROLUS DURAN.

Do you know whether that restless impetuous Joe Francia who bores one with repeated visits is in Paris? I should like to see what he has been painting.

And now, dear Old Ben, I must close. Please divide our best love between your mother and yourself and

Believe me ever

Yr. very affect. old friend,

JOHN S. SARGENT.

In October he entered the studio of Carolus Duran, then the foremost portrait painter in Paris.

Few painters have reached success by steeper paths than Carolus Duran. He was born at Lille on July 4, 1837, and was of Spanish descent through his paternal grandfather. In his native town he was entered as a pupil of the painter Souchon, who in his student days had been a pupil of David. His promise was unmistakable, but his poverty was great. After bitter struggles he amassed just sufficient money to seek in 1858 the wider field of Paris. Here his talents were unrecognized; he was unable to earn a livelihood. He attended not at the École des Beaux Arts but at the Académie Suisse, where he met Fantin Latour, and where teaching meant, in the main, leaving pupils to work out their own salvation. He frequented the Louvre, and by copying well-known pictures for a few francs he was able to keep himself from actual want. His hope was fast failing. But he believed in himself, and he was gifted with a spirit not easily vanquished. At the blackest moment in 1860 he returned to Lille, where with his picture *Visite au Convalescent* he won the Wicar prize. With the money he set out for Italy. There in the monastery of Subiaco, in the neighbourhood of Rome, he shut himself up to study the elements of his art. Thence he returned to Paris to experience a further period of trial and discouragement. He could find no patron and he was unable to obtain orders.

He was now twenty-five years of age, of medium height, with regular and handsome features and dark eyes. His dark hair was parted in the middle with a curl thrown out on each side of his forehead, and he wore a Velasquez beard, which gave an outward sign of his Spanish origin. He did not falter in the will to succeed. In 1865 he was back at Lille painting portraits for 150 francs apiece. Then in 1866 he produced a picture, *L'Assassiné*, strongly marked by the influence of Courbet and now in the museum at Lille, which was purchased for 5,000 francs. This picture proved the turning-point in his career. The canvas shows a group of peasants gathered about a stretcher on which lies the body of a murdered man. In the grouping of the onlookers, in the record of their emotions, varying from horror to mere curiosity, and in the concentration of interest brought about by the light on the victim there is a robust and dramatic power—but the picture denotes no departure from the prevailing French tradition.

The purchase of the picture enabled Carolus Duran to visit Spain. Here he fell under the influence of Velasquez. After six months he returned to Paris, dominated by his impressions of the Spanish master, whose works he had assiduously copied. In 1869, under this new inspiration, he painted *La Dame au Gant*, a portrait of Madame Duran. With this picture his reputation was established. He moved from success to success, becoming the most popular portrait painter in Paris. Fortune, as if to atone, now showered on him prosperity and success. He became a dominant figure in Paris life. Never free from a certain affectation (had he not changed his name from Charles Durand to Carolus Duran?) and with an air which was slightly flamboyant, he was the victim of not a few caricatures and popular gibes. His habit of caracoling like a riding master in the Bois de Boulogne on a prancing barb earned him the title of Caracolus Duran; his skill at billiards that of Carambolus Duran. His mastery of the guitar, his proficiency with the foils, his good looks, his sumptuous home in the Champs Elysées, were interpreted at times as a love of ostentation and excited the envy and criticism of those outside the circle of his friends.

In 1874, the year in which Sargent entered his studio, he held an exhibition of his portraits. It is mainly as a portrait painter that he survives to-day, though he worked in other fields as well.

In France Carolus Duran was the favourite of the critics. He was acclaimed as a colourist; his portraits were applauded for their incisive force, for the skill with which he laid emphasis on revealing characteristics, for his power of detaching the sitter from superfluous accessories and *décor* and bringing him into a relation personal with the spectator.

He was the portrayer of the society of his time, of its silks and its fashions, its moods and its temper. It was a world that thought well of itself and its equipment, an atmosphere that was at least on the surface untroubled and serene. Duran does not dive too deeply into its significance. Men of letters and science, politicians and leaders of the fashionable faubourgs, pass before him and are arrested on his canvases—easy, representative, distinguished people, smooth and deliberate in their outlook on the world. The tradition of "Académisme" is there, but it is altered, relieved of many of its conventions and some of its dulness.

The *atelier** was "run" by some American students, who made a fixed charge to cover expenses. Duran, very much as a surgeon at a hospital, gave his services for nothing. That was the general practice, to which the well-known studio of Julien was one of the few exceptions. A painter would look to a return for his services in the prestige of his studio, and the missionary work done on his behalf by his students. In all cases the advancement of art was a sufficient pretext. The pupils of the *atelier* Duran worked in a studio on the Boulevard Montparnasse. A model would be drawn on Monday and painting would begin on Tuesday. Twice a week, generally on Tuesday and Friday, Duran himself would descend from Olympus to review the work of his pupils. The visit was a very formal affair. Nothing was omitted that could add prestige to the occasion. The Master's entry was the signal for the pupils to rise in their places; then while they stood beside their easels he would approach one or other of them, and after a moment's inspection of their work and without turning round, hold out his hand for the brush or pencil

* Mr. Joseph Farquharson, R.A., and Mr. C. M. Newton, both at one time in the *atelier*, have kindly supplied me with the facts.

with which the pupil stood ready: having made his corrections he would pass on to a neighbouring easel. His observations were brief and his commendations exceedingly rare. On one occasion a newly arrived pupil standing by his easel and seeing Duran's hand extended after an examination of his work, in the customary way for brush or pencil, assumed that the gesture had a congratulatory purpose. He accordingly seized the Master's hand with undisguised pleasure. The mistake was not forgiven. The sanctity of the routine had to be protected from shocks of such a kind. Shortly afterwards the offending novice left to achieve distinction in a career remote from art. One day a week the whole class would adjourn to Duran's own studio, where, with the awe in those days more easily inspired, they would watch the Master at work. No great cordiality seems to have existed between Duran and his pupils. They were there to learn and he was there to teach, and that was the beginning and end of it.

During Sargent's first year of attendance R. A. M. Stevenson (1847–1900) was a pupil. Stevenson, after graduating at Cambridge in 1871, had been studying at the École des Beaux Arts, Antwerp. Robert Louis Stevenson has described his cousin Bob in "Talk and Talkers" under the guise of "Spring Heel'd Jack." An *atelier* presided over by Carolus Duran was no place for spring heels. The conversation of "R. A. M." was iconoclastic and revolutionary, "glancing high like a meteor and making light in darkness"; to Academism it was sedition. It kept Duran uneasy. Thirty-two years later Sargent was asked by Mr. D. S. MacColl to exert his influence in obtaining a pension for Stevenson's widow. He wrote as follows:

My dear MacColl,   *Nov.* 21, 1916.

   Your schemes seem to be always of the best and I will be delighted to help in this one if I can. To begin with I shall at once read the book,* which I am sorry to say I have not done. But even without this book I think he has the greatest claim to public gratitude for his admirable teaching.

   * R. A. M. Stevenson, "Velasquez."

LUXEMBOURG GARDENS AT TWILIGHT.

Minneapolis Institute of Art.

Throughout his life he gave his extraordinary powers and talent to the purpose of letting others into the secret and there must be many who are grateful. . . .

Yours sincerely,
JOHN S. SARGENT.

Later he wrote again:

MY DEAR MacCOLL,

. . . I am afraid you would be disappointed in the slightness of my acquaintance with R. A. M. Stevenson and of my recollections of him in the old days, when for a year I was with him in Carolus Duran's studio which he left long before I did. Really my principal impression was that of having all my boyish ideals on art smashed by him (a good riddance) and being horrified by his free thought and independence—of course later on I saw the truth of what he used to say—unfortunately I have hardly ever met him for the last twenty years, but I appreciate him now much more than I did when we were thrown together.

I am very glad that the pension is granted to his widow. At your suggestion and Colvin's I wrote to Balfour who replied after he had read the book, saying that it was settled. He thought the book very interesting and seemed particularly pleased that "hating Burne Jones' work as he must have done" he had been so sparing of censure. I was afraid that the allusion to that school and to the attitude of the cultivated person towards art would have made him send the widow to Botany Bay.

Yours sincerely,
JOHN S. SARGENT.

It is evident that in his student days Sargent shared the apprehension excited in the studio by this brilliant free-spoken lover of the arts. To Duran, at any rate, it must have been a relief when Stevenson with "his gusts of talk and thunderclaps of contradiction" passed out into the freer air of Barbizon and Grez. All the same, Stevenson's "Velasquez" was one of the few criticisms on painters for which Sargent had any liking. Indeed, Stevenson and Fromentin were the only two among deceased critics to whom I ever heard him refer.

"En art tout ce qui n'est pas indispensable est nuisible" was one of the precepts which Duran had formulated after his study of Velasquez. It became one of the texts of his studio. "Mon but a été toujours celui-là: exprimer le maximum au moyen du minimum" was the later variant of the same idea. "Cherchez la demi-teinte" he would add, "mettez quelques accents, et puis les lumiéres." But above all, to his pupils his advice was "Velasquez, Velasquez, Velasquez, étudiez sans relache Velasquez." He urged them to make copies of the pictures of Velasquez in the Louvre, not laborious copies, but copies "au premier coup." In painting a picture he would retreat a few steps from the canvas and then once more advance with his brush balanced in his hand as though it were a rapier and he were engaged in a bout with a fencing-master—these gestures were often accompanied by appeals to the shade of Velasquez. Those who watched Sargent painting in his studio will be reminded of his habit of stepping backwards after almost every stroke of the brush on the canvas. and the track of his paces so worn on the carpet that it suggested a sheep-run through the heather. He too, when in difficulties, had a sort of battle cry of "Dæmons, dæmons" with which he would dash at his canvas.

It was, then, to such a workshop and under such a master that Sargent at the age of eighteen was admitted as a pupil, and the question arises, What did Sargent owe to the teaching of Duran? The question is best answered by remembering Duran's precepts and seeing how far they are reflected in Sargent's art. It has already been shown how Duran insisted on the study of Velasquez and the omission in art of all that was not essential to the realization of the central purpose of a painting. He had himself travelled far from the sharp contrast of values by which he had dramatized his picture L'Assassiné. He had got rid of his tendency to be spectacular. From Velasquez he had learnt to simplify. His teaching was focussed on the study of values and half-tones— above all, half-tones. Here lies, he would say, the secret of painting, in the half-tone of each plane, in economizing the accents and in the handling of the lights so that they should play their part in the picture only with a palpable and necessary significance. Other things were subordinate. If Sargent excels in these respects, it is sufficient to recall the fact that they formed the core of Duran's instruction. There is no need to put his influence higher. Few pupils in painting who have the talent to absorb their master's teaching fail in the long run to outgrow his influence and to progress beyond and outside it on lines of their own.

Sargent himself always recognized his debt to the teaching of Duran. At the height of his fame, when looking at a portrait by a younger painter, he observed to Mr. William James: "That has value. I wonder who taught him to do that. I thought Carolus was the only man who taught that. He couldn't do it himself, but he could teach it." Again, when Mr. James asked him how to avoid false accents he said: "You must *classify* the values. If you begin with the middle-tone and work up from it towards the darks—so that you deal last with your highest lights and darkest darks—you avoid false accents. That's what Carolus taught me. And Franz Hals—it's hard to find anyone who knew more about oil-paint than Franz Hals—and that was his procedure. Of course, a sketch is different. You don't mind false accents there. But once you have made them in something which you wish to *carry far*, in order to correct them you have to deal with both sides of them and get into a lot of trouble. So that's the best method for anything you wish to carry far in oil-paint." Mr. George Moore, in one of the most illuminating essays in "Modern Painting," said: "In 1830 values came upon France like a religion. Rembrandt was the new Messiah, Holland was the Holy Land, and disciples were busy dispensing the propaganda in every studio." The religion had no more ardent apostle than Carolus Duran.

Chapter IV

IF we attempt to define the artistic influences with which Sargent was in contact in Paris, we are confronted with the difficulty that in a summary it is necessary to make use of labels and employ hard-and-fast designations for tendencies which are in their nature elusive, and do not lend themselves to precise definition. It is a subject which only the expert can approach with confidence. But labels, if they lack the precise assistance offered by a signpost at cross-roads, serve to give a general idea of the nature of the country. They are useful as indications, and we need not press the question too far whether the work of any particular painter comes strictly under the label which is applied to him. This is more particularly the case where French art in the decade 1870–80 is concerned. That was a period of fluidity in artistic tendencies, and, if we take it in conjunction with the immediately succeeding years, a period in which the art critics burnt their fingers with a recklessness that has few parallels. Nor, if we remember the fate of the "refusés" in Paris and of Whistler in London can it be said that the Academicians did much better or even as well. Whatever else may be said of the period, it can certainly be pointed to as a warning against dogmatism in art.

Here, however, it is not a question of criticism or even of explanation, but of recalling the names of the artists then at work and the tendencies for which they stood. One distinctive school, with Theodore Rousseau (1812–67) as its foremost founder, had been at work since 1830 and was now drawing to its close. During the decade 1870–80, Millet (1875), Corot (1875), Diaz (1876), Daubigny (1878) died, the surviving leaders of the Barbizon school, of those "plein-air" painters, who influenced by Constable and Bonington had freed French landscape painting

30

from its formality and its studio adjustments, and brought it into closer contact with the moods of nature and the changing aspects of earth and sky. Windows had been opened, air and light had entered in. Under the influence of these workers, set pieces, staged effects and classic ruins had given place to the notation of landscape seen with a more direct vision. For the first time the quality of impermanence in cloud or sun, stillness or storm, became part of the nature painter's subject. A moment before the scene had been different, a moment later it will have changed again. A new aspect of beauty had been transferred to canvas, together with a new vision and a new craft, and here, since such parallels recur and may be found also in the case of Sargent's art, it is worth pointing out that even such an individual school as the Barbizon painters had characteristics shared by the literature of the day.

And it would be well to remember that the Barbizon school, though not ordinarily associated with the Romantic Movement, did not escape a certain infiltration of the Romantic spirit. As we look at their landscapes we are made aware of an ulterior significance, we become more and more conscious of a spiritual significance afloat in the representation of the scene. A woodland scene by Diaz or Daubigny is invested with a peculiar melancholy, a *fête champêtre* would do violence to the spirit which haunts it, we feel that birds of no common plumage lodge in its branches, that here it is the horn of Roland rather than the woodman's axe that will be heard in the dells of the forest; again, in a painting by Millet the peasants tilling the fields seem not so much labourers toiling on the land as members of a religious order fulfilling the dictates of a pious foundation; or again, the borders of a lake, the banks of a river by Corot in his later years being visions of a spiritual world unprofaned by man.

Side by side with the Barbizon school there had grown up the school of the "Realists." The leader was Gustave Courbet (1819–77), a rich and vigorous personality, abounding in force and originality, well equipped to impose his views and head a revolution whether in the studio or behind a barricade.

A man of the people, wearing wooden shoes, with the physique
of a blacksmith and the profile of an Assyrian, deep and jovial
in his laughter and a convinced republican, he was within an
ace of being shot as an insurgent in 1848, and in 1871 was sen-
tenced by court-martial to six months' imprisonment for his
share in the destruction of the Column Vendôme—though his
action here was dictated by the desire to save the larger evil of
the destruction of the Louvre. To make art a living force, "fit
for democracy," and turn it from embellished renderings of
classical subjects and the effete pageantry of bygone ages, was
his declared purpose. His theme was the world as it is, without
the gloss of *ce vil idéal*; rich, abundant, teeming with significance,
to be rendered as a painter sees it, without the intrusion of
drama, moral values or shadowy subjective associations. "Mettez vous en face de la nature, et puis peignez comme vous sen-
tirez, parbleu," was his advice to students. His own method of
painting was to work on dark red or brown grounds, reserving
the light to the last. It was never his scheme to begin with the
middle tints and scale up to the high lights and down to the
dark shadows, the method which was advocated and practised
by Sargent. But it was only after years of toil that Courbet
found favour with the critics, and was accepted by the public,
though by that time he had formed a coterie of disciples. Of
these the most eminent was Manet (1832–83). Edouard Manet
was the pupil of Couture, a teacher who was the slave of rule
and tradition, and devoted his talents to the production of idealized renderings of classical and historical subjects, the "grand
art," in fact, of the time. By 1863 Manet had broken away
from Couture and his revolt marked the beginning of a new
era in art. For it was in that year that the committee or jury
of the Salon rejected with true academic instinct certain pictures
considered revolutionary in their tendencies, raising thereby such
a storm of protest among the younger artists that the Emperor
was begged to intervene. He visited the Palais de l'Industrie,
and the committee proving obdurate he ordered that the rejected canvases should be exhibited in a separate room divided
by a partition from the Salon.

REHEARSAL OF PASDELOUP ORCHESTRA AT THE CIRQUE D'HIVER.
Boston Art Museum.

This was the origin of the famous Salon des Refusés. Here were shown works by Fantin Latour, Bracquemond, Jongkind, Cazin, Chintreuil, Cals, Colin, Harpignies, Legros, Jean Paul Laurens, Camille Pissarro, while Whistler was represented by his *Girl in White*, rejected the previous year by the Royal Academy, and Manet by *Le Déjeuner sur l'Herbe*. The exhibition was derided by the critics. It was parodied at the Variétés as the "Club des Refusés" and known in the Boulevards as the "Exposition des Comiques." *Le Déjeuner sur l'Herbe* (now in the Louvre) set Paris by the ears. It was attacked not only for the novelty of its technique but also, and here the public were able to join in, for its subject: two men in the bourgeois costume of the day picnicking under some trees with a nude woman as one of the party, while a second woman was seen bathing in the background. This was so violent a departure from the idealized assemblages engaged in a court function or illustrating an historical or classical episode, to which the walls of the Salon had grown accustomed, that protests poured in from all sides, and when Manet replied his subject was the same as Giorgione's, he was answered that he had failed to idealize his figures as Giorgione had done, and the distinction was good enough for a public deaf to reason. Had not Gustave Flaubert been prosecuted for the publication of "Madame Bovary" in 1857? The die-hards of the Romantic Movement were still in possession. Manet became one of the most abused men in Paris; hardly a voice was heard in defence of his art; Gérôme stigmatized his pictures as *cochonneries*, and when *L'Olympia* was exhibited in the Salon of 1865 the clamour burst out again. Zola, who praised Manet's work, was included in the demonstration of hostility. But Manet's faith in himself remained unbroken, and with *Le Bon Bock* exhibited in 1873 a change began; nobody spoke again of his pictures as *cochonneries*.

Meanwhile the critics had found fresh game and were busy with a group of painters with whom Manet was beginning to be associated. The principal figures in this "revolutionary" group included Claude Monet, Pissarro, Sisley, Cézanne, Berthe

Morisot, Degas, Renoir, and in a less degree Boudin* and
Lépine. On April 15, 1874, under the title of "Société
anonyme des artistes, peintres, sculpteurs et graveurs," they
opened an independent exhibition in the Boulevard des
Capucines. Claude Monet showed a picture entitled *Impression: Lever du Soleil*. The word "Impression" was seized
on by a writer in the *Charivari*, and henceforth Impressionism
was looked upon as a convenient subject for ridicule. The
Impressionists became a target for the critics, their work was
described as "anarchist rubbish," they were scoffed at for their
theory and ridiculed for their technique. But jibes do not
kill, they continued to exhibit their pictures. The battle was,
therefore, raging in the seventies at the time when Sargent
entered the studio of Carolus Duran.

In this abbreviated record of the movements in painting
during these years, no mention has been made of Ingres, who died
in 1867. Mr. MacColl has described his work as "realism
within Raphaelism," and as a painter he stands somewhat outside
the more obvious classifications. Though he was looked up to
as one of the greatest of French artists, his immediate influence
was merged and is not easily traced in subsequent movements.
He was too remote from the current life of the day. Even
Degas, whose aim it was at first to follow the direction given to
painting by Ingres, is drawn early in his career to other sources
of influence, notably to Manet and the Japanese. But no French
artist was more or as much admired by Sargent. Two artists
so dissimilar it would be difficult to name. On the one hand,
Ingres, with serenity in his delineation of form, and with repose
and beauty in his lines, but often nerveless and inept in his colour,
and shunning the agitation and movement of light: on the other,
Sargent, forcible in his execution, concerned with the play and
reflection of light, and on the look-out for the intricate aspect
of things; the exponent of an art that is alert, vibrating, and
vital with colour and the spirit of life. But when the contrast

---

* Of Boudin, Claude Monet has said: "Je peux dire que Boudin a été mon Initiateur,
qu'il m'a révélé à moi-même et ouvert la bonne voie. Et le premier pas quelle importance!" See "Chez Claude Monet," Marc Elder, Bernheim-Jeune, 1924.

is exhausted, there remain the draughtsmanship, the genius for composition and the fluent strength and elegance of line of the French master. It was these that Sargent was never tired of extolling. When in 1914 he visited Paris with Professor Tonks to see the exhibition of the collected work of Ingres, he pointed to *Jupiter Enthroned* as the picture in which the highest gifts of the artist were most completely combined.

From this brief survey it may be gathered that in Paris in 1874 there were at least three schools of painting: the Independents, who included Impressionists or Luminists, towards whom the Realists were inclining; the Academicians; and lastly those who, like Carolus Duran, were dominated by the influence of Velasquez. The three schools, if schools they can be called, were divided by partitions of no great strength. That between the school of Duran and the Academicians permitted of considerable intercommunication; that between the school of Duran and the Independents was, it is true, more solid, but at the same time not so high as to make it impossible to look over at what was being done on the other side. Reflections from the Luminists diffused themselves across the barrier, but as the art of Sargent shows, they were allowed only a limited scope in their operation and kept in strict subjection. From letters he wrote it will be possible to gather his own view with regard to this very point.

Chapter V

THE echoes of Sargent's first years in Paris come to us faintly and the lights are fitful. At eighteen years of age he is still slight in build, a little shy and awkward in manner, reserved (as he remained throughout his life) in conversation, but charming, fresh, unsophisticated and even idealistic in his outlook on the world, engagingly modest and diffident, speaking perfect French, hardly aware yet of his gifts, and bound by a romantic devotion to his sister Emily and his parents. All testimony agrees. And so he crosses the threshold of his career. From the first he was a worker of astonishing capacity. He would breakfast every morning with his sister Emily at seven so as to arrive at the studio before eight, and on Mondays in order to secure a good place for the week he would start earlier. At five o'clock in the evening he would leave the studio and go to the École des Beaux Arts, where he remained till seven. Dinner over, he would go to the studio of Bonnat and attend a class which lasted from eight to ten at night. On Sundays he worked at home, dining with his family and bringing fellow-students into the radius of that encouraging milieu. Among these were Caroll Beckwith, Frank Fowler, Russell, Edelfeldt the Finnish painter and Alden Weir. With all this he found time for music and for reading.

He was rarely to be seen except in the Latin Quarter. He was immersed in his work. Paul Helleu, then a fellow-student, remembers him as always dressed with distinctive care in a world which still affected the baggy corduroy trousers tight at the ankle, the slouch hats or tam o'shanters, and the coloured sashes associated with the Latin Quarter. He was a striking figure as he strode down the Rue Bonaparte to the École des Beaux Arts, and already a little noted and recognized as one of the very few whose future could be looked on as definitely assured. The Latin Quarter at this time was the Latin Quarter of Murger's "Vie de Bohème" and Du Maurier's "Trilby." In the intervals of study it invited and even expected a somewhat excessive devotion to the lighter sides of Paris life. It was, in fact, the Latin Quarter of popular report. Sargent, according to all accounts, remained apart; not from any settled austerity of mind, but because he was absorbed in his work to a point of fanaticism. Never in the memory of the Latin Quarter had a harder worker been seen. He was too human to ignore and too ironic to condemn "l'existence debraillée des rapins," but it formed no part of his own career. He simply had not the time to spare; when he had, he could enjoy it. In March, 1875, he writes to Ben Castillo after a visit to Nice with Carolus Duran:

52, RUE ABBATRICE,
March 6th, 1875.

MY DEAR BEN,

A cold perspiration bursts out all over me when I recollect that more than a month has elapsed since I received your kind letter; but I can give several reasons for not answering it sooner; fits of slight illness, hard work and the Concours, now nearly ended.

We have had a few days of delightful sunny spring weather, which make my companions and me wild to go out into the country and sketch. On the night of Mi-Carême we cleared the studio of easels and canvasses, illuminated it with Venetian or coloured paper lanterns, hired a piano and had what is called "the devil of a spree." Dancing, toasts and songs lasted till 4, in short they say it was a very good example of a Quartier Latin ball. The whole quarter was out all night in the wildest festivity, quite surpassing anything I have ever seen in the Italian carnival. I enjoyed our spree enormously, I hope not too much; probably because it was such a new thing for me.

I am anxious to hear news of you and to hear how you like Cambridge and the University life.

We saw so much of other people in Nice that no time was left us for long talks together. Theodore senior is off to Algiers. My two friends left Nice unwell, and Carolus Duran took one of their vacant beds in my room. I came up to Paris with him three days later. I enjoyed Nice immensely. Now good-bye dear Ben. I hope to see you here in the spring.

Your affect.
JOHN S. SARGENT.

In the summer of 1875, the family gave up 52, Rue Abbatrice and moved to St. Enogat, near Dinard. Sargent remained
in Paris and joined Caroll Beckwith, sharing a studio with him
at 73b, Rue Notre Dame des Champs. In June he joined his
parents at St. Enogat. The coast attracted him, and two years
later he returned to the neighbourhood and painted one of
his earliest Salon pictures, *En Route pour la Pêche*. He was
charmed by the house his parents had taken and wrote to Ben
Castillo:

> MAISON LEFORT,
> ST. ENOGAT PRÈS DINARD,
> ILE ET VILAINE,
> *June 20th*, 1875.
>
> DEAR BEN,
>
> I am really ashamed at having left your letter so long unanswer-
> ed; as long as we were in Paris it was very difficult to find the time, but
> since our arrival here I confess there was leisure enough as the weather
> has been unfavourable for sketching. I wish you believed in the maxim
> "Whatever is, is right!" If *I* did I would thrust it at you.
>
> How glad you must be to be with your Mother again after all your
> hard work. I congratulate you sincerely for passing your examina-
> tions successfully. Mr. del Castillo said that you would pay a visit to
> Lue again this summer but I fear it is too great a distance for us to
> hope to see you here.
>
> We enjoy our little country house very much with its pleasant
> gardens and thoroughly rural entourage. I have reason to be contented
> and thankful for my quarters are charming. My bedroom is the most
> beautiful interior I have ever seen in anything short of a palace or a
> castle. It is furnished throughout in the mediaeval style. Its beamed
> ceiling and floor are of oak, its walls completely hung with stamped
> leathers and arras; the furniture is all antique and richly carved,
> especially the grand bedstead with canopy and bed posts, the immense
> wardrobe, and ebony cabinet. Then there is a great tapestried chimney
> piece, plenty of oil portraits, a few small choice casts such as a head of
> Goethe and a beautiful reduction of the Moses of Michel Angelo. This
> enumeration ends with the most charming detail of all; the windows.
> They are of lattice, that is to say, of small lozenges of glass, joined
> together by bands of lead, and from them you look right over and into
> the fig tree with its great shining green leaves and ripening fruit, then
> over the pear trees and cherry trees and flowers of the garden, to the
> wide cornfields, and over them to the sea.

WINEGLASSES.

There is much to paint, but it has poured ever since we have been here, so I have accomplished little as yet. Once more congratulating you on your brilliant success.

I remain,

Your very affectionate old friend,

JOHN S. SARGENT.

The spontaneity of his work at this time is striking. There is no sign of effort; it is perhaps immature, but the painting is easy as a signature and stamped with an individual character to be developed as time went on, but never to be radically altered. Impulse, execution, vision, indications of method, and immense facility are already there.

There is a notable sketch in oils of about this time.* It is signed, and it bears two dates, 1873 and 1874. It was signed and dated by Sargent as recently as 1923. If it is 1874 it was probably painted at Benzeval—the foliage is northern, the scene obviously French. The study is remarkable for its dexterity: an empty table covered with a white cloth stands in the trellised arbour of an estaminet garden; the sunlight makes a pattern through the trellis, and falls sharp and bright on the tablecloth; beyond are shrubs, silvery in the sunshine; and an enclosing wall shuts out the distance. Two glasses filled with red *vin du pays* stand on a metal tray on a side table and reflect the light. The scene is entirely commonplace; yet though uneventful it has all the quality of an episode. It shows a markedly French influence both in subject and treatment: a featureless *bosquet* of a lowly inn seen in vivid sunshine, the shadows light in tone, the foliage quivering in the glare, the commonplace suddenly invested with interest by art.

In 1875 Sargent painted the portrait of Benjamin P. Kissam in Paris. In May, 1876, he sailed with Mrs. Sargent and Miss Emily Sargent for America. It was his first contact with the United States. There is no hint of the impression he received, yet the situation was in some ways singular. He was an American by parentage, born and educated in the Old World, steeped in the culture of Europe, and now, at the age of twenty for the first time,

* Now in the possession of Sir Philip Sassoon.

he was introduced to his native country. The contrast in many
ways must have been sharper than it would be to-day. The
great American collector had hardly got to work, the piecemeal
transfer across the Atlantic of European collections of art had
hardly begun. It was only by visiting Europe that a citizen of
the United States could obtain any idea of the history of painting;
naturally the studios of Paris were crowded with Americans.
Painting in America was seeking a definite lead, feeling its way,
and waiting for that directing impulse which was to come to it
from Paris. An American citizen coming to the United States
with an artistic training must have noticed symptoms of its
civilization which were profoundly interesting; at the same time
he was bound to be aware of activities lacking the graces of
the Old World. American citizenship had from early days influenced Sargent's outlook on the world. Now for the first time
he was among his countrymen: the occasion struck an answering
chord in his disposition. Henceforward, wherever his residence
and whatever the conditions of his calling, it was to America that
he felt bound, not only by the ties of race, but by fellow-feeling.

Chapter VI

IF a choice of all the wonders of the "Arabian Nights" had been offered the Sargent family, assuredly they would have chosen the "Enchanted Horse." Even in America, where it might have been expected that anchorages would be found, they continued to move, ignoring distances and never omitting to see anything that had the least claim to interest. Altogether they were four months in America, and in that period they managed to see Philadelphia, which included several short visits at country houses belonging to relatives, Newport, Chicago, Saratoga, Niagara, Lake George, Quebec and Montreal, ending up with Washington and New York. It was the year of the Exhibition at Philadelphia, which coinciding with the speeding up of large fortunes did a great deal to start the fashion of collecting famous works of art. Sargent was entirely taken up with the examples of Japanese and Chinese art. It was just the moment when in Europe, and more especially in France, Oriental painting was influencing the modern school of artists. The Paris Exhibition of 1867 had given an impetus to the enthusiasm for Japanese technique. Everywhere collectors were hunting for the works of Hokusai, Outamaro and Harunobu. In the studios, Japanese artists were taken as models of reticence and economy in the statement of a fact, and as creating spatial atmosphere by means of a few lines. By the time Sargent was at work in Duran's studio the impulse from Japan had already passed into French painting, and its message had been extracted and absorbed. At the Philadelphia Exhibition he had before his eyes a further proof of what might be learnt from the East.

During his visit to America he seems to have done little painting. A water-colour *Below Niagara*, a sketch of Admiral Case's daughter and a portrait of his father's sister, Mrs. Emily Sargent Pleasants, a reproduction of which is given opposite p. 44 are among the few works which can with any certainty be attributed to this period. On the journey back across the Atlantic, during a storm in which their vessel the *Algeria* was caught, he did a study of waves. This is one of the few occasions on which he took the sea as a subject for a picture, often though he painted water in fountains or lakes or canals. Yet with the exception of Turner it would be difficult to name any painter who has rendered so convincingly the restlessness and weight and iridescence of moving waters or made them such a prominent feature in their work. In his study of the Atlantic, the force and volume of the waves, the desolate iteration of crest and trough, and the dark anger of the storm are dramatically contrasted with the thin white track made on the waste of waters by the vessel and the frail platform from which the sketch is taken. The eye is carried over the welter of waves to the horizon. It is a picture with distance, a thing comparatively rare in Sargent's landscapes.

The beauty he sought lay in the relation of light to clearly discerned objects, to things near by and of ascertainable texture and form. It is exceptional to find in his pictures that lyrical quality which from Turner to Wilson Steer has been associated with distance in landscape. Dramatic oppositions in light and colour are to be seen in their strength at a short range of vision, and it is such oppositions that appealed to Sargent. If horizon lines had in them a note of monotony and panoramas an element of vagueness, there was the further consideration that the vagueness of distant panoramas involves subdued tones, and that fact may have made him reluctant to treat such subjects. Training and temperament may have disposed him to a preference for what was strong in tone. By temperament he was buoyant, active and alert, dreaming no dreams, little given to contemplative moods, and when once his genius had matured he inclined definitely to what was clear and affirmative, pronounced and explicit. That mood of pensiveness which is suggested by far-flung horizons, distant hills and remoteness in space was foreign to his nature.

Commending some amateur work in which he had found more

AN ATLANTIC STORM.

merit than he expected, he once said: "He does what is in front of him, he doesn't shirk the difficulties and like most amateurs go wandering into distances." * It would not be true to say that Sargent never "wandered into distances," but certainly his preferences lay in other directions.

But the reasons which we may find to explain any special characteristic in Sargent's landscapes are of little moment; the important fact is that he has left behind him a series of water-colours that for volume, variety and beauty is not easily matched.

In October, 1876, the family were back in Paris. That autumn Sargent painted *Gitana* and *Rehearsal at Cirque d'Hiver*. The following year he sent his first picture to the Salon, a portrait of Miss Watts. It was well received by the critics. Henry Houssaye described it in *La Revue des Deux Mondes* as "Un charmant portrait de jeune miss par M. Sargent, d'une claire harmonie, et duquel on ne peut reprocher que des mains fuselées."

He was very little in Paris during the summer of 1877. He was for two months at Cancale with Eugène La Chaise, then after picking up Caroll Beckwith in Paris they all three stayed at the Sorchans' country house near Lyons. In August Sargent joined his family at Bex, in Switzerland. Wherever he was, he painted; his output was continuous.

His painting is acquiring distinctive character. It diverges from the work of Duran and Bonnat, and carries that work into a different order of vision and execution. Form is involved with light, facts are curtailed, structure and action are indicated rather than stated, the atmosphere is clear and the shadows luminous, even the darkest passages carrying reflection. To borrow the terms of literature, the effect is produced without rhetoric, without one inessential adjective; the language is nervous and exact, with the rhythm and cadence of the finest prose. His work is allied definitely and from the first to the Realists, but his realism is lifted and illuminated by the mystery and variety of shadow and light. In the early landscapes a silvery and delicate quality is noticeable, which later was to give place to more robust colouring in his rendering of scenery—a

* The amateur was Mr. Winston Churchill.

change which accompanied his gradual reversion to a preference for Southern landscape with that emphasis and exultant assertion of light characteristic of the South.

In 1878 there was exhibited at the Salon a ceiling painted for the Louvre* by Carolus Duran which contained a head of Sargent by Duran and a head of Duran by Sargent. Duran approved so highly of Sargent's share in the work that he consented to sit for the portrait which was hung in the Salon of 1879.

It had an immediate success and it was widely reproduced, even figuring on the cover of *L'Illustration*. But the process of being outrun by the disciple is never agreeable to the master. The legend goes that Duran felt acutely his pupil's progress, that he, later on, invaded the Louvre with ladder and palette and removed Sargent's head from the ceiling. The legend may be dismissed. The head still occupies its place in the design, but the jealousy with which Duran watched his pupil's triumphs is notorious. The contrast with his own bitter struggles was in itself a source of provocation.

Sargent's handiwork appears in another French picture painted in the year 1880. Georges Becker (1846–1909), the French painter, was commissioned by M. de Freycinet's Government to paint a picture of the review at Longchamps, held on July 14. Becker invited Sargent to assist him, and the two painters worked together in a tent on the field of the review, with sentries to restrain the curiosity of a prying crowd. This picture I have been unable to trace.

Sargent's fellow-students at this time included Walter Gay, Templeman Coolidge, Ralph Curtis, Charles Forbes, Robert Hinckley, Stephen H. Parker, Elliot Gregory, Chadwick and Harper Pennington, all American by birth. Mr. Albert Belleroche† was also a student at the time. Among his French colleagues were Lobre and the portrait painter Helleu, his lifelong friend.

---

* Now to be seen in Room XIX.

† Mr. Belleroche wrote an account of Sargent's lithographs in *The Print Collectors' Quarterly*, February, 1926. Only six lithographs by Sargent are known to exist. Proofs of these are in the British Museum: (1) "Study of a Young Man" (seated), (2) "Study of a Young Man" (drawing), (3) "William Rothenstein," (4) "Albert Belleroche," (5) "Albert Belleroche" (head only), (6) "Head of a Young Woman."

MRS. EMILY SARGENT PLEASANTS.

When the two first met Sargent was twenty-two and Helleu eighteen. He astonished Helleu with his knowledge of French literature and his command of the French language; his conversation, in fact, was indistinguishable from that of a cultured Frenchman. Helleu at the time was a struggling student, and often unable to pay for a meal. Sargent seems to have suspected this to be the case. One day he climbed up to Helleu's small studio in the Rue de la Grande Chaumière, at a moment when Helleu was in the depths of despair about his work and his prospects. The pastel which he had just finished had set the final seal to his discouragement, and it was resting on the floor when Sargent, the successful young painter, opened the door. There was at once a new atmosphere. There was a magnetic quality of encouragement in his mere presence. "That is a nice thing," he said in a thoughtful way, pointing to the pastel, "Charming, charming. The best thing you've ever done, *mon petit* Helleu." Helleu protested: "Oh, no, I was just thinking what a horror; I'd just torn it off the easel when you came in."

"Because you've been looking at it too long, you've lost your eye. No one ever paints what they want to paint, but to me who can only see what you've done, not what you're aiming at, this is a charming thing I must have for my collection."

Helleu was enchanted—he would be proud if Sargent would accept it.

"I shall accept gladly, Helleu, but not as a gift. I sell my own pictures, and know what they cost me by the time they're out of hand. I should never enjoy this pastel if I hadn't paid you a fair and honest price for it." Thereupon he drew out a note for one thousand francs. Helleu, who had never even seen a thousand-franc note, felt as if the heavens had opened. Thousand-franc notes were not so often handled in those days. Later it dawned on him that the note must have been brought for the special purpose. It was the turning-point in his career. Sargent had set him on his feet. Helleu says he constantly helped his less fortunate competitors. He was equally generous with money, though it expressed itself in action shyly and by stealth, with encouragement and advice, or in improving the work of others with his own pencil or brush. His success stirred no envy, fortune seemed to have chosen him for her own, his days were cloudless, and his friends numerous and faithful.

At this time Helleu was conspicuous among his friends. The two were often seen breakfasting together at the restaurant Livenne, sharing a table with Rodin and Paul Bourget—Rodin, a raw vigorous youth of no general culture, uttering occasionally winged reflections on art; Bourget lively, eager, ranging over and illuminating every topic, his speech shimmering with grace and wit and directing his conversation chiefly to Sargent; Sargent himself, vigorous, robust, full of humour and of theories minted in the practice of his art, his ideas quickened by culture and success, warmed the company with his laughter, which was sometimes ironic and sometimes sprang from the depths of his nature. Sargent was a good eater and lived on a generous scale; but he could accept rough and scanty fare and discomfort when in pursuit of his calling, and for days on end he lived in a shed among the Carrara Mountains, travelling to his work in a basket slung on ropes across a wide ravine, and subsisting on the food of the workers. Cold, heat, mosquitoes, inadequate rations affected him no more than they would the hardiest big-game hunter in Africa, or the most thick-skinned salmon-fisher in Norway. Painting was more than an art to Sargent, it held the exhilaration of a sport as well; his quarry was a suitable subject, his trophy the creation of a thing of beauty.

Chapter VII

SARGENT'S picture *En Route pour la Pêche* in the Salon of 1878, received "honourable mention." It was his second exhibited work. His age was twenty-two.

In the autumn of 1878 he spent several weeks at Capri. From there he wrote to Ben Castillo:

CAPRI (*paper*),
Aug. 10*th*, 1878 (*date added by Ben*).

DEAR BEN,

By this time I fancy the Latin Quarter is deserted of all our mutual friends and that you are rarely to be seen within its bounds. The week contains no more Friday afternoon.

I got a letter from Beckwith the other day which informed me of the movements of the different fellows. Why didn't you join them in their walking tour? By the way I never saw the joke at all myself, but the question comes natural to me just now as I am inclined to think that companionship a great object. If it were not for one German staying at the Marina, I should be absolutely without society and he is in love and cannot talk about anything but his sweetheart's moral irreproachability. We are going over to Sorrento in a day or two to visit her, and I have agreed to keep her husband's interest rivetted to Vesuvius, Baiae, Pozzuoli and other places along the distant opposite shore.

Naples is simply superb and I spent a delightful week there. Of course it was very hot, and one generally feels used up. It is a fact that in Naples they eke out their wine with spirits and drugs, so that a glass of wine and water at a meal will make a man feel drunk. I had to take bad beer in order not to feel good-for-nothing. I could not sleep at night. In the afternoon I would smoke a cigarette in an arm-chair or on my bed and at five o'clock wake up suddenly from a deep sleep of several hours. Then lie awake all night and quarrel with mosquitoes, fleas and all imaginable beasts. I am frightfully bitten from head to foot. Otherwise Italy is all that one can dream for beauty and charm.

It is however true that the "Vandalia" is at Naples. Cap. Robson was very polite and asked me to lunch on board on Tuesday, but at lunch time I was sailing past the Vandalia's bows in the Capri market boat, packed in with a lot of vegetables and fruit. There is a steamer from Naples and Capri, but it has no particular day for going, so that if one comes to the quai of Sta. Lucia every morning as I did with one's luggage, one is sure of getting off in less than a week.

I am painting away very hard and shall be here a long time. So if you write soon, as I should like, address *Capri* otherwise P.R. Naples. With love to Mrs. Castillo and Wm. Durel.

Your affect. old friend,

JOHN S. SARGENT.

There were living on the island, besides the enamoured German, several French and three English artists, one of whom —Mr. Frank Hyde—had a studio in the old monastery of Santa Teresa. Mr. Hyde had never met Sargent and had never seen his work, but hearing that an American artist had arrived and was staying at one of the inns, he called and found him with no place to work in, but perfectly content and revelling in the beauty of the island. Mr. Hyde invited him to come and work at the monastery. There he provided him with a famous model called Rosina, "an Ana Capri girl, a magnificent type, about seventeen years of age, her complexion a rich nut-brown, with a mass of blue-black hair, very beautiful, and of an Arab type." Sargent made many studies from her, one of which, the property of Miss Sargent, was exhibited at the Royal Academy in 1926, and will be found reproduced opposite. During the remainder of his stay he resided at the Marina Hotel; here he imported a breath of the Latin Quarter, entertaining the artists on the island and organizing a fête in which the tarantella was danced on the flat roof of his hotel, to an orchestra of tambourines and guitars. But no entertainment in the Latin Quarter could compete with the figures of the dancers silhouetted against the violet darkness of the night under the broad illumination of the moon, the surrounding silence, the faint winds from the sea, and a supper when the stars are giving place before the first orange splash of day. Bonnet, Sain, Doucet, Chatrau, Frank Hyde and others were the guests of Sargent on that occasion.

In 1879 he exhibited *Dans les Oliviers Capri* and *Portrait*

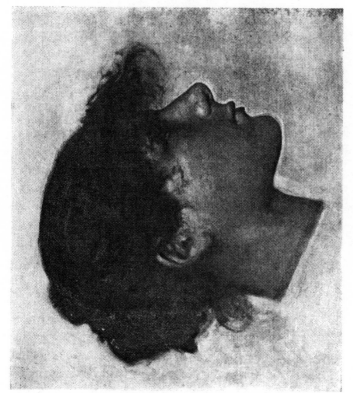

HEAD OF ANA-CAPRI GIRL.

de Carolus Duran. *Dans les Oliviers* was the replica of a picture he had already sold and sent to New York. The portrait of Duran is influenced more than most of his early pictures by the manner of Duran himself. Brown predominates, the tones are rather sharply contrasted, the treatment has less distinction than usual, is even not without a commonplace element; the guitarist, the dandy with elegant cuffs of ruffled lawn, the riding school and the fencing class, seem to be summarized in the rather florid and obvious model. It is the portrait of an eminently successful man, pleased with himself and perhaps not unaware that in posing to a pupil he was paying him a singular and liberal compliment. The picture seems to anticipate the comment made by Duran when someone congratulated him on his pupil's success: "Oui mais Papa était là!" Though the portrait received no mark of Academic approval it was a popular picture and did a great deal to consolidate the painter's reputation in Paris. In 1879 he painted also *Luxembourg Gardens at Twilight, Portrait of Robert de Civrieux with Dog* and *In the Luxembourg Gardens.*

In the autumn he paid his second visit to Spain, in the company of two French painters, MM. Daux and Bac. The party rode through the Ronda Mountains to Gibraltar. Here, in addition to painting, he made researches into Spanish music and folk-songs, subjects in which he and Vernon Lee were alike interested. On his return to Paris he wrote to her:

> You wished some Spanish songs. I could not find any good ones. The best are what one hears in Andalusia, the half African Mela-guemas and Soleas, dismal, restless chants that it is impossible to note. They are something between a Hungarian czardas and the chant of the Italian peasant in the fields and are generally composed of five strophes and end stormily on the dominant, the theme quite lost in strange fioriture and guttural roulades. The gitano voices are marvellously subtle. If you have heard something of the kind you will not consider this mere jargon.

At his studio in Tite Street he used in later years to entertain himself and on occasions try to entertain his guests, or beguile the tedium of a sitting, with a gramophone and records of Spanish music. "That stuff," speaking of Spanish folk-songs, he said,* "is at the bottom of all good music." It may indeed be of interest to some to know the four pieces which he preferred, even sending for them from Boston in 1916, so that Mrs. Gardner might have the benefit of them. They were:

> Malaguemas Fandangerillo Catalan por Juan Breda.
> Malaguemas estito Juan de Mellizo por Juan Breda.
> Farrucae, cantada por la Nina de los Peinas por Juan Breda.
> Guillans cantados por Pavon.

In January, 1880, he paid his first visit to Morocco. From Tetuan he wrote to Ben Castillo:

> HOTEL CENTRAL,
> TANGIER,
> *Jan. 4th,* 1880.

Unchanging friend and dauntless correspondent it is very creditable of you to have written to me after such a long hiatus. But instead of cursing so malignantly why don't you guess that I have been doing so much jogtrotting on atrocious horses and mules that I can't sit down to write, and that the temperature in these tropical regions is such that one's fingers refuse to hold the pen. This is an exaggeration.

The other day on a ride from Ceuta to Tetuan we essayed a most tremendous storm of hail and rain that made us shiver and set our half naked Arabs shaking in the most alarming way, but now the weather is beautiful and the temperature just what it ought to be. We have rented a little Moorish house (which we don't yet know from any other house in the town, the little white tortuous streets are so exactly alike) and we expect to enjoy a month or two in it very much. The patio open to the sky affords a studio light, and has the horseshoe arches arabesques, tiles and other traditional Moorish ornaments. The roof is a white terrace, one of the thousand that form this odd town, sloping down to the sea. All that has been written and painted about these African towns does not exaggerate the interest of at any rate, a first visit. Of course the poetic strain that writers launch forth in when they touch upon a certain degree of latitude and longitude—is to a great extent conventional; but certainly the aspect of the place is striking, the costume grand and the Arabs often magnificent.

* H. F. Stewart, "Memoirs of Francis Jenkinson," p. 80.

I regret the many months spent in Spain in the rain and bad weather that quite spoiled the trip as far as painting and enjoyment goes. When you carry out your plan of a visit to Spain, be sure to go in the spring; one loses too much by going there in December.

Best love to your people,

Your affectionate friend,

JOHN S. SARGENT.

This expedition to Spain and Morocco resulted in several of his well-known works—among them *Fumée d'Ambre Gris, The Alhambra, The Court of the Lions, Spanish Beggar Girl, Spanish Courtyard, El Jaleo* and the *Spanish Dance*, which, like so much of his early work, are now only to be seen in America.

El Jaleo was subsequently bought by Mr. T. Jefferson Coolidge, who told Mrs. Gardner that the picture should one day be hers. She had seen the picture at exhibitions, and satisfied herself that it would be shown to best advantage with the light coming from below. Anticipating the day when the picture would be hers, she built an alcove in her music-room at Fenway Court, framed in a Moorish arch, and along the floor arranged a row of electric lights which would reproduce, as far as possible, the conditions under which the picture had originally been painted. Mr. Coolidge, when he saw these preparations, accelerated his generous intentions and handed the picture over to be installed in this flattering environment.

Sargent was back in Paris in time to start with Helleu and Ralph Curtis for a tour in Holland, and to return before the opening of the Salon. It was his first opportunity of studying Franz Hals in his native country and in the fulness of his power. The impression was never forgotten. Indeed, Hals henceforward has to be reckoned as one of the formative constituents in his art. Many years later, to Miss Heyneman who was seeking advice from him, he said: "Begin with Franz Hals, copy and study Franz Hals, after that go to Madrid and copy Velasquez, leave Velasquez till you have got all you can out of Franz Hals."

Though preferences necessarily change in kind and degree and too much importance should not be attached to an artist's *obiter dicta,* it is of more than passing interest to note that once when discussing genius in painting he said that the four painters who in his opinion possessed it in a superlative degree were Rembrandt, Titian, Tintoretto and Raphael, and upon Velasquez being suggested, added that no painter exceeded Velasquez in technical skill, but that he was less gifted in his power to interpret "spiritual qualities."

While in Holland the party visited Scheveningen, and here Sargent did a sketch in oils of his friend Ralph Curtis, seated among the sand dunes. It is painted in a low key, soft in tone and delicate in colour, done obviously "au premier coup," and shows unmistakably that he was in these years inclining to the modern French school of painting.

In the same year, 1880, he exhibited at the Salon a portrait of *Mme. E. Pailleron,* the wife of the French author M. Edouard Pailleron and daughter of M. Buloz, then director of *La Revue des Deux Mondes,* also *Fumée d'Ambre Gris,* a study for which was shown at the Exhibition at the Royal Academy in January, 1926.

Chapter VIII

IN the late summer of 1880 Sargent went with his family
to Venice to the Hotel d'Italie, Piazza San Moisé. After
a few days he found a studio at the Palazzo Rezzonico,
Grand Canal, in which several American and French artists
were already installed. The Palazzo had become a sort of
barrack for artists, with some of the amenities of a palace and
the gaiety of the Latin Quarter. Here he worked during the
remainder of his stay.

Tiepolo, whom he considered as the first of decorative artists,
and Tintoretto were the painters whose works claimed his
attention at this time. He was soon a well-known figure in
Venice; daily he could be seen in a gondola, sketching with his
sister Emily, herself an accomplished water-colourist, in one of
the side canals, painting some architectural feature in the full
glory of sun and shadow, or seated with his easel on one of the
lesser piazzas making a study of a church façade, doorway, window,
or of any one of the thousand effects which Venice offers in
unique abundance. His art is seldom concerned with the actual
life of the place, its people, its ceremonies or customs; what he
sees is the Venice fashioned magically in stone, the glint on its
waters, the reflections on its walls, its gondolas, the spars and
sails of its shipping thrown against the background of a church,
or its dazzling sky mirrored on the dancing facets of an agitated
canal. He paints here, there and everywhere with a deliberate
nonchalance in the choice of his topics, taking things as they come;
discovering things as it were by accident, but seeing them with
an intensely personal outlook, more nearly concerned, in fact, with
how he sees and how he paints than with the associations of what
he sees. In Spain he had been caught by the "spirit of place" and
he had seemed for the time to enter into and become part of what
was in its essence racial and bone of its bone. Spanish dancing

53

had appealed to his love of the natural—to his pleasure in something at once vivid, elementary and pictorial. The subject itself had excited him with its grace and wildness, its colour and its attitudes. He had mixed with the people, not as a student observer, but on a basis of equality, catching the spirit and human significance of what he saw. But here in Venice it is as though he were setting out on the course he was to follow through his career; he is no longer interested in the people and their mode of life, his visual attention is absorbed by the surroundings in which they are merely negligible incidents. Henceforward it becomes more and more rare to find among his sketches any record of episodes characteristic of a people or a race or of the commerce of their daily lives; the *vox populi* seems to fall on deaf ears. But meanwhile he is shaping his own convention. He has his own individual way of looking at the world, and he is slave to no tradition. Problems of light and shadow were exercising the painters of the day in Paris, and in these he was experimenting, feeling his way to the solution which he ultimately evolved.

He stayed on in Venice through the late autumn, moving, when his family left, to 290, Piazza San Marco, All' Orologio, but retaining his studio at the Rezzonico. He exhibited at the Salon of 1881 four portraits—namely, *Portrait de M. R. S.* and *Portraits de M. E. P.*, and the portrait of Miss Burckhardt catalogued as *Mlle. L. P.*, and also known as *The Lady with a Rose*, of which Henry James wrote: "It offers the slightly uncanny spectacle of a talent which on the very threshold of its career has nothing more to learn. . . . The picture has this sign of productions of the first order, that its style would clearly save it, if everything else should change—our measure of value of its resemblance, its expression of character, the fashion of dress, the particular associations it evokes." Few of Sargent's portraits have so summarized the spirit of youth; none, perhaps, has rendered so exquisitely its unfolding fancies and aspirations and its inexperience. Here is a picture in which temperament has played a part; it is something more than the intellectual conception of a great painter. The delicate modelling of the head, the freshness of the colouring, the half-tones of the flesh, the ease which the artist has imported into a pose which leans to the artificial, and the mastery shown in the painting of the dress, mark it out as one of his most distinctive achievements. It invites comparison with Duran's *Lady with the Glove*, and measures how far the pupil had advanced beyond the highest effort of his master.

In June, 1881, Sargent was writing from Paris to Castillo in a spirit of youthful elation:

> Just a few frantic arabesques to acknowledge the receipt of your pleasant letters and communicate my plans. In the first place I have got a 2ieme *medaille* at the Salon and am *hors concours* and a great swell. I accept your congratulations. It is for that portrait of a Chilian lady (Mme. R. S.) that I was painting last summer Avenue du Bois de Boulogne.

Later he was in London staying with Mr. Joseph Farquharson, R.A., in Porchester Gardens, "to paint two heads" and see his parents and sisters off to America. Back again at 73, Rue Notre Dame des Champs, he reports that he is "painting portraits and getting along very well with the Spanish dancers" (*El Jaleo*) the picture which was to be famous in the Salon of 1882, and for which he had made several studies when in Spain.

That summer he sent some sketches to Vernon Lee. They had arrived in some disorder.

> As for the sketches (he wrote on receiving her acknowledgement) having arrived "*en compote*" I should think they could easily be cured by Heath Wilson, if he will take the trouble. I am convinced that the likeness of Miss Robinson is horrid and that she hates me and will never allow me to make amends. It is really hideous. Let Heath Wilson retouch it with a hot poker, and put an umbrella into it and open the umbrella. Your portrait might be varnished with light varnish. Verni Sochnee for instance. Don't let D or any of his boys varnish it: they have some wondrous prescription for making a picture blaze under a thick coat of enamel like a panel of a new carriage; "au surplus charmants garcons."

The letter which follows was written after reading Vernon Lee's volume of essays "Belcaro." In the essay "In Umbria" she had discussed the relation of an artist to his work. "Can a pure and exquisite work be produced by a base nature?" was the question she propounded. Her answer had been very decidedly in the affirmative. She had attacked the doctrine of Ruskin and contended that artistic talent achieved its end independently of creed or sentiment—a theme which she had illustrated by the case of Perugino, the professional purveyor of religious art, whose pictures had been dictated by a purely commercial instinct and bore no relation to his inner beliefs.

March 24th, 1882.

My dear Violet,

I have put off writing to you till I had read your book (Belcaro), and lately I have had very little time. I am quite delighted with it and I think it is a book that will do a great deal of good, and I hope it is very much read, for your view of art is the only true one. Of course your book is addressed to a public entirely different from *me,* for instance. To me the conclusions you come to, or the feeling you start from, are altogether natural and self evident, and need no debating; and the chief interest of the book to me is to know that you possess the right idea. The arguments you used and the process of convincing I watch as an outsider, not having any doubts myself. I think your theory of the all-importance of beauty and its independence of or its hostility to sentiment applies admirably to the antique, and to the short great period of art in Italy. It is certain that at certain times talent entirely overcomes thought or poetry. In decadence, this occurred to an outrageous extent. It is another question and I suppose a matter of personal feeling whether that state of things is more interesting than another; Whether Raphael in his cartoons at Hampton Court is more admirable than in the Sposalizio, or whether he is more admirable at all than Botticelli. There are some like Dürer and Rembrandt and the French Millet who are very "inquiètants" for one who thinks as you do, for their talent is enormous too and they have "intimité." Perhaps we will have a chance to skirmish together, for I think very likely I will go to Florence this summer. With love to all your circle,

Your old friend,

John S. Sargent.

His two pictures in the Salon of 1882 were singled out by the critics for unqualified praise. "Before the portrait" (*Mrs.*

SPANISH WOMAN.

Austin), Jules Comte wrote, "one does not know which to admire most, the simplicity of the means which the artist has employed or the brilliance of the result which he has achieved." Henry Houssaye declared that *El Jaleo* was the most striking picture of the year. Thus at the age of twenty-six Sargent, an American, was being hailed in Paris as the author of the two outstanding pictures of the Salon. If it be true that art knows no nationality (did not Whistler say that you might as well talk of English mathematics as of English art?), the same might have been said, at any rate in 1882, of criticism, for here was a foreign artist, little more than of age, measuring himself beside the established favourites of Paris, beside Duran and Bonnat, Bougereau and Dagnan Bouveret, Bastien Lepage, Besnard, Boldini and the Impressionists, and being acclaimed as the most successful painter of the year. He was soon receiving as many commissions as he could execute, charging for a full length eight thousand francs, for a half length five thousand, and for his subject pictures and landscapes anything from two to four thousand.

In the late summer of 1882 he was again in Italy, staying in Venice with the Curtises, the parents of his friend Ralph Curtis, at the Palazzo Barbaro, where in 1896 he painted the *Venetian Interior*, his diploma picture at the Royal Academy. In the autumn he was in Rome and Florence and visited Siena. Here, as Ralph Curtis wrote, the early art of Italy started in Sargent a strong sympathy for the Pre-Raphaelite painters; so much so that in 1884 Curtis had some misgiving lest Sargent, when he migrated to London, might allow his genius to be drawn towards this already over-tilled, if not exhausted field of painting.

In 1883 Sargent exhibited at the Salon his picture of tne Boit children under the title of *Portraits d'Enfants*, and was criticized for "its four corners and a void" and the abbreviated execution, but the most captious acknowledged the beauty of the figures of the children, shown under a strong light upon a background of deep shadow relieved by a faint indication of light through a small window. What strikes the observer, in spite of the rather scattered composition, is the unity of the general impression, and this arrests his attention before his eye begins to take in the detail. The field of vision is occupied by delicately adjusted masses of light and dark, and then as the eye changes its focus, the skill with which the painter has modulated his degrees of definition from the child seated in the foreground to the children further removed and the just-suggested objects in the background becomes strikingly apparent. Henry James in "Picture and Text" declared it to be an achievement "as astonishing on the part of a young man of twenty-six as the portrait of 1881 was astonishing on the part of a young man of twenty-four."

At the end of 1883 Sargent changed his address from 73, Rue Notre Dame des Champs to 41, Boulevard Berthier, and at the beginning of 1884 he went to pay his usual visit to his parents, who for the last few years had been spending their winters at Nice. In March, 1884, he was present in London at a dinner given by Edwin Abbey and Alfred Parsons to the American actor Lawrence Barrett.

A GAME OF CHESS.

Chapter IX

IN 1883 Sargent had begun a portrait which was to have a good deal of influence on his career. As far back as 1881 he had met Madame Gautreau in Paris society, where she moved rather conspicuously, shining as a star of considerable beauty, and drawing attention as one dressed in advance of her epoch. It was the period in which in London the professional beauty, with all the specialization which the term connoted, was recognized as having a definite rôle in the social hierarchy. Madame Gautreau occupied a corresponding position in Paris. Immediately after meeting her, Sargent wrote to his friend del Castillo to find out if he could do anything to induce Madame Gautreau to sit to him. "I have," he wrote, "a great desire to paint her portrait and have reason to think she would allow it and is waiting for someone to propose this homage to her beauty. If you are 'bien avec elle' and will see her in Paris you might tell her that I am a man of *prodigious talent*." The necessary preliminaries were arranged, and the disillusionment seems to have begun quickly, for after the first few sittings he wrote to Vernon Lee from Nice on February 10 (1883): "In a few days I shall be back in Paris, tackling my other 'envoi,' the Portrait of a Great Beauty. Do you object to people who are 'fardées' to the extent of being a uniform lavender or blotting-paper colour all over? If so you would not care for my sitter; but she has the most beautiful lines, and if the lavender or chlorate of potash-lozenge colour be pretty in itself I should be more than pleased." In another letter, and again to Vernon Lee, he wrote: "Your letter has just reached me still in this country house (Les Chênes Paramé) struggling with the unpaintable beauty and hopeless laziness of Madame Gautreau."

Even when the picture was nearing completion he was assailed by misgivings. "My portrait!" he wrote to Castillo, "it is much changed and far more advanced than when you last saw it. One day I was dissatisfied with it and dashed a tone of light rose over the former gloomy background. I turned the picture upside down, retired to the other end of the studio and looked at it under my arm. Vast improvement. The *élancée* figure of the model shows to much greater advantage. The picture is framed and on a great easel, and Carolus has been to see it and said: 'Vous pouvez l'envoyer au Salon avec confiance.' Encouraging, but false. I have made up my mind to be refused."

The picture was accepted for the Salon of 1884. Varnishing day did nothing to reassure the painter. On the opening day he was in a state of extreme nervousness. It was the seventh successive year in which he had exhibited. Every Salon had seen the critics more favourable, the public more ready to applaud. But without suggesting that the critics and public of Paris are fickle, it is probably fair to say that popularity, fame and reputation are more subject to violent fluctuations there than in other European capitals. This, at any rate, was to be Sargent's experience. The doors of the Salon were hardly open before the picture was damned. The public took upon themselves to inveigh against the flagrant insufficiency, judged by prevailing standards, of the sitter's clothing; the critics fell foul of the execution. The Parisian public is always vocal and expressive. The Salon was in an uproar. Here was an occasion such as they had not had since *Le Déjeuner sur l'Herbe, L'Olympia* and the Exhibition of the Independents. The onslaught was led by the lady's relatives. A demand was made that the picture should be withdrawn. It is not among the least of the curiosities of human nature, that while an individual will confess and even call attention to his own failings, he will deeply resent the same office being undertaken by someone else. So it was with the dress of Madame Gautreau. Here a distinguished artist was proclaiming to the public in paint a fact about herself which she had hitherto never made any attempt to conceal, one which had, indeed, formed one of her many social assets. Her resentment was profound. If the picture could not be withdrawn, the family might at least bide its time, wait till the Salon was closed, the picture delivered, and then by destroying, blot it as an unclean thing from the records of the family. Anticipating this, Sargent, before the exhibition was over, took it away himself. After remaining many years in his studio it now figures as one of the glories of the Metropolitan Museum in New York. The scene at the Salon is described in a letter written by Sargent's friend and fellow-painter, Ralph Curtis, to his parents. It will be noticed that at a certain point Sargent's forbearance gave way and that his pugnacity, which has already been referred to, burst out:

MY DEAR PEOPLE,

Your paper will be ordered this a.m. Yesterday the birthday or funeral of the painter Scamps (John Sargent). Most exquis. weather Walked up Champs E. chestnuts in full flower and dense mob of " tout Paris " in pretty clothes, gesticulating and laughing, slowly going into the Ark of Art. In 15 mins. I saw no end of acquaintances and strangers, and heard every one say " où est le portrait Gautreau ? " " Oh allez voir ça "—John covered with dust stopped with his trunks at the club the night before and took me on to his house where we dined. He was very nervous about what he feared, but his fears were far exceeded by the facts of yesterday. There was a grande tapage before it all day. In a few minutes I found him dodging behind doors to avoid friends who looked grave. By the corridors he took me to see it. I was disappointed in the colour. She looks decomposed. All the women jeer. Ah voilà " la belle ! " " Oh quel horreur ! " etc. Then a painter exclaims " superbe de style," " magnifique d'audace ! " " quel dessin ! " Then the blageur club man—" C'est une copie ! " " Comment une cope ? " " Mais oui—la peinture d'après un autre morceau de peinture s'appelle une copie." I heard that. All the a.m. it was one series of bons mots, mauvaises plaisanteries and fierce discussions. John, poor boy, was navré. We got out a big déjeuner at Ledoyens of a dozen painters and ladies and I took him there. In the p.m. the tide turned as I kept saying it would. It was discovered to be the knowing thing to say " étrangement épatant ! " I went home with him, and remained there while he went to see the Boits. Mde. Gautreau and mère came to his studio " bathed in tears." I stayed them off but the mother returned and caught him and made a fearful scene saying " Ma fille est perdue—tout Paris se moque d'elle. Mon genre sera forcé de se battre. Elle mourira de chagrin " etc. John replied it was against all laws to retire a picture. He had painted her exactly as she was dressed, that nothing could be said of the canvas worse than had been said in print of her appearance dans le monde etc. etc. Defending his cause made him feel much better. Still we talked it all over till 1 o'clock here last night and I fear he has never had such a blow. He says he wants to get out of Paris for a time. He goes to Eng. in 3 weeks. I fear là bas he will fall into Pre-R. influence wh. has got a strange hold of him he says *since Siena.*

I want him to go to Seville and do the tobacco girls with me in Nov. Says he will—nous verrons.

It would be wearisome to quote at any length the criticisms which appeared. Extracts from *La Revue des Deux Mondes* and *L'Illustration* will suffice to show at once the fallibility of even the most enlightened, and also the antagonism which the picture roused. In *La Revue des Deux Mondes* Henry Houssaye wrote:

> Nous allions, oublier, le grand succès au Salon; car il y a succès et succès; le portrait de Mme. . . . par M. Sargent. Le profil est pointu, l'oeil microscopique, la bouche imperceptible, le teint biafard, le cou cordé, le bras droit desorticulé, la main desossée; le corsage decolleté ne tient pas au buste et semble fuire le contact de la chair.* Le talent au peintre se retrouve seulement dans les reflets miroitants de la jupe de satin noir. Faire d'une jeune femme justement renommée pour sa beauté, une sorte de portrait-charge, violà à quoi mênent le parti pris d'une exécution lachée et les éloges donnés sans mesure.

In *L'Illustration* Jules Comte, one of the most authoritative critics of the day, expressed himself as follows:

> Quelle amère désillusion nous attendait devant l'oeuvre du peintre. . . . Sans doute, nous retrouvons de la grace dans les attaches, surtout dans celle du cou, qui est delicieuse, et la pose ne manque pas de souplesse, mais comment a-t-il pu songer a peindre ainsi Mme. X . . . sèche, rèche, anguleuse? On dirait, en face de ce profil sans ligne, un papier decoupé, et encore quelle decoupure. . . . Pas l'ombre de dessin dans la bouche; le nez n'est ni modelé, ni fait seulement; pas de plans dans ce visage plaque, et quel teint, et quelle couleur . . .
>
> Jamais nous n'avions vu pareille déchéance d'un artiste qui avait semblé donner plus que dès esperances. Mais voilà, on n'a pas le temps de reflèchir, on veut aller vite, et on arrive a n'être plus capable de subir des influences. Il y a deux ans, on parlait de GOYA à propos

---

* Albert Woolf wrote in the *Figaro* in reference to the dress: "One more struggle and the lady will be free."

MADAME GAUTREAU.
Gardner, Fenway Court Museum.

de M. Sargent, qui revenait d'Espagne: nous ne savons où il est allé depuis lors; mais on dirait qu'il n'a plus regardé que de l'imagerie japonaise.

De Fourcaud, writing in the *Gazette des Beaux Arts*, said that anyone standing before the picture could in a very little time fill ten pages with the adjectives, violent and contradictory, which were pronounced by the spectators. Détestable! Ennuyeux! Curieux! Monstruéux! he gives as examples. He goes on to say that the critics fell into three divisions: those who exclaimed in pious horror at the decolletage, those who recognized the picture as evidence of modernity and applauded the artist's courage, and, lastly, those who condemned the picture for the monochrome colour of the flesh tints. De Fourcaud himself recognizes the picture as a masterpiece, not only for the extreme serenity and rhythm of the lines, but for the summary it presents of the psychology of a professional beauty, who, if regarded and treated only as such by the world, ends by being less a woman than as it were a canon of worldly beauty, dressed, posed and with her whole outlook adjusted to the supreme purpose of the rôle to which society has condemned her. That indeed, is what the artist has achieved in this masterly portrait.

Here, perhaps, in sheer beauty of line he has approached as near to Ingres as at any time in his career. If we could eliminate the content of the picture and reduce it to the outline in which the figure, the dress and the poise of the head are contained, we should have before us a drawing of free and flowing lines, rhythmic as the stem of a flower.

Sargent, who was now twenty-eight, had been working for ten years in Paris. The Salon of 1884 was to have been a culmination of his efforts. He had painted what is now recognized as a masterpiece, displaying excellences which he was perhaps never to surpass. It had been received with a storm of abuse. Paris, which had been smooth and well-disposed and encouraging, had turned, and like a child splintering a plaything, had dealt a violent blow at its recognized favourite. He was not in the least in doubt about his art, but he was always sensitive to atmosphere, always easily affected by an unsympathetic environment. Paris had awakened suddenly one May morning in an uncongenial mood, its friendliness hidden in clouds; the accord which had prevailed between painter and public was at an end. Was it worth while to try and readjust the relation and reconcile the differences? Was the disappointment accentuated by the unwitting offence given to a reigning beauty? We do not know. A certain mystery hangs over the whole affair. Sargent was undoubtedly mortified and sore; that, at least, is clear. Perhaps a combination of reasons was urging him to take advantage of the opening which offered itself in London. However that may be, it was to London that he made up his mind to migrate.

Seven years later, in 1891, the same lady was painted by Gustave Courtois. He, too, chose to represent her with her face in direct profile, but turned so that her eyes look to the left side of the canvas. He, too, portrayed her with very much the same openness of attire that had aroused such a storm in 1884. But seven years had brought a change in the way such things were regarded. The picture, which now hangs in the Luxembourg, was accepted by the public without comment, its propriety was unquestioned. The pious protests of 1884 were silent before the revolutionized fashions of 1891. Only one further communication seems to have passed between Sargent and his offended model. In 1906, as the following letter to Major Roller shows, Madame Gautreau had very much modified her opinion of the picture:

PALAZZO BARBARO,
VENICE,
Oct. 3rd, 1906.

MY DEAR ROLLER,

 I think I know what Mme. Gautreau wants to see me about. She wrote me last year of a matter of vital importance—it was that the Kaiser who was such a dear, thought her portrait the most fascinating woman's likeness that he has ever seen, and that he wishes me to have an exhibition in Berlin of my things. I wrote that I was abroad and couldn't manage it. But to tell you the truth, I don't want to do it. It is a tremendous trouble for me to induce a lot of unwilling people to lend me their "pautrets" and Berlin does not attract me at all.

ON THE THAMES AT CALCOT.

So if you are taken into Mme. Gautreau's confidence, and I wish you would tear your shirt for it, please discourage her from giving me the K.K. command.

Yrs. sincerely,
JOHN S. SARGENT.

In 1916 the picture was exhibited at the San Francisco Exhibition, and in January of that year Sargent wrote to his friend Edward Robinson, the well-known director of the Metropolitan Museum:

31, TITE STREET,
CHELSEA,
Jan. 8, 1916.

MY DEAR NED,

. . . The permission to communicate with the Museum when I have something that I think worthy of it, makes me venture to suggest to you, rather than to the Trustees, a proposition for what you may think of it. My portrait of Madame Gautreau is now, with some other things I sent from here at the San Francisco Exhibition and now that it is in America I rather feel inclined to let it stay there if a Museum should want it. I suppose it is the best thing I have done. I would let the Metropolitan Museum have it for £1,000. . . . Let me know your opinion. . . . If Madame Gautreau should not stay in America I think she had better come back here with the rest of my things.

Yrs. ever,
JOHN S. SARGENT.

Fortunately, owing to the generosity of Sir Joseph Duveen, the Tate Gallery possesses a study of the same subject, but whether this was done before or after the picture in the Metropolitan Museum I have been unable to discover. Several drawings of Madame Gautreau's profile were found among Sargent's sketches. She is also the subject of another oil-painting now at Fenway Court, and bequeathed, with her other possessions, to the United States by Mrs. Gardner.*

* See p. 62.

Chapter X

IN the same year (1884), while Madame Gautreau from the walls of the Salon was like the goddess Clotho spinning the fate of Sargent's future destiny, his portrait of Mrs. Henry White, exhibited in the Royal Academy, was exciting even more than usual contradiction among the critics. Opinion fluctuated between the extreme condemnation of *The Athenæum*, which described the picture as "hard, metallic, raw in colour, and without taste in the expression, air and modelling," and the praise of R. A. M. Stevenson, which, though delivered later, represented, as did all that came from his pen, what may be considered the more instructed view of the time. Stevenson found in the picture "that large and noble disposition which we admire so much in the old Masters." "The wavering silhouette," he continued, "of the figure, now firmly detached from and now sliding off into its surroundings, may be followed with pleasure even if held upside down. It falls into a perfect scheme of decorative effect, and yet it relieves from its environment with all the consistency and variety of truth." Mrs. White was the wife of Mr. Henry White, first secretary to the American Embassy in London; she occupied a prominent position in that society of Mayfair, through which Sargent was so soon to paint his way. The portrait was hung in the dining-room of Mr. White's house in Grosvenor Crescent, and there, where it formed the subject of constant discussion, not always well-informed but none the less dogmatic, it fulfilled a missionary and educational purpose, making the name of Sargent familiar to many and gradually enrolling supporters to a new canon of taste in portraiture.

The portrait created that gap in the fence which is so helpful to wealthy patrons of painting seeking for a lead across country which they can follow with security. It seemed at that time as

66

abrupt a departure from the smooth conventions of the portraiture of the day as might a Cézanne from a Birkett Foster. The highest praise, perhaps, to which in social circles it was at first considered entitled was the indefinite pronouncement that it was "chic personified in paint." By degrees, however, it won its way and gave a decisive lead, bringing many applicants to Sargent's door. It is worth contrasting the two portraits of this year, that of Madame Gautreau in Paris and that of Mrs. White in London, because they represent two currents in Sargent's painting, to one or other of which he had still definitely to commit himself. The beauty of Madame Gautreau's portrait lies, as has been suggested, in the delicacy and rhythm of the lines, and the sculpturesque and plastic forms which they embody. It is one of the very few of Sargent's pictures in which there is any trace of the Italian influence of which he was so much aware at this time, and which, if rumour speaks correctly, he was ready to admit to a share in his development. In the extreme simplification of the design and in the sensitive line of the profile it is perhaps not fanciful to detect a suggestion of the manner of Piero della Francesca. The picture, which is daring and original, owes little to contemporary Paris influences. Mrs. White's portrait, on the other hand, has for its dominant theme the effect of light on the subject painted, on the planes and ordered tumult of the dress, on the background and accessories, on the features of the model. The form of the furniture is hinted at rather than defined. Sargent has, in fact, in this picture incorporated just so much of the method of the Luminists as he was to carry with him through the rest of his work as an artist. It represents the direction in which he was tending; it is the first presage of his London as distinguished from his Paris manner. He was to revert, in certain instances, to his earlier vision; but from 1884 we can date the growth of his ultimate method of expression. Did the reception accorded the Gautreau portrait influence his outlook? Nothing seems more improbable; complete sincerity was his most prevailing characteristic. Just as his spoken word was the accurate reflection of his character and thought, so his painting was the inevitable means by which he expressed what he saw; from neither would the clamour of opinion have deflected him in the slightest degree.

In the summer of 1884, after leaving Paris, he painted the picture of the Misses Vickers which was exhibited at the Salon in 1885, and sent to the Academy in 1886. Sargent owed his introduction to the Vickers family to an amateur sculptor and painter named Natop, then working in Paris. The Vickers, quick to appreciate the talent of the painter, became the first English patrons of his art in England. He was invited to Lavington Rectory, which the Vickers had taken, near Petworth, and here he made a study of the children with white lilies, also *The Dinner Table*, with at it Mr. and Mrs. Albert Vickers, and a portrait of *Mrs. Albert Vickers*.* Everything connected with country life in England was new to him. The climate, the windy skies, the sedate and tranquil landscape, the flowers and vegetation, the placid summer light—all came upon him with the interest of novelty, but without witchery or enticement. The impression made by the trees and scenery of England roused in him no enthusiasm; at the moment his vision was occupied with the gardens and the large white lilies; and his astonishment at the growth of rambling cucumbers was such that he was unable to demur to the suggestion that he must till then have thought they grew in slices. From Lavington he went to Bolsover Hill, Sheffield, the home of another branch of the family, where he remained for three weeks painting the Misses Vickers. At the Academy the picture is authoritatively stated to have been rejected by the judging committee, and only accepted on an intimation from Herkomer that he would resign unless the picture was recalled and hung "on the line." It also obtained a majority in a *plebiscite* instituted by the *Pall Mall Gazette*, as the worst picture of the year. It was the painter's first important attempt at a group, and represents three sisters, resembling in this respect his pictures of the Hunters, the Wyndhams and the Achesons. Here, as in the

---

* His only English portrait before this date was *Mrs. Wodehouse Legh* (Lady Newton), painted in Paris.

STUDY OF SWANS.

Hunter and Wyndham groups, he has portrayed the three sisters seated. In none of his other pictures has he succeeded more admirably in producing an entirely natural and familiar arrangement without its being in the least commonplace. No adventitious accessory is introduced. Nothing takes the eye from the grouped figures. It is no formal study. The sisters seem simply to have subsided into those attitudes, precisely as they might have done had no painter been present. This naturalness is more noticeable here than in his later groups, where the arrangement of the figures sometimes looks like a device to produce a required effect. Here the background is no more than the necessary *repoussoir* for the figures; details are repressed; a deep shadow fills the back of the canvas, broken by a subdued light in the right-hand corner, which, as in the picture of the Boit children, comes from a window at the end of the room. As a matter of fidelity to fact it may be questioned whether it is possible for the light of day to illuminate the figures as it does, without dispelling a good deal of the obscurity in the room—a criticism equally applicable to the picture of the Boit children, but one to which there are obvious answers.

In November, 1884, Sargent was at Bournemouth doing a portrait of Robert Louis Stevenson. "Sargent," wrote Stevenson, "has been and painted my portrait: a very nice fellow he is, and is supposed to have done well; it is a poetical but very chicken-boned figure-head, as thus represented."

In the winter of that year he was back again in Paris. There he was at home among the painters. Degas, Renoir, Sisley and Pissarro were among those he saw most often, but Claude Monet was the artist of all others with whom he was on the most friendly terms. The common meeting-ground was the gallery of M. Durand-Ruel, then at 16, Rue Lafitte. Pissaro, at this time under the influence of Paul Signac and Seurat, was breaking away from the Impressionists, and in a lapse which was to prove temporary, was painting in the *pointilliste* or *néo-impressioniste* manner. At the Durand-Ruel gallery this method excited lively debates. It met with little approval, and Renoir would greet Pissarro with the ironic salutation of "Bon jour, Seurat." They agreed only in the condemnation of official art, and as to this, unanimity prevailed. Apart from the painters, he saw little of the French; his associates were the Burckhardts, the Boits, William Dana, Julian Story and Miss Strettell (Mrs. Harrison). At the Louvre, where he was a constant visitor, he studied Rubens and the Primitives.

Early in 1885 he moved to London and engaged a studio at 13, Tite Street (subsequently renumbered as 33, Tite Street), of which he took a twenty-one years' lease in 1900. It was the first step in his career as a painter in London. 13, Tite Street had previously belonged to Whistler, who had decorated it with a scheme of yellow, so vehement that it gave a visitor the sensation of standing inside an egg.* At the beginning of 1885 Whistler had moved his studio from Tite Street to 454, Fulham Road.

Beyond Henry James and the American artists then painting in England Sargent knew few people. He was taking a venturesome step. In Paris he had left behind him that cosmopolitan world from which his sitters had been principally drawn. He was little known in England either personally or by reputation, and what was known about him placed him rather in the position of an accused or, at any rate, of a suspect. Did he not come equipped with the French artistic outfit, and was not all French art suspect? Whistler had been bad enough, and here was another American, also trained in the studios of Paris, bringing with him, in all probability, the intolerable provocations of French technique; and, moreover, it was distaste for Paris rather than preference for London that had induced Sargent to change his scene. The citadel that he had set out to capture was not easy. He was twenty-eight years of age, his frame more solid than of yore, and of athletic build, his face now fuller but handsome and distinguished in feature and expression. His hair and beard were dark; his complexion was ruddy. His eyes were of a vivid grey-blue with a reflective intensity in them when his interest was aroused like one musing upon the page of a book. A musician, a linguist, widely read in the literature of both

* E. R. and J. Pennell, "The Life of James Whistler," i., p. 300.

England and France, and as deeply proficient in the history and theory of art as he was in its practice, he was well equipped for winning his way and overcoming opposition and prejudice. His attitude towards his own talents was marked by slightly amused humility, probably less noticeable during the ardours and aspirations of his youth than later, which, having its root in an innate modesty and genial irony, can never have been entirely absent. Seriously as he regarded art, and high as he put an artist's calling, he had neither the arrogance of the dedicated spirit, nor the pretensions of the prophet. G. F. Watts, R.A., said of himself that his aim was to do for modern thought what Michael Angelo had done for theological thought; such a purpose would have been inconceivable to Sargent, passionately absorbed though he was in painting. His object was to record with the utmost skill attainable the thing as he saw it, without troubling about its ethical significance or, indeed, any significance other than its visual value. Perhaps for this reason he was least successful, when towards the end of his career he was pushed by circumstances into painting to meet a particular demand, to play the part of a laureate on canvas, and to celebrate subjects of the Great War not so interesting to the eye of the painter as exciting to the historian, poet or patriot. But at the outset of his London career no such problems presented themselves. He was there to paint in his own way with only one task before him, to put at the service of art his own vigorous and accomplished technique.

Chapter XI

SARGENT'S acquaintance with Gloucestershire and the west of England began at Broadway. In 1885 (he had then been settled in Tite Street some six months) he went with the American artist Edwin Austin Abbey for a boating expedition on the Thames from Oxford to Windsor. At Pangbourne Sargent, who was a fine swimmer, dived from the weir and "struck a spike with his head," Abbey wrote, "cutting a big gash in the top. It has healed wonderfully well, but it was a nasty rap. It was here that he saw the effect of the Chinese lanterns hung among the trees and the beds of lilies. . . . After his head was bound up he knocked it a second time and reopened the wound." * Abbey insisted on Sargent coming to Broadway to recover, and so in September, 1885, Sargent took up his residence at the Lygon Arms, the seventeenth-century inn in that village. He carried with him a sketch of the effect he had noted on the river. It was the origin (so far, at any rate, as the arrangement of light) of the picture *Carnation, Lily, Lily Rose.*

In those days Broadway had not added to its serpentine length a tail of modern dwellings; the traveller from the vale of Evesham to the Cotswolds was met, at his entrance into the village, by the sight of Russell House, with its tithe barn and old-world aspect.

In 1885 the Millets and Abbey were sharing Farnham House, which lies a few paces higher up the village street. Of this place Sir Edmund Gosse wrote:† "The Millets possessed on their domain a mediæval ruin, a small ecclesiastical edifice, which was very roughly repaired so as to make a kind of refuge for us, and there Henry James and I would write, while Abbey and Millet painted on the floor below and Sargent and Parsons tilted their easels just outside."

* E. V. Lucas, "Life of Edwin Austin Abbey," i., p. 151.
† "Letters of Henry James," i., p. 88.

72

Here in 1885 a group of friends, united by intellectual and artistic interests, foregathered: Edmund Gosse, Henry James, Alfred Parsons, Fred Barnard, Sargent, Abbey, Millet and others. Henry James, then forty-two, had been resident in England since 1876. He had just completed "The Princess Casamassima" and the "Bostonians," which was appearing in the *Century Magazine*.

After many wanderings he had settled in London, and was slowly accustoming himself to the intellectual atmosphere of England, which after the vivacity and *raffinement* of Paris had seemed at first "like a sort of glue-pot." Since 1881 Henry James had been writing in Paris appreciative reviews of Sargent's work. In 1884 he wrote to William James: "I have seen several times the gifted Sargent, whose work I admire exceedingly, and who is a remarkably artistic nature and a charming fellow." Their friendship had therefore begun before their meeting at Broadway. But Henry James was not the only man of letters in the party who had learnt to appreciate Sargent's work. In 1880 Sir Edmund Gosse, as a young author and critic, had been sent to Paris by John Morley to write about pictures and statues in the Salon, for the *Pall Mall Gazette*, and he had contributed an article to the *Fortnightly Review* on the same subject. He, too, had recognized the genius of Sargent. Up to this time (1885) Sargent's exhibits at the Academy,* and his pictures at the Grosvenor Gallery, had been received with a very tepid measure of approval by the critics. *The Spectator*, writing of the *Misses Vickers*, perhaps went further than most of its contemporaries. "And yet," its critic wrote, "when it is all done what good is it? . . . no human being except a painter can take pleasure in such work as this . . . but genuine lasting pleasure can no man take in what is essentially shallow, pretentious and untrue." To find himself now at Broadway with two distinguished men of letters devoted to his cause, and among fellow-countrymen and enthusiastic admirers, must have seemed to Sargent like sailing into port.

Those who saw the study of the Vickers children at the

* *A Portrait* (1882), *Mrs. Henry White* (1884), *Lady Playfair* (1885).

Academy in 1926 will have realized that it obviously contained the first suggestion for the picture *Carnation, Lily, Lily Rose*. It was painted at Lavington Rectory in 1884. Two children are seen working in a garden, with tall white lilies, similar to those in the final picture, growing in the background. The vision must have remained latent in the painter's mind, and been evoked by the scene witnessed on the river, the mauve light, produced by twilight and Chinese lanterns, and the white frocks of the two children. Sargent was resolved to paint this scene. At first he took as his model Mrs. Millet's small daughter, aged five, covering her dark hair with a fair golden wig and sketching her in the act of lighting a Chinese lantern at the moment when the sun had set and a flush still hung in the sky. While engaged on the sketch he saw the two Barnard children, then aged seven and eleven, who, with their parents, were living in a house near by. They were of a more suitable age, and their hair was the exact colour Sargent wanted; he asked Mrs. Barnard to let the children pose. It is the Misses Barnard who figure in the picture.

Never for any picture did he do so many studies and sketches. He would hang about like a snapshot photographer to catch the children in attitudes helpful to his main purpose. "Stop as you are," he would suddenly cry as the children were at play, "don't *move!* I must make a sketch of you," and there and then he would fly off, leaving the children immobile as Lot's wife, to return in a moment with easel, canvas and paint-box.

The progress of the picture (Sir Edmund Gosse writes), when once it began to advance, was a matter of excited interest to the whole of our little artist-colony. Everything used to be placed in readiness, the easel, the canvas, the flowers, the demure little girls in their white dresses, before we began our daily afternoon lawn tennis, in which Sargent took his share. But at the exact moment, which of course came a minute or two earlier each evening, the game was stopped, and the painter was accompanied to the scene of his labours. Instantly, he took up his place at a distance from the canvas, and at a certain notation of the light ran forward over the lawn with the action of a wag-tail, planting at the same time rapid dabs of paint on the picture, and then retiring again, only with equal suddenness to repeat the wag-tail action. All this occupied but two or three minutes, the light rapidly declining, and then while he left the young ladies to remove his machinery, Sargent would join us again, so long as the twilight permitted, in a last turn at lawn tennis.*

These brief sessions every evening went on from August till the beginning of November, and when the evenings grew more chilly Sargent would dress the children in white sweaters which came down to their ankles, over which he pulled the dresses that appear in the picture. He himself would be muffled up like an Arctic explorer. At the same time the roses gradually faded and died, and Marshall and Snelgrove had to be requisitioned for artificial substitutes, which were fixed to the withered bushes. Sargent could be charming with children, natural and easy, without condescension or an appearance of talking down to their level. But he was no indiscriminating worshipper of childhood, and sentimental generalizations on the subject found him an unsympathetic hearer. When harassed by the persistence and too untutored flutterings of an uncongenial child he has even been heard to murmur a regret "for the good old days of Herod." At Broadway for the Christmas festivities of 1886, a cousin of the Barnards, aged nine, was introduced at dinner, immensely trimmed and polished for the occasion. Sargent, beaming down on him, said: "So young and yet so clean." The felicity of the immediate reply, "So old and yet so artistic," secured for the precocious boy a staunch friend. To the Barnard children he was devotedly attached, and the friendship formed with them as children ran rejoicingly through his entire life. Here at Broadway he was drawing rather drastically on their endurance and patience. But he got them interested in the picture, and each day's preparations were an event.

In November, 1885, the unfinished picture was stored in the Millets' barn. When in 1886 the Barnard children returned to Broadway the sittings were resumed.

One of the difficulties was the provision of the necessary flowers. When the Millets moved into Russell House a flower bed was cut in the garden and the country was ransacked for roses, carnations and lilies. Sargent, chancing on half an acre

* Letter from Sir Edmund Gosse to the author.

of roses in full bloom in a nursery garden at Willersey, said to the proprietor: "I'll take them all, dig them up and send them along this afternoon." The letter of which a facsimile is printed opposite shows the artist's own sense of his task. The whole episode illustrates his thoroughness. He left no stone unturned, he suffered no obstacle to bar his passage, where his art was concerned. When abroad in the same spirit he would cross a glacier, skirt the edge of a chasm or climb a precipice to gain a coign of visual vantage. And yet, even in 1885, in the midst of these activities, he appears to have entertained the thought of giving up art. On this point we have the testimony of Sir Edmund Gosse.

> At this time (Broadway, 1885), I saw more of him than at any other time, and if I have anything worth relating it was gathered during these enchanted weeks. In the first place I must say that the moment was a transitional one in the painter's career. He was profoundly dissatisfied with Paris, though I am not sure that I know why. He was determined to shake the dust of it off his shoes. He was certainly unwilling to settle in America, and he looked in vain (for the moment) for any genuine invitation to stay in England. His sitters were all American birds of passage: I recall the Vickers family who kept him copiously occupied. In this juncture, it will perhaps be believed with difficulty that he talked of giving up art altogether. I remember his telling me this in one of our walks, and the astonishment it caused me. Sargent was so exclusively an artist that one could think of no other occupation. "But then," I cried, "whatever will you do?" "Oh," he answered, "I shall go into business." "What kind of business?" I asked in bewilderment. "Oh, I don't know!" with a vague wave of the hand, "or go in for music, don't you know?"

Sir Edmund was impressed by Sargent's comments on pictures; they

> "showed the extreme independence of his eye. For instance," he continues, "although I believed myself intelligently occupied with contemporary art, and rather proud of my acquaintance with the latest French painting, Sargent's trenchant criticisms quite knocked me off my legs. At that time English taste accepted Gérome's elegant nudities without reserve, and Sargent instructed me that they were all sugar and varnish. But even more surprising to me were the liberties he took with the painters who were the immediate darlings of the Parisian œsthetic press, such as Henner and Rolland

and that meteoric genius the unfortunate Bastien-Lepage, much worshipped in the innermost American circles. "Tricks!" Sargent succinctly defined the famous optical concentration of Bastien-Lepage. But most revolutionary for me, was his serene and complete refusal to see anything at all in the works of Alma Tadema, then in the zenith of his fame. "I suppose it's clever," he said, "of course it *is* clever—like the things you do, don't you know, with a what d'you call—but of course it's not art in any sense whatever," with which cryptic pronouncement I was left awed and shaken. These judgments on fellow-artists were, doubtless, exacerbated by the crisis Sargent was himself passing through, but they were wholly sincere, and they were pronounced without a trace of animosity or passion. Sargent's dislike of Alma Tadema's painting here expressed was accompanied with the highest deference to his knowledge and opinion. There were few artists for whose artistic judgment Sargent entertained such cordial respect, none that he was more ready to consult as a critic. His own practice of painting at this time, interested me, especially as, though I had lived much with artists, the manner of it was quite unfamiliar. Sargent started a new canvas every morning, painting for a couple of hours at a time with the utmost concentration. I do not think that he had worked much in the open air before. He was accustomed to emerge, carrying a large easel, to advance a little way into the open, and then suddenly to plant himself down nowhere in particular, behind a barn, opposite a wall, in the middle of a field. The process was like that in the game of musical chairs where the player has to stop dead, wherever he may happen to be, directly the piano stops playing. The other painters were all astonished at Sargent's never "selecting" a point of view, but he explained it in his half-inarticulate way. His object was to acquire the habit of reproducing precisely whatever met his vision without the slightest previous "arrangement" of detail, the painter's business being, not to pick and choose, but to render the effect before him, whatever it may be. In those days, when "subject" and "composition" were held in much higher honour than they are today, this was a revolutionary doctrine, but Sargent was not moved. His daily plan was to cover the whole of his canvas with a thin coat of colour, so as to make a complete sketch which would dry so rapidly that next morning he might paint another study over it. I often could have wept to see these brilliantly fresh and sparkling sketches ruthlessly sacrified.

One of Sargent's theories at this time was that modern painters made a mistake in showing that they know too much about the substances they paint. Of course, Alma Tadema with his marble and his metal, was the eternal instance of this error. Sargent, on the other hand, thought that the artist ought to know nothing whatever about the nature of the object before him ("Ruskin, don't you know—rocks and clouds—silly old thing!"), but should concentrate all his powers on a representation of its appearance. The picture was to be a consistent vision, a reproduction of the area filled by the eye. Hence, in a very curious way, the aspect of a substance became much more real to him than the substance itself. An amusing little instance occurs to me. He was painting, one noon of this radiant August of 1885, in a white-washed farm-yard, into which I strolled for his company, wearing no hat under the cloudless blue sky. As I approached him, Sargent look at me, gave a convulsive plunge in the air with his brush, and said "Oh! what lovely lilac hair, no one ever saw such beautiful lilac hair!' The blue sky reflected on my sleek dun locks, which no one had ever thought "beautiful" before, had glazed them with colour, and Sargent, grasping another canvas, painted me as I stood laughing, while he ejaculated at intervals, "Oh! what lovely hair!" The real colour of the hair was nothing, it existed only in the violet varnish which a single step into the shade would destroy for ever."

The unfinished picture of the children had not been named, but one evening while Sargent was at his easel in the garden, a visitor asked what he intended to call it. Sargent happened to be humming the words of a song which they had been singing the previous evening, "Have you seen my Flora pass this way"; one line of it was, "Carnation Lily, Lily Rose," and that line answered the question.

Music had played a large part in the life of the colony at Broadway. "We have music," Edwin Abbey wrote, "until the house won't stand it. Sargent is going elaborately through Wagner's trilogy, recitatives and all: there are moments when it doesn't seem as if it could be meant for music, but I dare say it is. I've been painting a head. Sargent does it better than I do and quicker, but then he is younger." Miss Strettell (Mrs. L. A. Harrison) had joined the party in 1886, and was a power-ful unit in the ranks of the Wagnerians. She and Sargent would play duets by the hour, and came to be known in consequence as "the co-maniacs." "We have really had a gay summer," Abbey wrote, "prentending to work and sometimes working (for there are numberless places with easels in them to hide away in—if you really *do* want to work—until four, and then tennis until

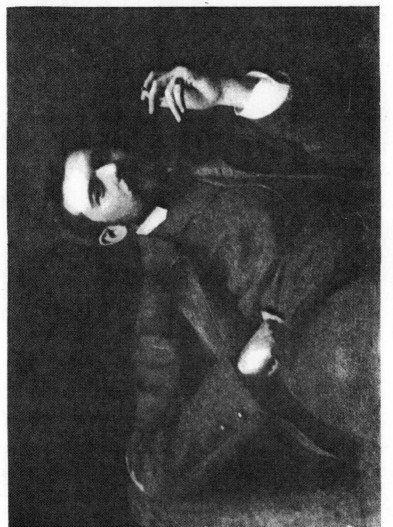

JOHN S. SARGENT, ÆTAT. 30.

dinner-time, and after dinner dancing and music and various cheering games in the studio—but mostly dancing."

It was at Broadway that Sargent made a full-face drawing of Henry James. The drawing, which pleased no one, was a complete failure and was destroyed, Sargent saying it was "impossible to do justice to a face that was all covered with beard like a bear." The following year he did a fine profile, reproduced first in the "Yellow Book" and then as the frontispiece of Mr. Percy Lubbock's edition of Henry James' "Letters." In the same year, 1886, he painted the portrait of Sir Edmund Gosse, exhibited at the Memorial Exhibition of the Royal Academy, 1925.

In October, or late September, 1885, Sargent had interrupted his residence at Broadway by a second visit to Robert Louis Stevenson at Bournemouth. Stevenson had just returned from an expedition to the West Country, during which he had been laid up for several weeks at Exeter by a severe hæmorrhage. Back once more at "Skerryvore," he was confronting illness with all his vivacious gaiety and courage. He had just published "Prince Otto," and at the moment he was finishing "The Strange Case of Dr. Jekyll and Mr. Hyde," writing "Olalla" as a Christmas story, and laying the foundation of "Kidnapped." Of the two men, Stevenson, born in 1850, was the elder by six years. It was their last meeting. When Sargent returned to Bournemouth with his parents in 1888, Stevenson had left for San Francisco and the South Seas. There is no record to show whether it was chance or design which led to their meeting and to Sargent's painting the two portraits of him. Probably Henry James brought it about.

Stevenson, at the time of Sargent's visit, was taken up with a criticism of himself by William Archer, which had appeared in a magazine called *Time*. He regarded it as unjust in certain particulars, and it goaded him into setting forth one aspect, at any rate, of his own philosophy of life.

Can you (he wrote to William Archer) conceive how profoundly I am irritated by the opposite affectation to my own, when I see strong men and rich men bleating about their sorrows and the burthen of life, in a world full of "cancerous paupers" and poor sick children and the fatally bereaved, ay, and down even to such happy creatures as myself, who has yet been obliged to strip himself, one after another, of all the pleasures that he had chosen except smoking (and the days of that I know in my heart ought to be over). I forgot eating, which I still enjoy, and who sees the circle of impotence closing very slowly but quite steadily around him. In my view one dank, dispirited word is harmful, a crime of lèse-humanité, a piece of acquired evil; every gay, every bright word or picture, like every pleasant air of music, is a pleasure set afloat: the reader catches it, and, if he be healthy, goes on his way rejoicing; and it is the business of art so to send him, as often as possible.

Some hint of the vitality of this way of taking life speaks in the debonair and whimsical figure that Sargent has caught in the very moment of movement. Here is nothing "dank" or "dispirited," no thought of a closing "circle of impotence"; but a being, who, while lean and haggard with illness, is still for venture and conquest and "as full of spirit as the month of May"— his eye as bright as though he had just seen the Rajah's diamond or heard the call of Silver's parrot. We see him with invention quickening in his brain, his spirit astir with fancy and antic wit; a vivid personality revealed with the intimacy that perhaps a sketch can best attain. R. A. M. Stevenson described the picture as "instinct with life and gesture, to a degree perhaps impossible to render by closer and more explicit workmanship," and Robert Louis himself wrote about it to W. H. Low on October 22, 1885.

Sargent was down again and painted a portrait of me walking about in my own dining-room, in my own velveteen jacket, and twisting as I go my own moustache: at one corner a glimpse of my wife, in an Indian dress, and seated in a chair that was once my grandfather's but since some months goes by the name of Henry James's, for it was there the novelist loved to sit—adds a touch of poesy and comicality. It is, I think, excellent, but is too eccentric to be exhibited. I am at one extreme corner: my wife in this wild dress, and looking like a ghost is at the extreme other end: between us an open door exhibits my palatial entrance hall and part of my respected staircase. All this is touched in lovely, with that witty touch of Sargent's: but of course it looks damn queer as a whole.

The picture was exhibited at the New English Art Club in 1887, and it is now in the possession of Mrs. Payne Whitney.

ROBERT LOUIS STEVENSON.

Chapter XII

THE Broadway days were a beneficent interlude in Sargent's career. When he had severed his links with Paris, but had not yet forged new ones with London, he found there a sheltered corner and an atmosphere of security and encouragement. His position was not unlike that of Henry James, when he, a few years earlier, settled in London. Like James, Sargent was a stranger in a strange country, his art little known, his public not formed, his work not quite in line with recognized standards.

In 1876 Henry James had written to his brother:

at a time when my last layers of resistance to a long encroaching weariness and satiety with the French mind and its utterance has fallen from me like a garment. I have done with 'em for ever, and am turning English all over. I desire only to feed on English life and the contact of English minds. Easy and smooth-flowing as life is in Paris, I would throw it over tomorrow for an even very small chance to plant myself for a while in England. If I had but a single good friend in London I would go there.

Nine years had seen Henry James securely established, and in spite of the "glue-pot" atmosphere of social England, he felt his environment was congenial to the pursuit of his art. His experience was of profit to Sargent. Sargent could also draw encouragement from the artistic status of Abbey, Millet and Boughton. London is not easily taken by storm, its walls need more than a blast of trumpets before they will fall, but once a recognition has been won, a stranger probably has a better chance of being appreciated in London than in any other city in the world. From Holbein to Sargent, painter after painter from across the Channel has established himself in England, found a host of patrons, and built up fame and fortune. Taste in England is often shy of new developments in art; when once it has conquered its shyness, it is never niggardly in approbation. It throws off its insularity and reserve. Artists and public applaud with generosity and without regard to nationality or origin. This may have been less true of the eighties, but even then, if the innovator in art could survive the blows levelled at him by the upholders of conservative and academic standards he could safely count on receiving a generous measure of praise. Whistler, who had accompanied innovation and delayed his own recognition by a fierce fusillade of provocative wit, was beginning to come into his own, and in 1885 had been elected to the British Society of Artists. Anything, however, that made acclimatization to English life easier was to the good. That is what Broadway did for Sargent.

Spending as he did so many months there, it is surprising that he should not have painted the countryside more often. He was so deeply immersed in the technique of painting and so readily responsive that it might have been expected that he would have found many subjects in the neighbourhood. But with the exception of three or four small canvases, one of which, entitled *Broadway*, was hung at the Academy Exhibition of 1925, nothing survives to show that he was ever outside London. What is the explanation? From the first, accustomed to sharp contrasts and a uniformly clear atmosphere, to the challenge of stable and high-keyed values, his eye was perhaps too little adjusted to the subtle effects of English landscape, its fleeting impressions of light and shade, its delicate relation of values and its subdued distances. English scenery does not proclaim its glories, but whispers its enchantments, and yields its secrets only to those whose sensibilities are tuned by association, sentiment and training to respond. Its waters do not glitter and sparkle in fierce sunlight; its trees do not push skyward, secure from winter storms; it is not rich in terraces and marbles gleaming under blue skies and transparent air; white oxen do not plough the fields; its most brilliant colours are tempered by an atmosphere enchantingly its own. Landscape, indeed, is as national as customs, modes of thought and language itself, and no cosmopolitan has the key. It may, indeed, be questioned whether any painter from Titian to D. Y. Cameron or any poet from Dante to Robert Bridges has rendered the landscape of a country other than his own in terms that completely express just that element of vision which is special to the native outlook. The Frenchman, when he sets out to paint the Thames Valley, or the Englishman when he takes the Loire for his theme, is not speaking his native tongue. He is a translator. We need only instance Turner in Switzerland, Bonington and Richard Wilson in Italy, Monet in England.

We are in the habit of attributing to scenery the qualities implied by the words grand and awful, romantic, melancholy, picturesque or smiling, and there is also scenery which is sentimental, with a special psychology of its own. It is the psychological significance which only the supreme artist, who is also the native artist, can capture. Need we then be surprised that Sargent, a stranger to this country, with a temperament taught by habit to mature artistically only in the full definition of sunny scenes, should have found little in this visible world of England to excite his sympathy? His American descent, though filtered through the studios and galleries of the Continent and diluted by the educational ingredients of Europe, was nevertheless a factor to be reckoned with. And with such a descent we do not as a rule connect the mood of pensiveness and "poetic reverie" that we associate with English landscape.

The forms "netted in a silver haze," the colours, the half-tones and dim tinted stains of English landscapes, the

Farms, granges, doubled up among the hills,
And cattle grazing in the watered vales,

the scenes, in fact, that have inspired the painters and poets of England had small appeal for Sargent as an artist. For one thing, he cordially disliked the quality of English light. The most successful picture which he painted out of doors in England, he succeeded in painting only with the assistance of a Chinese lantern. But in this canvas, by taking the half light and hues of failing day and by adding a reflection from the artificial illumination, he obtained a subtlety and delicacy of colouring reminiscent of his earliest work, and produced what will always rank as one of his great achievements.

On the other hand, in his picture *Broadway* already referred to he cannot be said to have given a true rendering of English landscape. He has imported into his scheme of colour and his treatment of the tones a Southern atmosphere. The emphatic handling gives an air of finality, as if the scene always had been and always would be the same, as if no season could alter its texture, no cloud subdue its colour. It is, in fact, deficient in some of the special qualities which have been noted as characteristic of English scenery. But Sargent has sometimes a startling way of confounding summary judgments. A few yards from the picture *Broadway* was hanging at the Academy a picture painted at Whitby in 1896. A grey sea, a cloudy day, brown fishing-boats in the middle distance under full sail—here was the very atmosphere of the English coast; here was a composition that murmured the poetry of the sea, quiet and serene, with mystery in the colour, the open sky and the movement of the ships. It is as if he had recalled his manner of a bygone time to show that the lyrical element was within his range. There is also the picture *Home Fields*, painted in 1885, now in the Detroit Institute of Art, which is said to reproduce that coolness of colour and treatment so uncommon in his landscapes. But of such moods his painting offers only widely scattered evidence. His picture *Game of Bowls at Ightham Moat*, painted when he first came to England, may also be cited. Here he has caught English scenery, not at its best by any means, but in a grave and dreary mood, low in key and tone, but not lacking in truth either of colour or general effect. Moreover, the game goes forward as though the players themselves were affected by the opacity of the atmosphere.

Sargent was curiously indifferent to the trees and woods of England; the trees to him were not

> Those green robed senators of mighty woods
> Tall oaks, branch charmed by the earnest stars,"

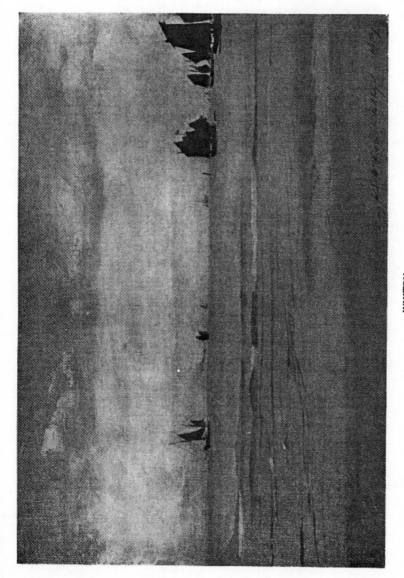

WHITBY.

but, as he once described them with their spreading skirts of ver-
dure in the park of Sutton Place, "old Victorian ladies going perpetually to church in a land where it is always Sunday afternoon."

> The mythic oaks and elm trees standing out
> Self poised upon their prodigy of shade

had no charm for him. He left them alone. But there is no
reason to regret that he passed English landscape by. The field
for his genius was and remained the countries where the atmosphere lent no mystery to what he saw, where subjects he wished
to represent stood out in all the opulence of form and colour.
"You speak of Lord Byron and me," wrote Keats in one of his
letters. "There is this great difference between us. He
describes what he sees, I describe what I imagine." Sargent
described what he saw. He painted, if such an expression may
be allowed in this connection, straight from the shoulder. Both
in his water-colours and oils he transposes beauty of fact into a
key of his own, direct, emphatic and suggestive, often satisfying
in design, and rich in colour and decorative value. When he
paints in Italy he does not paint fiction or romance; in his renderings of Venice we shall find little sense of the past, we shall look
in vain in his cypress groves for the vision of a hamadryad or in
his fountains for the glimpse of a naiad; all is rich and vivid and
open to the day, painted with a fine sincerity of mind, the work
of a painter who felt the immediate impression of the moment
with an intensity that called for an instant response. There is
no "sigh for what is not," no reaching out for what is "before or
after," the visible subject is recorded with consummate facility
and accomplishment, with a swiftness and decision that exclude
hesitation, with an effect that has an air of inevitableness, and
abundant in vitality. Years of study and tireless work had made
him the master of means wherewith he was able to say exactly
what he had to say, whether by indication or description.

Chapter XIII

WHEN the decade of the eighties began, the direction of painting in England, for the most part, was in the hands of the Academicians then at the height of their power. The Pre-Raphaelite brotherhood had come to an end; no distinct movement had taken its place. Orthodoxy, as dictated from the walls of the Academy, held the field. Nonconformity was unorganized and looked at askance, alike by the elder painters, the public and the critics. The younger artists trained in Paris, when they returned with new methods and revolutionary ideas, could find no outlet for their art; the Academy turned its back, the critics were hostile, the public as a whole would have none of their handiwork.

But the forces of revolt had been gathering. In 1877 Sir Coutts Lindsay opened the Grosvenor Gallery with the avowed intention of giving painters a chance, whose works had "previously been imperfectly known to the public." To the first exhibition Millais, Alma Tadema, Watts, Poynter, all sent pictures, and while it is true that works by Holman Hunt, Rossetti, Burne-Jones, Walter Crane and Whistler were also shown, it was clear from the first that the Royal Academy was again to be a dominating influence. Whistler was represented by several pictures, one of which, *The Falling Rocket*, was to be famous in the Law Courts. It was upon this picture that Ruskin made on July 2, 1877, in "Fors Clavigera," his famous comment: "I have seen and heard much of cockney impudence before now, but never expected to hear a coxcomb ask two hundred guineas for flinging a pot of paint in the public's face."

Whistler, regarding this as a libel, took proceedings against Ruskin. The case was heard in November, 1878. Burne-Jones, Frith and Tom Taylor, the art critic of *The Times*, were called for the defence, and at the conclusion of the hearing Whistler was awarded one farthing damages, the judge, Baron Huddleston, ordering that each party should pay his own costs. The hearing gave Whistler a rare opportunity of exercising his wit, not a little to the discomfiture of Sir John Holker, the Attorney-General, who conducted the case for Ruskin as if he had been briefed, not by an æsthetic prophet, but by the Philistines themselves. One feature of the trial, which Lord Justice Bowen, who was junior counsel for Ruskin, used to detail with a wit no less polished than Whistler's, was the introduction into court of a Titian as an exhibit, designed to demonstrate to the jury what constituted "finish" in a painting. But the jury, fogged as they were by the display of other works of art, and the course which the case had taken, imagined they were being shown, not a Titian, but a Whistler, and would have none of it.

The stress laid throughout on what was called "finish" in a picture defines in a measure the artistic standard of the day. "Finish," indeed, might well be used as summarizing several of the principal qualities then considered essential in a picture. It was against this aspect of art, quite as much as against the subjects considered suitable to the walls of the Academy, that those influenced by French painting were protesting, as yet not very effectively.

The Pre-Raphaelite Movement, which began shortly before 1850, may be said to have come to an end about 1870. It was as definitely British in its origin as any school of painting that has flourished in England, and it was sincere. In conversation with Sir Edmund Gosse, Sargent claimed in addition for the Pre-Raphaelites that they "were passionate in their art." With Ruskin as its prophet, Millais (1829-96), Holman Hunt (1827-1910) and Dante Gabriel Rossetti (1828-82) as its originators, and Ford Madox Brown (1821-93) as a principal ally, it aimed not merely at truth of representation, but at an emotionalism which was opposed to Classicism and vapid genre painting which the public confidently expected to see on the walls of the Academy. The founders of the movement sought for moral and poetic themes in the Bible, in Dante, and in the poetry of Keats, Tennyson and Coventry Patmore. The same care and finish was bestowed on every item, whether of leaf, blade of grass, wine-glass, table, cornfield or dining-room; though every object was selected with a premeditation inconsistent with Realism in its proper meaning. *Past and Present*, by Augustus Egg, and the *Last Day in the Old Home*, by Robert Martineau, may be taken as illustrations. These are themes which might have been chosen by Hogarth, but whereas Hogarth would have imparted to them a quality and character true in their universality, the later Pre-Raphaelites have treated them with a sentimentally moral convention.

They record on canvas the Victorian mood. We see "respectability" confronted with a crisis, and behaving just as, from our knowledge of the tradition, we should expect; that is to say, in accordance not so much with the precepts of human nature, as after the pattern imposed by the conventions of the day.

Nothing, at any rate, could be further removed from the realism of Sargent. They represented a point of view which was the very antithesis of his own; deliberate and studied emotion never entered into his art. He was the last man in the world to tolerate sentimentality. Yet it is true that one of his favourite pictures was *Take Your Son, Sir*, by Ford Madox Brown, and that he entertained a deep admiration for Rossetti. Indeed, he owned a small engraving of Rossetti's, *The Meeting of Arthur and Guinevere*, which hung on the landing of his studio, and pointing to this on the very last occasion I saw him he said: "That is the difficult thing to do, anyone can paint, but to design a group so that it will—well, do in sculpture—that's what counts. Rossetti could do it." This was in 1925 when he had been for some time taken up with sculpture, and had executed some small bronzes, including Leda and the Swan, two figures from the nude, a Dancer, Death and Victory, Jove, a figure of Psyche and this very composition of Rossetti's. But in his art he certainly gave no outward sign of kinship with the Pre-Raphaelites; his appreciation, in fact, remained academic.

In technical methods, too, Sargent and the Pre-Raphaelites were as the Poles apart. The technique of the Pre-Raphaelites consisted in a "painting largely transparent, like water-colour

JAVANESE DANCER.
National Gallery, Millbank.

over a white ground, so that in brilliancy the effect is that of water-colour on white paper."* Their pictures were painted in many cases inch by inch, with minute and careful touches, copal varnish was used by them; they aimed at uniform brilliance in colour. To this the large, free and rapid brush-work of Sargent was entirely opposed, but difference of outlook and method never hindered him from admiring schools of painting other than his own.

When he came to London the influence of the Pre-Raphaelites had ceased since many years to be an active force in painting, only traces of it were to be seen here and there. As a recognized school, Pre-Raphaelitism had passed away.

The art situation in London was as different as possible from that which he had found ten years ago on entering the studio of Carolus Duran. In Paris there were recognized schools of painting, each with its accomplished masters. There, dogmatism had been forced to give way before search and enquiry and new ideas. Academism, if not actually dethroned, had ceased to command the deference necessary to authority. In London nothing of the kind had happened. The Grosvenor Gallery was, it is true, carrying on a separate existence, but the Academicians were year by year tending to crowd out all heterogeneous exhibitors; the advance-guard of Modernism was being outmanœuvred.

To a young foreign artist accustomed to the enthusiastic daring and variety of Parisian painting, English Academic art must have seemed cold, slightly devitalized and over-formal— whether his eyes dwelt upon Leighton's gentlemanly and accomplished renderings of classical and mythological subjects, Watts' ethical sermons in paint, Tadema's slick and careful studies of make-believe Greek and Roman life, or Poynter's correct and elegant studies in a similar field. Even the genius of Burne-Jones must have struck him as timidly remote, seeking "out of sight the ends of being and eternal grace," and pursuing beauty through the romantic by-ways of an exotic world. Millais, perhaps alone among the leading artists, could be cited as a

* See D. S. MacColl, "Nineteenth Century Art," pp. 129–130.

colourist and draughtsman combined. But Millais, now showing little trace of Pre-Raphaelitism with its minute adherence to visible facts, was adopting a different technique and applying it to approved Academy subjects, such as *Cherry Ripe* and the *North-West Passage.*

By 1885, when Sargent took up his residence in Tite Street, authority was about to lose the vigour of its hold. It was already being said that "the Royal Academy would be quite good if it wasn't for the Royal Academicians." The inadequacy of the Grosvenor and the hostility of the Academy were compelling the younger spirits to take the matter into their own hands. London was every year receiving a number of young artists who, having finished their studies in Paris, were bent on finding for themselves the opening for their art which was denied them at Burlington House. In 1886, accordingly, after many meetings and the surmounting of many difficulties, the New English Art Club, a group of some fifty young artists, "all more or less united in their art sympathies," as the catalogue stated, opened their first exhibition at the Marlborough Gallery. Sargent had been invited to contribute and sent a small Impressionist *Study*, and a portrait of *Mrs. Barnard.* Others connected with the movement in its early stages were Professor Brown, Jacques Blanche, G. Clausen, Alfred East, Mark Fisher, Walter Sickert, T. C. Gotch, Maurice Grieffenhagen, Arthur Hacker, Sir John Lavery, Alfred Parsons, J. J. Shannon, Wilson Steer, Adrian Stokes, Edward Stott, H. S. Tuke and later Professor Tonks. Lord Leighton predicted that the movement would last three years; the New English Art Club still continues to hold its annual exhibition. The common bond of this group of painters was French influence—and if any element of what is best in French art and theory has passed into English painting it should be remembered that the pioneers in England were the New English Art Club, at whose first exhibition Sargent was a contributor.

Almost at the same time a new movement was starting in Scotland. There, as in England, while there were artists who painted with distinction, the general trend was toward sentimental genre pictures. Portrait painting, too, had become more and more literal, smooth and exact, and landscape more and more conventional, formal and obvious. The Academy was doing nothing to discountenance these general tendencies; on the contrary, Scottish Academism standardized the evils which the younger painters were trying to combat. The banner of revolt was raised in Glasgow, and the honour of giving birth to the "Glasgow school" fell to the great commercial centre of Scotland. It was here that towards 1880 W. G. MacGregor and James Patterson were joined by James Guthrie, E. A. Walton, George Henry and Joseph Crawhall, a young painter from Newcastle. In 1884 this group of painters received an accession of strength in John Lavery and A. Roche, just then fresh from Paris. The general characteristics of the group have been summarized by Mr. Caw in his volume of "Scottish Painting." "Prettiness," he writes, "and sentimentality and subject in the old sentimental sense were condemned, and broad powerful painting, full in tone and true in value was cultivated." Just as "values" had been the watchword in France since 1830, so now they were becoming correspondingly important in the art of Scotland.

Landscape painting was carried on at Cockburnspath, a centre established by Sir James Guthrie in East Lothian, and here the revolutionary forces gathered in much the same way as half a century earlier the French landscape painters, in a similar spirit of innovation, had made Barbizon their headquarters. The common relation between the members of this group lay in a general resolve to seek emancipation from the traditions of which the Academy was the janitor and guardian. To this end, in varying degrees, they followed other tendencies in painting; the Barbizon school, the school of Manet, Bastien Lepage, Whistler and through him the Japanese, Velasquez and Franz Hals, and the great Italians, were all eagerly sought as guides.

The outlook that resulted was essentially cosmopolitan. Realism and Impressionism each played its part, but personal characteristics, as was inevitable in a group each member of

which had his own idea of how to combat stereotyped pictur-
esqueness and anecdotalism, in the end prevailed. Different lines
of radiation and progress from a common centre were gradually
discovered, and each painter began to travel along his own road.

The critic of *The Times*, writing of the Academy Exhibition
in 1882, indirectly expressed the prevailing antagonism to the
French school of painting. Writing of what he called the
Idyllic School he said:

> This idyllic school as it has been called was simply the offspring
> from the work of such men as Mason, Pinwell and Walker, and had it
> not been for the early and almost simultaneous deaths of those artists
> it would have struck permanent root in our art. This as it seems to us,
> is the mine of feeling which needs working, this is the healthy direction
> in which our artists should be encouraged to tread. But with perhaps
> the exception of Jules Breton and Josef Israels, the influence of all
> continental Schools is against any such method.

This extract shows that both the critics and the public were
more exercised about the subject-matter of pictures than questions
of technique and method. In England the Romantic Movement
had been dying very slowly, and at the beginning of the eighties
Realism, cradled and nourished in France, was still regarded as a
dangerous and insidious force, inconsistent with, if not destruc-
tive of, great art. The plea of *The Times* critic on behalf of
the Idyllic School was a summons to a rearguard action to
drive back the invaders. In literature, too, Realism was drifting
across the Channel. The year 1880 had seen the publication
of "Les Soirées de Medan," containing *Sac au Dos* and *Boule
de Suif*. In the early eighties Maupassant (1850-93) was
challenging the popularity of Zola (1840-95), while Alphonse
Daudet (1840-97), the Goncourts and M. J. K. Huysmans were
all contributing to the ascendancy of Realism. In England the
death, in 1881, of George Eliot, Carlyle and Borrow brought
an epoch to a close. The way was opening for the new influence.
George Moore, "Mark Rutherford" and George Gissing were,
each in his own manner, proclaiming the new era. Thus side
by side with the painters returning from Paris, the younger

writers in England were giving support to the same influences already dominant in France.

While the interaction of literature and painting may easily be overstated, there is always a tendency for the same point of view to permeate both branches of artistic expression. At a given time one art may be in advance of the other, but in the end the two will be found, for at least a while, to be moving concurrently abreast. The Classic, Romantic and Realistic Movements have each in turn become a principal factor in both pictorial and literary art. Art cannot escape the influence of life. And if this be true, it is often the portrait painter who first reflects contemporary influence. We can see at a glance that the society painted by Goya differs from the society painted by Velasquez; that the men and women on the canvases of Watts and Millais are of a different order from those who figure in the work of Reynolds and Gainsborough. This is due, not only to the methods of the painters and the fashions of the sitters, to technique and dressmaking, but to the circumstances and conditions of the particular epoch. A portrait painter therefore interprets not merely those he paints, but through them he interprets the society in which they live, move and have their being. Sargent for twenty-five years was engaged in portrait painting in London, and, as in the case of every great portrait painter, it will be found that not a few of the characteristics common to these years are summarized in his portraits. In the eighties the way was open for new talent, for a painter like Sargent, whose natural gifts had been disciplined in the studios of Paris, and who could bring to the art of portrait painting originality, unrivalled powers of execution, and a certain daring in representing and interpreting his fellow-men, without departing, however, too violently from tradition.

Chapter XIV

IN April, 1885, after a winter of work in London, Sargent joined his family at Nice. Two letters to Miss Strettell (Mrs. Harrison) show his preoccupation at this time with music.

BAILEY'S HOTEL,
GLOSTER ROAD,
April 3, '86.

MY DEAR COMANIAC,

I have just got a note from Mrs. Fraser which makes me remain stupid, as you say at a certain watering place which you so often advertise. I am to go with you and Mrs. Liszt to the Liszt concert "dont l'ivoire a le trac." You must ask him to play even without his notes.

I suppose I am indebted to Comyns Carr for this treat which I hope I may repay by a series of amiable processes. . . . I have begun two portraits and am getting them well under way before leaving for Paris about the 15th to finish them when I return 15th May. I shall see you I suppose at (illegible) little play . . . and I will rejoice for are we not the two Comaniacs and is not Wagner our strait Jacket? He is.

Yours sincerely,
JOHN S. SARGENT.

ARTS CLUB,
May 17, '86.

DEAR COMANIAC,

. . . Richter's plans are now known. "The Grand Wagner Night" is on June 7th and June 10th same programme 2nd Act of Tristan and almost entire 3rd Act of Siegfried with Malten, Gudehns, Henschel etc. The concerts before contain nothing for us and the last one is Beethoven Missa Solemnis. How are you enjoying Porto Fino? "Will it wash?" as Violet Paget says of Venice. Since that remark I have not written to her.

I am very well hung at the Academy and Grosvenor and cheerful on that score. Most of my friends are out of town Abbey and Millet at Broadway, Mrs. Playfair and Mrs. Harrison at Aix.

Yours ever,
COMANIAC.

STUDY OF CROCODILES.

In the summer of 1886 he again visited his family, who were living at Gossensass, then no more than the hotel and a few chalets, near the newly opened railway on the Brenner. Gossensass may be remembered as the spot chosen by Ibsen in which to spend the summer months between 1883 and 1893, and as the scene, in 1889, of his meeting with the young Viennese lady Miss Emilie Bardach, who suggested the heroine of the "Master Builder."* Ibsen was then sixty-one. Nine years later he wrote: "That summer at Gossensass was the most beautiful and the most harmonious portion of my whole existence. I scarcely venture to think of it and yet I think of nothing else. Ah! forever!" Ibsen was certainly there at the time of Sargent's visit, but there is no record of their becoming acquainted. These visits meant no pause in Sargent's output of work. He would arrive at the station loaded with canvases and sketch-books, bristling with the equipment for *plein air* sketching, and with these piled up round him in a fly he would draw up at his destination dominant and smiling. No infatuated fisherman, arriving beside a chalk stream on a summer evening, could be more on the tiptoe of expectation than Sargent on these occasions. To the end of his days he had the supreme gift of being able to look forward, with the certainty of discovering excitement in new scenes and places. He habitually took thought for the morrow, but not of the anxious kind; it was thought rich in anticipation of what the next day would bring forth. Few artists can have rejoiced as much in the exercise of their calling; certainly none can have practised it with more singleness of purpose. But it was away from his portraits, on the canals of Venice or the plains of Palestine, in the passes of the high Alps or among the dancers of Spain, or the fountains and cypresses of Italy and the gardens of Sicily, or, again, at Capri or Corfu, or on any one of the countless journeys that he made with friends, that his spirit was most at ease and serene—anywhere, in fact, where he could "make the best of an emergency" as he called painting a water-colour. And an emergency was seldom wanting. Mrs. de Glehn recalls

* Edmund Gosse, "Ibsen" (1907), p. 169.

how on a hot day in Italy, having missed a connection at a
junction, the party had to wait a considerable time. The rest of
them had no thought but how to keep cool, but Sargent at once
unpacked his easel and in the great heat he brought off one of his
most brilliant studies of white oxen outside the station. This
is a typical instance of his zeal, which coined even the accidents
of life into opportunity.

In the late summer of 1886 he was back again at Broadway,
finishing *Carnation, Lily Lily Rose*.

In 1887 he was invited to go to America to paint the portrait
of Mrs. Marquand, but he was reluctant to relinquish the hold
he was acquiring in London; orders had been coming in quicker
than he expected. He was beginning to find unlooked-for sympathies in his new surroundings, and while critical opinion was
still very divided about his work, he was everywhere recognized
for better or for worse as a new force in painting. This year
(1887) he was represented in the Academy by *Carnation, Lily
Lily Rose* and his portrait of *Mrs. William Playfair*, and in
the exhibition of the New English Art Club by the sketch of
Mr. and Mrs. R. L. Stevenson and *The Portrait of a Lady*.
He had also painted Dr. William Playfair, Edith Lady Playfair,
Mrs. Charles Inches and Mrs. Charles Fairchild. When, therefore, the invitation to visit America arrived, he named a price
which he believed would be deterrent, but his offer was accepted.
It was never easy to him to refuse; it was always distasteful to
him to disappoint. Within the limits of fidelity to his art, it
was his way to think more of what others wanted than of what
was most attractive to himself. His mild subterfuge having failed,
he resolved on his second expedition to the U.S.A. In July
he was at the Henley Regatta with a party of friends staying for
a week at the Shiplake Inn, and this "outing" was repeated again
in July, 1888. On this second occasion Alfred Parsons was host
at the Red House, Shiplake.

In a letter to Claude Monet Sargent expresses admiration
for a picture by that Master which he had recently bought,* and
described efforts of his own to paint Thames scenery.

* The picture *Rock at Treport* was sold at the Sargent sale, July, 1925.

Mon cher Monet,

C'est avec beaucoup de mal que je m'arrache de devant votre délicieux tableau pour lequel "vous ne partagez pas mon admiration" (quelle blague!) pour vous redire combien je l'admire. Je resterais là devant pendant des heures entières dans un état d'abrutissement voluptueux ou d'enchantment si vous préférez. Je suis ravi d'avoir chez moi une telle source de plaisir.

Vous, ne dites rien de votre projet de venir, à Londres à l'automne. Il me serait presque agréable de le savoir remis parceque je serai absent en Amérique. J'ai des commandes de portraits là bas et une occasion très agréable d'y aller passer deux mois. Je pars le 17 Septembre.

Quoique j'ai beaucoup travaillé dernièrement sur la Tamise je n'ai rien comme résultat. C'est un peu parceque ce sacré projet de voyage me rendait impossible l'achèvement de mon tableau, et puis les difficultés matérielles faire des gens en bateau sur l'eau, entre bateaux etc.

Je vous envoie ce que j'aurais du vous envoyer il y a longtemps. Si vous trouvez des difficultés à toucher . . . les banquiers Drexel, Harjes et Cie 31 Bd. Haussman connaissent ma signature.

Cher Monet je vous remercie et je vous aime. Comme artiste, alors, je vous adore.

JOHN S. SARGENT.

Je ne suis pas gris.

Sargent considered that Claude Monet had exercised a greater influence on art than any modern painter, and some letters written several years later give his reasons; for the moment, however, it is worth noting that in 1888 he was expressing his admiration for Monet in terms of warmest eulogy.

On September 17 Sargent sailed for America. He remained there during the winter 1887-88. It was just the ordinary experience of strenuous work, mostly carried out at Boston where late in December, at the St. Botolph Club, Newbury Street, there was an exhibition of some twenty of his pictures. These included *El Jaleo* (shortly before this date purchased by the Hon. Jefferson Coolidge), portraits of *Mrs. Marquand, Mrs. Inches, Mrs. Brandegee, Mrs. Boit, Mrs. Gardner,* and the picture of the *Boit Children,* as well as some of his smaller studies done in Italy.

It was the first occasion on which America had had the chance to realize that in Sargent they could claim as a countryman a painter of the first rank. The vigour and freedom of his work, its directness of statement and sincerity, its brilliant variation from the stereotyped conventions of the day, and its masterly and summary adaptation of means to a given end, made a profound impression on the American public. Henceforward his position in the United States was assured.

American appreciation, the sense of being a prophet in his own country, probably brought him as much solid satisfaction as the whole volume of praise and fame which was bestowed on him in Europe. America, indeed, was a much more constant motive for his actions than was generally supposed. His decorative work at Boston—and it is but only one instance of many—was prompted by this national allegiance, and to this has to be added his constant desire that America should be the home of so large a share of his best work. When the Metropolitan Museum acquired the portrait of Madame Gautreau, when *El Jaleo* was installed at Fenway Court, and when Boston bought the great series of water-colours which now adorns the Museum of that city, he was keenly pleased. Though his nationality was not apparent on the surface, and though he was not bound by close personal associations, the idea of his country and of his obligations as an American citizen never left him.

In 1887 he did six illustrations for Miss Strettell's (Mrs. Harrison's) "Spanish and Italian Folk Songs." It is to be regretted that the book is out of print on account not only of the illustrations admirable in design and quality, but for the beauty of the translations themselves.

In the early part of 1888 Sargent was back in England. His family had spent the winter in Florence, where his father had been struck down by a paralytic stroke. In the spring it was decided to bring him to England, and a house was leased for the summer at Calcot, Reading. Such time as he could spare from his work in London Sargent now spent with his family at Calcot. In the winter they moved to Bournemouth, to a house near Skerryvore, the former home of R. L. Stevenson. It was here, in April, 1889, that FitzWilliam Sargent died.

Since his seizure at Florence Sargent's father had been an

THE MORNING WALK.

invalid, his contacts with the world broken, his memory affected, and his capacity for movement gravely impaired. Sargent watched over him with a "lovely happiness of temper" and constant solicitude. The last months of the father's life were eased by the ministering care of the son. Yet Sargent did not, as a rule, suffer invalids gladly; by nature robust, he was so seldom ill himself that he was inclined to think others were apt to surrender too easily. When, in later years, he was subject himself to inroads of influenza he was singularly obstinate in working up to the last possible moment, then only to pursue unaided methods of salvation in the austere surroundings of his Tite Street bedroom. But those whose memories of him go back to 1889 recall vividly the rare quality of the tenderness with which he soothed the last months of his father's life. Before his father's death he had taken the vicarage at Fladbury, near Pershore, and there the succeeding summer was spent by the family. His visitors were Vernon Lee, Miss Anstruther Thomson, M. and Madame Helleu, Miss Flora Priestley, Miss Strettell, Alden Weir, the Richardsons, Judge Patterson and Major Harold and Mrs. Roller, as well as the colony from Broadway some nine miles distant. Here Sargent painted two portraits of Miss Priestley, and one of *M. and Madame Helleu in a Canoe*.

There is no doubt that in 1888 and 1889 Sargent was definitely experimenting in Impressionism. He was busy painting the play of light on sunlit water, catching the exact flicker, the ripple of the reflections, and their fleeting effect on objects within range. He made several studies of his sister, Mrs. Ormond, under these conditions; one a full-length, *Fishing*, was shown at the Memorial Exhibition at Burlington House, another is reproduced opposite p. 100.

These pictures show a delicacy of touch and a tenderness of colour which give place to other qualities in his later work. The charm we see here is not the charm we are accustomed to look for in the work of subsequent years. It is more intimate and personal, more subtle and pervasive. Broken touches, here and there broken colour, lightness of key, harmony of tone, unity of effect, and contrast reduced to its lowest terms—the characteristics, in fact, associated with Impressionism are found in the studies of this period. He was at the time under the influence of Monet's picture of the *Rock at Treport*, then in his possession and referred to in his letter; but that influence waned. Sargent turned away from this phase of his painting, and by 1890 he had reverted to the style with which he was more familiar. The picture of Mrs. Ormond* justifies the wish that there had been other interludes in his career of a like kind; not certainly at the expense of his greater manner, but as occasional pieces, as lyrics set in drama, or idylls in a book of odes.

Sargent has invested the figure of a young woman sauntering on a sunny day beside a river in the month of June with all the poetry that such a subject can suggest. Her beautifully modelled head is framed by her open sunshade, the light from the water is reflected on her face, and seems to move as it plays on the inner surface of the sunshade; the frame thus formed is completed by the gloved hands, one of which holds the stick of the parasol while the other grasps one of the corners of the sunshade. The figure of a girl in a white dress, the foliage, the still water, the meadow beside which she walks are bathed in sunlight. As she moves "over the gleam of the living grass," she communes with her inner thoughts, her lips slightly parted, her mind detached from the scene of which she forms a delicate and illumined feature.

This year, 1889, he exhibited at the Academy portraits of *Sir George Henschel*, *Mrs. George Gribble*, and *Henry Irving;* at the New English Art Club, *A Morning Walk*, and *St. Martin's Summer*, and at the New Gallery the well-known picture of Miss Ellen Terry as Lady Macbeth. In reference to his portrait of Ellen Terry he wrote to Mrs. Gardner as follows:

33, TITE STREET,
CHELSEA, S.W.,
Jan. 1st, '89.

DEAR MRS. GARDNER,

  Am I in time to forestall the conclusion that I forget my friends? I should dislike such a reputation and being a very bad correspondent I seem to invite it. Horrible injustice! It shows the utter inanity of logical inferences.

* Exhibited at New English Art Club, 1889.

M. AND MADAME HELLEU.

You know several of the people whom I am painting now, so I shall talk shop. Henschel, Miss Huxley, Ellen Terry; if one can say one is painting, when sittings resolve themselves into sitting by the fire or at the piano with lamps at two in the afternoon. There ought to be a Tower Eiffel here with studios at the top. Miss Terry has just come out in Lady Macbeth and looks magnificent in it, but she has not yet made up her mind to let me paint her in one of the dresses until she is quite convinced that she is a success. From a pictorial point of view there can be no doubt about it—magenta hair!

I am going to Paris in the Spring for the Jury of '89 and to paint a portrait or two. Will you be there in March or April?

With best wishes for a happy New Year,

Yours sincerely,

JOHN S. SARGENT.

The dress for Lady Macbeth was designed by Mrs. Comyns-Carr, who relates on the first night of the play Sargent shared her box and, on the appearance of Ellen Terry on the stage, exclaimed with that lingering intonation so familiar to those who knew him, "I say!" It was a sign in him, unpretentious in itself as a schoolboy's expression of delight, that he had been "bowled over."

He also sent six portraits to the United States Section of the Paris Exhibition; for these he was awarded a medal of honour and made Chevalier of the Legion of Honour.

When Sir George Henschel wrote to express his thanks for his portrait, he received in reply a note which shows the gracious turn Sargent could give to such acknowledgments.

I must tell you (he wrote) what a great pleasure it has been to me that my venture at painting you has resulted in such a generous expression of satisfaction on your part and Mrs. Henschel's, greater than I have ever met with—and that with my means I have given you the pleasure that you always give me with yours and I should be quite satisfied with my portrait if I created in you the sentiment of sympathy which prompted me to do it.

A later letter to Sir George Henschel shows his consideration for younger artists. He was always ready to let them draw on his knowledge and also his resources—as if it were a matter of course they should, or, at any rate, keen pleasure to himself.

Sir George had asked him to look at the work of a young artist friend; Sargent wrote:

33, TITE STREET,

MY DEAR HENSCHEL,   (*No date*).

. . . very good naturedly brought his pictures here. The larger portrait of a man in an Inverness cape has a great deal of style and arrangement as well as extraordinarily thorough and minute drawing. You will I think see he is working in the right direction— I do decidedly—for it is evident that he has a much better sense of form than of colour and he is right in turning his attention to drawing. To try for colour (of which he seems to have no sense at all) would probably handicap him in his drawing and he had much better go on sacrificing everything to form and get the very most he can out of that. He ought to guard against his things having a certain photographic look. Please do not let him know that I have made this sort of report to you. He might think what I say about colour rather discouraging and unfair and whether consciously or not he is doing what I advise.

In the late summer of 1889 he was painting in Paris. It was the year of the Universal Exposition. In the following letter to Claude Monet he refers to his picture of the Javanese dancer:

PARIS,

MON CHER MONET,   *Jeudi.*

Quelle idée ! J'ai été horriblement occupé et je manque de timbres postes: voilà qui explique mais n'excuse pas mon silence. J'aurais du répondre à une aussi gentille lettre qui était tout à fait en harmonie avec ma façon de penser—c'est des félicitations banales qui m'auraient fait rire de votre part.

Je voudrais bien pouvoir m'arrêter à Giverny mais les Javannaises me retiennent ici jusqu' au dernier moment qui est déjà passé du reste. Il-y-a plus d'une semaine que je devrais être en Angleterre.

Apropos du Olympia, j'ai vu Boldini qui donnera mille francs: j'ai en ami parlé à Roll et à (illegible). Les deux approuvent et Roll donnera quelque chose mais (illegible) dit qu'il ne peut pas. Je n'ai pas vu Duret en personne. Je reste encore quelques jours ici.

Venez en Angleterre plus tard, mon addresse de Londres pour les lettres.

Bonne poignée de main et je vous en prie ne soyez jamais inquiet de mon affection.   JOHN S. SARGENT.

As the letter shows, he was interesting himself in the purchase of Manet's *Olympia* for the Louvre.

CLAUDE MONET SKETCHING.

Chapter XV

IT is commonly said that when Sargent grew tired of portrait painting he turned to decoration and began his work for the Boston Library. But when he undertook this work he was only thirty-four and he was occupied with it for the best part of thirty years. Before its completion he had undertaken, in 1916, further decorative work at the Boston Museum of Fine Arts which he finished in 1921, and in 1922 he painted the two decorative panels in the Widener Memorial Library, Cambridge, Massachusetts, in commemoration of Harvard's share in the War. It was therefore within a very few years of his arrival in England that he turned to decoration and many years before he had reached his culmination as a portrait painter.

The Boston Public Library was designed by the famous architectural firm of McKim, Mead and White, of New York, and the member of the firm principally responsible for the form and structure of the building was Charles Follen McKim, born in 1847. The building is constructed in the style of the Italian Renaissance.

The trustees of the library before 1890 had resolved that it should be decorated internally in a manner worthy of the architecture, which has made it one of the best-known civic edifices of the United States.

It was agreed to invite the co-operation of Sargent, Edwin Abbey and Puvis de Chavannes. In January, 1890, Sargent with his sister Violet arrived in America; Edwin Abbey and Stanford White had preceded them. In the spring of 1890 the architects McKim, William Rutherford Mead, and Stanford White, together with St. Gaudens, who had been commissioned to carry out certain sculptural groups for the building, began the negotiations on behalf of the trustees. St. Gaudens at the time was engaged on a medallion of Miss Mead, the future Mrs. Abbey. He wrote the following letter to Abbey:*

DARLING,

McKim, White, Sargent, thee and I dine at the Players Wednesday night this week at 7.30. D.V., so help me God. But, be Jasus, McKim don't want any other fellows round, although I tried to (get) the whole crew together as we had agreed. The photos will be on hand. If you can't come, let me know right away. The Medallion looks like hell. I thought I had done a good thing, but it makes me sick.

ST. G.

It was after this dinner that the following letter was written by Charles McKim to Mr. Abbott, President of the Board of Trustees:

57, BROADWAY,
NEW YORK,
May 9th, 1890.

McKIM, MEAD AND WHITE,
    Architects.
CHARLES F. McKIM.
WM. RUTHERFORD MEAD.
STANFORD WHITE.

MY DEAR ABBOTT,

Let me explain my despatch of today. I received one morning a little over a week ago an excited note from St. Gaudens, stating that Abbey had just returned from Boston and was at that moment dining with him. It appears that while there, Abbey had gone over the Library and was so impressed that on his return he could talk of nothing else. This at least was the substance of St. Gaudens's note.

It appeared also that Sargent had expressed himself strongly interested in it, and knowing the policy of your Board in favour of mural decoration should the opportunity offer for it, St. Gaudens proposed boldly that we should meet at "The Players" Club the following Wednesday evening and dine with him and talk over a scheme to be submitted to the Trustees. You can imagine how joyfully this news with such substantial assurances of interest and approval from men like Abbey and Sargent and St. Gaudens, and how delighted we were to accept his invitation to meet them at dinner. Only Abbey, Sargent, St. Gaudens and McKim, Mead & White were present. After

* E. V. Lucas, "Life of Edwin Abbey," p. 228.

STUDY FOR "THE ARCHERS."
Boston Decorations.

dinner, the plans of the Library were spread out and the mural possibilities of the walls and ceilings of the halls and galleries forming the special library collections discussed. Abbey was vastly interested in the Shakespeare collection while Sargent's interest in the direction of Spanish literature was a most natural one. The interest of the occasion was much enhanced by the presence of several hundreds of carbon prints from the Masters, covering the whole period of the Renaissance. The works of Baudry and Puvis de Chavannes were also discussed.

Finally Abbey with the spontaneity which characterizes him could resist no longer and seizing his pencil sketched out almost in a moment, upon a sheet of brown wrapping paper, which happened to be at hand, two compositions for the Shakespeare Room, representing at one end "Comedy" seated opposite "Tragedy" under a ceiling divided into "Sonnets." These two allegorical figures were placed in repose over the central door-ways of access and exit from the room and were surrounded each with numerous figures proper to the subject. It was impossible to restrain our admiration as he went from one thing to another, talking as he drew, and it was good to observe the pride which Sargent evinced in the powers of his brother-artist. The next day Abbey came here at four o'clock and stayed for two hours or more for the purpose of obtaining accurate measurements of the wall surface and ceiling to be covered, and the disposition of the various vaultings. I gave him three arrangements; one representing an assumed collection requiring a space the length of two windows, one representing the length of three windows, and one representing five windows in length. The last with the barrel vault (with square ends), the first two groined (with penetrations).

Last night I dined with him and his wife at St. Gaudens's and learned that he had actually made a study in oil since our meeting at "The Players" Club, which St. Gaudens and I are going to see today. To make a long story short, we propose if you approve, to descend upon you in Boston some time during next Wednesday, with the sketches which have been made at our request, and take dinner with you and talk this matter over.

Abbey sails immediately for Capri with his bride of two weeks. St. Gaudens and I are very anxious that you should meet and know him, hence the sudden dispatch. The suggestion to ask Mr. Brooks, Mr. Brimmer and others at the same time, was, in order to render the occasion more interesting, as well as to create, if possible, public support of a policy which has not yet been carried out on this side of the ocean. Of course we do not expect anything from the City, but I am convinced that any space which you may see fit to allot to Abbey and to Sargent can be paid for privately. *I already have some promising assurances of this!*

No such brilliant opportunity has come within my recollection and I feel sure that it will appeal to you all in the way it deserves.

Sincerely yours,

CHARLES F. McKIM.

S. A. B. ABBOTT, ESQ.

Towards the middle of May, 1890, the whole party went to Boston and there met the Trustees of the Library and settled the final terms of the great undertaking. Sargent was given and accepted the commission to decorate the corridor or special libraries floor at the head of the principal staircase; a task which was to tax his imaginative and intellectual resources for twenty-six years, and to evoke in him also a talent for the plastic arts and modelling in relief. The apartment is 84 feet long, 23 feet wide, and 26 feet high, lit from above with a vaulted ceiling.

It forms a spacious landing and encloses the head of the marble staircase. Abbey, at the same time, undertook the decoration of the distributing room, involving a frieze of 180 feet in length and 8 feet in height. His first intention was that the frieze should have for its theme "subjects taken either altogether from Shakespeare, or one each from some typical writer of the various countries of Europe." Later this was altered to a single subject, "The quest and achievement of the Holy Grail," divided into fifteen scenes.

It will be noticed that as late as May, Sargent was still thinking of getting his subjects from Spanish literature. Why then did he turn from a theme with which he was already familiar, and launch upon a subject so vast and complex as that he ultimately chose? It may well be that in the symbolic figures of an abstract theme he saw and welcomed an escape from the concrete, and from the literalness and limitations of portraiture. Decoration was a phase of art in which he had himself made no experiments. It is true that he had studied Tintoretto and Tiepolo and the great Venetian decorators, and had been a pupil of Carolus Duran when that artist had painted a ceiling for the Louvre, but he had done nothing of the sort himself.

Confronted now with the alternative of taking scenes from the pictorial literature of Spain, or choosing some scheme of his own, he turned to religion. The subject required faculties and qualities not usually associated with Sargent's art. For once he was not dealing with the visible and tangible world, but rather a thing so abstract as a movement of thought. The progress of that movement had to be interpreted, symbolized and legibly translated into painted form. It was a daring scheme. He must have seen in a flash of intellectual vision the possibilities of the idea. His mind must have been already stored with learning sufficient, at any rate, to enable him to visualize vaguely the opportunities or imagery provided by such a theme. But it was with no fervour of religious enthusiasm that he approached it. To Sargent the evolution of religion was a subject which could be viewed with detachment; he approached it without bias or preference. He was no mystic drawing near to some sacred shrine, no devout enthusiast working by the light of an inward revelation, but a painter aware that here was a subject with a significance lending itself to interpretation in decorative pictorial designs. His imagination was fired, but as when he was told he had revealed the moral qualities of a sitter he said, "No, I do not judge, I only chronicle," so in his Boston decorations he must be understood as treating objectively and dispassionately the images suggested by his theme.*

Though the agreement with the trustees was come to in May, 1890, the contract was not signed till January 18, 1893, when they undertook to pay fifteen thousand dollars, and the painter to complete the work by December 30, 1897. In 1895 the scope of the scheme was very much extended. Mr. Edward Robinson raised a subscription of a further fifteen thousand dollars, and for this sum Sargent agreed to decorate the side wall of the Sargent Hall and to enter into a contract to that effect. He was much exercised about the decoration of the tympana or lunettes, holding that it was inadvisable to settle as to these before the side wall had been completed. But

* At the end of the chapter will be found the titles of the subjects included in the decorations.

then, had the subscribers paid their money in the belief that the tympana were to be painted? Did they regard them as part of the bargain, or would they allow them to be dependent on the general effect and only painted if needed as part of the decorative requirements when the side wall was finished? These questions were very agitating. It was just the sort of difficulty most calculated to perplex the conscientious mind of Sargent. On the one hand was his scrupulous desire to fulfil to the letter what might be the expectations of the subscribers, on the other his recognition that the tympana might be the better for being left alone. In the end, and after a voluminous correspondence, he was persuaded by Mr. Robinson to regard himself as having a free hand; his scruples were set at rest, and when the time came for forming an opinion he went ahead with the tympana as part of the scheme. This second contract was signed December, 1895.

Having settled on his subject, "The development of religious thought from paganism through Judaism to Christianity," Sargent there and then began to make studies. At the end of May, Abbey, then on his way to England, wrote:*

> I wonder how John is getting on, and whether you have built him a beautiful model yet. I went into his studio a day or two before I sailed and saw stacks of sketches of nude people, saints, I dare say, most of them, although from my cursory observations of them they seemed a bit earthy. You will surely get a great thing from him. He can do *anything*, and don't know himself what he can do. He is latent with all manner of possibilities and the Boston people need not be afraid that he will be eccentric or impressionistic, or anything that is not perfectly serious and non-experimental when it comes to work of this kind.

Sargent had entered on this entirely new phase of his career at the age of thirty-four. Those who saw the exhibition at the Academy in 1926, and bore in mind that another exhibition of his paintings was being held in America, were astonished at the extent of his work. Few considered, or indeed knew, that concurrently with the work exhibited, he had during twenty-six years been engaged on this stupendous decoration at the Boston Library.

* E. V. Lucas, "Edwin Austen Abbey," i., p. 231.

When Abbey returned to England he sought for a place where he could work undisturbed; Broadway had disposed him towards the West Country. Wanderings through the counties of Oxford, Gloucester and Worcester finally brought him to Fairford, where in Morgan Hall he saw the very house he wanted. This was in the autumn of 1890. He entered into a lease for twenty-one years and at once began the construction in the grounds of a studio 64 feet long by 40 feet by 25 feet. There in November, 1891, Sargent joined him, and in cordial association carried out much of the preliminary work for the Boston Library designs.

Sargent meanwhile had remained in New York through the summer of 1890, pushing on with studies for his decorative scheme, and filling up the intervals with painting a number of portraits. The portraits of *Mr. George Peabody of Salem*, *Mr. and Mrs. and Miss Brooks*, *Senator Henry Cabot Lodge*, *Mrs. Francis Dewey*, *Mrs. Augustus P. Loring*, *Miss Katherine Pratt*, *Edwin Booth*, *Joseph Jefferson*, *Laurence Barrett* and a study of Carmencita singing, belong to this period.

It was also during this visit that he painted the well-known picture of *Miss Beatrice Goelet*, which with the portrait of the *Hon. Laura Lister* constitute Sargent's two most ambitious and successful renderings of childhood. Both pictures have been the subject of unmeasured praise. Both have been extolled as expressions of the spirit of childhood. Of the picture of the Hon. Laura Lister Mrs. Meynell goes so far as to say that "it takes its place with the most beautiful painted in all centuries." In America the Goelet portrait was the subject of discerning praise from the pen of Mrs. Van Rensselaer, and when later the same critic wrote an appreciation of Sargent's picture *Mother and Child* (Mrs. Davis and her son) she received from Sargent the following letter:

33, TITE STREET,
CHELSEA,
Dec. 15*th.*

MY DEAR MRS. VAN RENSSELAER,

I am sure you must be the author of an article that has been sent me from N.Y. in which Mrs. Davis' picture receives very high praise, because it seems to have touched a sentiment in the writer like what you expressed about the Goelet baby, and very few writers give me credit for insides so to speak. I am of course grateful to you for writing, but especially for feeling in the way you do, for it would seem that sometimes at any rate for you, I hit the mark.

Please believe me,
Yours sincerely,
John S. Sargent.

I feel as if I ought to have written a much longer letter to give you any idea of how much pleasure and what kind of pleasure you have given me.

The letter shows on the part of Sargent a greater sensibility to criticism than the public gave him credit for. As a matter of fact, praise, if it was discriminating, brought him the keenest pleasure. He was much too human and much too humble to pass it by or let it slip through his fingers; he clung to it with the inner satisfaction that belongs by habit to the diffident; and here was a point raised as to which he was sensitive. He was already perhaps a little tired of the hackneyed view that his portraiture was deficient in feeling, that he was a pitiless revealer of his sitter's defects. It was therefore something to the good that when he set out to paint childhood he could satisfy critics on the look-out for emotional quality in his work. No artist deficient in tenderness of feeling, no artist not gifted with the power of finely apprehending the particular significance of childhood could have painted these two pictures. They have not got the direct and winning artlessness of the children of Bronzino, Franz Hals, Holbein or Velasquez— it might even be said that in their childishness they are precocious, or should we say sophisticated—but they possess the same exquisite delicacy and distinction, the same subtlety of charm that we see in the *Fortune Tellers* or the *Lady Mary FitzPatrick* of Reynolds.

Sargent had a studio in New York in Twenty-Third Street, and here he painted the picture of *Carmencita*. Carmencita was a Spanish dancer recently arrived from Europe and holding the public of New York enthralled by her beauty and sensational

STUDY OF OXEN.

dancing. She consented to pose to Sargent. He soon found
that he had undertaken a perilous sitter. She was a primitive
and untutored creature, straight from the cabarets of Spain.
Civilization had put few fetters about her. She was reminiscent
of the sources from which his picture of *El Jaleo* had been
drawn. In mood she was wayward, now sullen and subdued,
then breaking into tempests of anger and impatience, ready to
smash anything that was to hand, or, again, sinking into an
entirely childish readiness to be diverted or amused. She made
no pretence of liking to have her portrait painted. She found
posing intolerable. Movement was the essence of her existence,
why forego it and be bored and insufferably constrained to please
an artist and be recorded on canvas? Sargent had to exercise
his ingenuity; "he used to paint his nose red to rivet her childish
interest upon himself, and when the red nose failed he would
fascinate her by eating his cigar. This performance was the
dancer's delight."*

Sargent was anxious that Mrs. Gardner should see this
"bewilderingly superb creature," and asked if she would give a
party at her house in Fifth Avenue. "Could you," he wrote,
"have her at your house in Fifth Avenue? If so, might I go
and see whether the floor or carpet would be good, and whether
there is a chandelier against which she would have to break the
head? It would have to be about twelve o'clock at night, after
the performance." In the end the party was given by Mrs.
Gardner at the studio of William Chase the painter, at Tenth
Street, New York. The fee paid to Carmencita was 150 dollars.
Mrs. de Glehn, then Miss Jane Emmett, was present with her
sister, and has described the scene. Sargent, whom she had never
seen before, was seated on the floor. The studio was dimly
lighted; at the end of the room was just such a scene as he had
represented in *El Jaleo*. Carmencita, a light thrown on her
from below, now writhing like a serpent, now with an arrogant
elegance, strutted the stage with a shadowy row of guitarists
in the background strumming their heady Spanish music. She
had arrived at the studio with her hair frizzled and her face

* W. H. Downes, "John Sargent," p. 31, citing H. J. Brock, *New York Times.*

loaded with powder and paint. Sargent, as her impresario for the occasion, smoothed her hair flat with a wet brush; he even applied a wash rag to her cosmetics.* This was carrying the office of stage manager too far; she resented it and boiled over. Tact was then required to cool her down and induce her to dance, but her "scenes" were short-lived. Before she had danced many steps Mrs. de Glehn saw her throw a rose at her painter as he sat in the half-light on the floor. He picked it up, and from his buttonhole it ratified the peace.

Some years later Carmencita came to London, and Sargent gave a party at 31, Tite Street, at which she danced in his studio. She was now married to the leader of her guitar orchestra, living in lodgings in Bloomsbury and dancing for a large salary at one of the music halls. Mr. Jacomb Hood,† who visited her, found her occupying, with her husband, a single bed-sitting-room and cooking together their meal on the fireplace; her portmanteau and one chair were the only seating accommodation. But she was no longer the Carmencita of New York. Time had abated her wildness, though not her beauty, and civilization had subdued the fire of her spirit, though not her grace—she was tamed—she danced at charity concerts, and in her steps she deferred to the standards of British conventionality.

The picture painted by Sargent was exhibited at the Society of American Artists at New York in 1890, at the Royal Academy in 1891, and at the Exhibition of American Art in 1919, and it now hangs in the Luxembourg. Carmencita stands with her right foot advanced, her right arm akimbo, in a dress of orange, black and silver, a silk scarf falls across her breast and is tied at the left hip, on which her left hand rests. The attitude suggests a challenge to the guitarists to play, to the audience to applaud. She is balanced on her feet with all the lightness of an accomplished dancer, in a moment the orange skirt will swirl, and the lissom figure spring into vehement action. In no other picture by Sargent is the suggestion of suspended movement so direct and convincing. In the treatment of the dress, as in the

* W. H. Downes, "John Sargent," p. 31, citing H. J. Brock, *New York Times*.
† Jacomb Hood, "With Brush and Pencil," p. 313.

fine portrait of Mrs. Leopold Hirsch (1902), there is a very definite reminder of Velasquez. The shimmer of silver, the notation of pattern, the suggestion of texture, the crispness of touch, are reminiscent of the portrait of Philip in the National Gallery. The dress rustles, the light plays in its folds, the whole figure is alert with vitality. If the pose verges on the theatrical, and the expression is wanting in the primitive emotions of *El Jaleo*, and if the tones of the flesh are less subtle than in some of his pictures, none the less it lives as a masterly expression of the artist's skill. Sargent himself expressed regret to Miss Heyneman that he should be represented at the Luxembourg by this picture. When asked why, he said: "After all, it is little more than a sketch."

When the picture was exhibited in New York an admirer offered £600. Sargent said to de Glehn: "I was unable to accept it as it had cost me more than that to paint." "Cost you more! how do you mean?" "Why, in bracelets and things." To such an extent had this capricious beauty to be coaxed before she would fulfil her promise to pose.

Chapter XVI

IN the autumn of 1890 Sargent and his sister, after a year's absence, returned to Europe, going direct to Marseilles, where they joined Mrs. Sargent and Miss Emily; the whole party proceeding together to Egypt and arriving at Alexandria on Christmas Eve. Thence they went to Cairo, where Sargent hired a studio and painted, among other pictures, the nude full-length of an Egyptian girl, now owned by Mr. Dering. Here they found Mrs. Farquharson and her stepson Mr. Joseph Farquharson, who were living on a dahebiah owned by Mrs. Farquharson's brother. After a month at Cairo, Sargent and his family, with the Farquharsons, embarked on one of Gage's steamers and went up the Nile to Luxor and Philae. Sargent himself with a dragoman made an expedition to Fayoum.

His main purpose in Egypt was to familiarize himself with the legend and myth, the history and archaeology, the symbols and religion of the country, and thus furnish himself with the material for the first stage of his Boston decoration. With his natural aptitude for mastering the essential, he came away at the end of this visit equipped with all the knowledge his exacting mind could require. The character and significance of the Egyptian gods, their relation to their time, their influence in history, the legends to which they had given origin, and the symbolism by which they were surrounded, had now only to be sifted and sorted in his brain, that they might be adapted for pictorial embodiment. Just as Gustave Flaubert had visited Carthage and settled down to master the archaeology necessary for "Salammbo," so had Sargent pored over the monuments and lore of Egypt that he might correctly interpret the spirit and significance of the pagan deities. His accuracy has never been questioned.

In April the family crossed over to Athens, whence Sargent

set out with a dragoman for Olympia and Delphi. Every morning he was in the saddle at 4 a.m., only ending the day's journey
when night again fell. He rode through miles of country
carpeted with wild flowers. Greece was displaying its beauties
and enchantments, and revealing its magic vistas in the allure-
ment of a golden spring. Long before his return to Athens he
had filled up every available corner of canvas and paper that
he had taken for oil and water-colour. From Athens the family
went to Constantinople. Here, by bribing an official, he
obtained leave to do a sketch of the interior of Santa Sophia,
and by the shores of the Bosphorus where the Judas trees
were in full bloom he did several water-colours. The study
of Santa Sophia* was made in the early morning, and is one of
the most purely atmospheric canvases which he painted. The
picture has charm and mystery, and probably few better examples
exist of his power for rendering the structure and spacing of
a building with the minimum of definition. In two other interior
studies, *St. Mark's, Venice: the Pavement*† and *Interior of the
Palazzo Ducale, Venice*,‡ he has succeeded equally well in
rendering structure, proportion and space; but in these the means
employed are comparatively matter of fact, they have not the
same atmospheric effect, the craftsmanship is consummate, though
they are less suffused with a mood. For that we must turn to
An Hotel Room,§ *My Dining-Room*‖ and the masterly picture of
Mr. and Mrs. Vickers, *A Dinner Table at Night*.¶ From Constantinople the family came west by Vienna, and in July (1891)
were at San Remo at the Villa Ormond. In August his sister
Violet was married in Paris to Monsieur Ormond. It was not
till the autumn of 1891 that he was back in England after an
absence, save for a brief visit in June, of two years. Mrs. Sargent
and Miss Emily spent that winter at Nice, and the following
winter in Tunis, returning to London in the spring of 1893.

* The picture owned by Mr. C. J. Conway was exhibited at the Royal Academy
Memorial Exhibition, 1926, No. 329.
† Owned by Miss Sargent.
‡ Owned by Viscount Lascelles, K.G., D.S.O.
§ Owned by Mrs. Ormond.
‖ Owned by W. G. de Glehn, Esq., A.R.A.
¶ Owned by V. C. Vickers, Esq.

It was then that a lease of 10, Carlyle Mansions, Cheyne Walk, was taken for Mrs. Sargent and Miss Emily, close to Sargent's own house in Tite Street. In the years to follow a large part of his home life was spent with his sister Emily.

In 1891 Sargent was represented in the Academy by his picture of *Carmencita* and a portrait of *Mrs. Thomas Lincoln Manson*. The critics were beginning to come over. They were falling into line with R. A. M. Stevenson and the public was following. Sargent was beginning to be recognized as the first of living portrait painters. In London he had formed many friendships: Professor Tonks, Mr. D. S. MacColl, Sir George Henschel, Mr. and Mrs. L. A. Harrison, Mr. and Mrs. Comyns-Carr, Mr. Frederick Jameson, Miss Heyneman, Wilson Steer, Sir George and Lady Lewis. He was a frequent visitor at Ightham Moat House, which had been leased by Mrs. Palmer, where he painted in 1889 the large picture of the "house party" playing at bowls, exhibited at the New Gallery in 1890.* Socially in London he was greatly sought after. He was becoming acclimatized to the conditions, beginning to feel himself at home, and being "licked into London shape" had proved a less trying process than he had anticipated. He, Whistler and Henry James were recognized in the nineties as stars of the first magnitude, and though Sargent and James equally and consistently shunned publicity like the plague, "renown" has a tendency to make things easy, to simplify the stranger's problems, and amplify his area of selection and choice. At the same time any one more completely unconscious of his prestige than Sargent can hardly be imagined. It coursed and eddied about his feet, but he never suffered it to throw him off his balance or to disturb the full and even measure of his working days.

In November, 1891, he joined Mr. and Mrs. Abbey at Morgan Hall, Fairford, and there for certain months in each year till 1895 he remained to share the studio and to pursue his Boston Library decorations. Mrs. Mead, the mother of Mrs. Abbey, was also of the party during the greater part of

* See *ante*, p. 84.

AT THE FORGE.

these years, and did much to enhance the contented spirit that reigned in this centre of strenuous work.

Before Sargent's arrival Abbey had written to Paris for assistance, asking that specimen drawings should be sent by students who were ready to join the studio at Fairford. Two students were chosen, James Finn and Wilfrid de Glehn (A.R.A., 1925). Between de Glehn and Sargent began one of Sargent's staunchest friendships.

Work would begin at nine or nine-thirty every morning and continue till dark, the studio being divided into a Sargent territory and an Abbey territory. An Italian named Colarossi came as model for Sargent, and one Demarco, "who had a very beautiful head," posed for Abbey.

Later on a younger model became necessary for Sargent's purposes, and an Italian named Inverno was chosen. This was the brother of Nicola d'Inverno, who subsequently in 1893 came to the studio as a model and remained in Sargent's service more than twenty years—Nicola will be remembered by everyone who visited the studio in Fulham Road. He used to pose for the frieze of the prophets and other portions of the decorative work and was constantly in attendance, assisting in the preparation of the "relief" work for the Boston Library, and looking after the mechanical accessories of the artist's work, accompanying Sargent abroad and taking charge of brushes, canvases and paints. Nicola, who had come from Clerkenwell and was in his spare moments a pugilist, used with Sargent to go by the name of the "Clerkenwell Chicken." Occasionally he would appear with a black eye as the trophy of an overnight contest, when Sargent would say: "Ah, I see we have met another man who is slightly the better." Sargent paid for Nicola's training at a gymnasium and would assist him financially when, as not infrequently happened, he was unsuccessful in some venture on the Turf. Nicola wrote his recollections of Sargent in the Boston *Sunday Advertiser*, February 7, 1926, and concluded: "Every hour I spent in his service will be a precious memory for ever. The world calls him a great, I know him to be a good, man."

One day a week, occasionally more often, Sargent, who kept

a horse at Fairford, would hunt either with the Heythrop, the Warwickshire or the North Cotswold Hounds. Those who only saw him in later years in London would hesitate to associate him with this particular form of activity and recreation, but it was a source of great enjoyment to him. In the first years of his London life he even kept a horse and rode regularly in the Row; and it is difficult to recognize him as the author of the following letter to Sir George Henschel, to whom, when he himself was leaving London, he lent his horse:

> I will give instructions about the mare's cribbing, she *must* either be muzzled or wear a cribbing strap, both of which she possesses. You will find the mare rather sluggish in the streets and inclined to gallop much too fast in the row. You had better use my saddle and bridle which has a very strong curb. She is shod by Messrs. . . . with a rational shoe and I would like her always to be shod by them.

This diagnosis of the mare's characteristics proved correct save on the one point of sluggishness in the streets, and when, like Hercules with Mr. Thornton in Mr. Sponge's "Sporting Tour," the mare showed tendencies to go through plate-glass windows, Sir George thought it time to return the horse to its owner. Sargent was fearless across country, but he was not an accomplished horseman. His departure to the meet was viewed with anxiety: his return in the evening hailed with relief. He had many falls. None displayed more nervousness than Colarossi, who so long as Sargent was absent at the hunt remained in a state of profound apprehension. Describing what used to occur Colarossi said, not without pride: "Sometimes he not come off the horse at all."

At one time Sargent took lessons at the Kensington Riding School, advised so to do by Mr. Joseph Farquharson, to whom he had confided his deficiencies in his early hunting days, saying that he had fallen off when his horse had jumped into a field and fallen off again when the horse jumped out of the field. As the result of these lessons a cavalcade including Mr. Jacomb Hood, Linley Sambourne, Shakespeare the singer, and Sir George Henschel would issue from the streets of London on Sunday mornings and clatter through Putney for a gallop in Richmond Park.

Sargent's hunting was responsible for one of the oddest episodes in his career. It was shortly before Christmas, 1891. Towards the end of the day he was riding homeward. He found himself in a field of winter wheat, a part of which he had to cross in order to reach a bridle path.

He was no agriculturist; he probably would have found it difficult to distinguish between a field of potatoes and a field of turnips. In all ignorance and innocence, therefore, he continued his way. His movements had been observed; through the twilight the owner of the winter wheat advanced upon him and without preliminaries launched out into a torrent of low abuse. Sargent was completely surprised. He dismounted, and as the man drew near began to apologize for his mistake, offering to make good any damage he had done. Far from being pacified by his courtesy, the farmer became more incensed. He worked himself into a frenzy of rage and loaded Sargent with every variety of threat and malediction. He was well known in the neighbourhood as a surly and foul-mouthed fellow, and Sargent, deeply agitated, mastered his temper and moved away, mounted his horse and rode home. That evening he described what had happened; Mrs. Abbey states that he was obviously in the grip of an agitating distress. At intervals he would return to the subject and discuss what he ought to do. For two days he was uneasy and silent and could do no work. Late on the second day he went out. Towards evening of that day Mrs. Abbey was returning from a walk. Her road led past the gate of the house where the farmer lived. As she approached, a figure walked rapidly down the path; drawing nearer she saw in the dusk that it was Sargent. When he joined her he exclaimed: "I've done it— I've done it." He was calmer than he had been at any time since the adventure. He went on to tell her that after looking at the thing from every side and turning it over and over in his mind he had settled what he ought to do; he had gone to the farmer's door, knocked, and when the farmer appeared, had said: "Come outside and defend yourself, I am going to thrash you."

The farmer called on his household to witness the assault, and then, answering the challenge, engaged in a struggle in the course of which Sargent appears to have carried out his threat. Such was the amazing story told as he and Mrs. Abbey walked home.

The farmer at once sought the help of the law. It was doubtful at first whether he would proceed by summons before a magistrate or by a civil action for damages. Sargent put the matter in the hands of Sir George Lewis. On January 21 Sir George wrote that the farmer had issued a writ for damages. He advised payment into court. £50 was considered adequate. The farmer accepted the sum, and proceedings went no further; and there, so far as Sargent was concerned, this curious episode ended. Later an unexpected turn was given to it by an invitation from the farmer to Sargent asking him to dine. Sargent declined, but as a reconciliation was in the air de Glehn and Finn took his place, and found the farmer if not ready to forgive, at any rate determined effectually to achieve forgetfulness by conviviality.

Legend has it that Sargent spent the interval between the insult and the assault in taking lessons in boxing. This scarcely needs denial; he spent the interval, it is true, in deep perplexity. His sense of justice, always lively, but balanced, had been outraged, but his indignation had cooled and had been replaced by a reasoned view of what under the circumstances it was right to do. He acted in a manner which was unspeakably distasteful to him, driven forward by the conviction that no other course was honourably open to him. It was in no spirit of revenge that he acted, it was probably with no sense of personal grievance, but on a conclusion of judgment arrived at on a point of honour. It was, in fact, the outcome of that rigid rectitude of mind which was habitual to him. We may look on it as evidence of character that he should have allowed the first heat of his anger to cool, and that then, after conferring with his conscience like any cadi seated under a tree, he should have thought himself bound to mete out retribution. His action, therefore, was no "wild form of justice," but a lively expression of the moral instinct embedded in his character.

HEBRAIC PORTION

North End of the Hall

Ceiling: Pagan religions of countries surrounding Palestine.
Lunette: Children of Israel, oppressed by pagan neighbours, expressing their dependence on the True God.
Frieze: The Hebrew prophets, typifying the progress of the Jews in religious thought, with final expectation of the Messiah.

IN THE EASTERN LUNETTES

Left: The downfall of paganism, as preached by Hebrew prophets.
Centre: The Hebrew ideal—the chosen people protected by Jehovah, through its observance of the Law.
Right: The Messianic era, foretold by Hebrew prophets.

CHRISTIAN PORTION

At the South End of the Hall

Lunette: Doctrine of the Trinity.
Frieze and Crucifix: Doctrine of the Redemption.
Ceiling and Niches: Doctrine of the Incarnation.

IN THE WESTERN LUNETTES

Left: Heaven.
Centre: The Judgment.
Right: Hell.

THE MEDIÆVAL CONTRAST

On the East Wall

Left Panel: The Synagogue.
Right Panel: The Church.*

* This analysis is taken from "Handbook of the Boston Public Library."

Chapter XVII

NEITHER Sargent's visits to America nor his work for the Boston Library had shaken his preference for London as a permanent home. The tie of allegiance to America was one thing, but Europe was necessary to his artistic life. From London he could easily visit his favourite countries and in Tite Street he was in close proximity to his mother and sister Emily.

When Sargent began his career as a portrait painter in London he was classed by the public and not a few of the critics as an Impressionist. This was inevitable. He hailed from the home of Impressionism; and London was still under the spell of "Finish."* If treatment was summary and abbreviated, and the subject suggested instead of stated with all possible explicitness, the painter was held in the early nineties to be sinning against the light. It was all very well to sow artistic wild oats in Paris, the harvest in London must be something to which the public was accustomed. Anything that showed a lack of "finish" was suspect. Sargent's bravura and vitality of technique were alone enough to stamp him in the popular mind as an Impressionist.

Few labels have led to more misunderstanding; applied in the seventies to a special aspect of painting, it was used later to cover qualities which had nothing to do with those which the word had been coined to describe. In Paris the word had a specialized sense; it did not denote that Impressionism common to much fine painting. It denoted a peculiar treatment of light, and was less concerned with focus, the relation of planes, and actual form.

In the following letters Sargent gives his own idea of the particular significance and value of Impressionism. The first letter, addressed to Mr. D. S. MacColl, was written in 1912:

* See *ante*, p. 87.

My dear MacColl,

I daresay I muddled what I said about Impressionism last night and perhaps this is a clear definition of what I think Monet would mean by the word, "The observation of the colour and value of the image on our retina of those objects or parts of objects of which we are prevented by an excess or deficiency of light from seeing the surface or local colour."

Of course to a very astigmatic or abnormal eyesight the whole field of vision might offer phenomena for the notation of an impressionist, but to the average vision it is only in extreme cases of light and dark that the eye is conscious of seeing something else than the object, in other words conscious of its own medium—that something else is what the impressionist tries to note exactly. . . .

Yrs. sincerely,

John S. Sargent.

The two letters which follow were written to Mr. Jameson, a close friend of Sargent and the author of a volume on art which forms the text of the letters.

31, Tite Street,
Chelsea, S.W.,
March 20th (1911 *or* 1912).

My dear Jameson,

I have been reading your book with great enjoyment, and feel as if my ideas and my vocabulary had gone through a very satisfactory spring cleaning and I like the opposition of your clear processes of reasoning and analysis as far as that will take one and the ultimate mystery that you lead one up to from the different directions.

There is one point only that I should quibble at and that is your use of the word *Impressionism* and *Impressionist*.

These words were coined in Paris at a particular moment when Claude Monet opened the eyes of a few people to certain phenomena of optics, and they have a very precise meaning which is not the one that you use them for, so that in the exact sense or to a Frenchman Watts' saying "All art is Impressionism" would be a misuse of words.

"Impressionism" was the name given to a certain form of observation when Monet not content with using his eyes to see what things were or what they looked like as everybody had done before him, turned his attention to noting what took place *on his own retina* (as an oculist would test his own vision).

It led to his doing 50 pictures of the same subject under varying degrees of light and the phenomena which he recorded would be more or less apparent when there was excess or deficiency of light and the fact that he is astigmatic accounts for his having an excellent subject for his own discoveries in this line.

A person with normal eyesight would have nothing to know in the way of "Impressionism" unless he were in a blinding light or in the dusk or dark.

If you want to know what an impressionist tries for (by the way Degas said there is only one Impressionist "Claude Monet") go out of doors and look at a landscape with the sun in your eyes and alter the angle of your hat brim and notice the difference of colour in dark objects according to the amount of light you let into your eyes—you can vary it from the local colour of the object (if there is less light) to something entirely different which is an appearance on your own retina when there is too much light.

It takes years to be able to note this accurately enough for painting purposes and it would only seem worth while to people who would wear the same glasses as the painter and then it has the effect of for the first time coming across a picture that looks like nature and gives the sense of living—for these reasons Monet bowled me over—and he counts as having added a new perception to Artists as the man did who invented perspective.

This observation or faculty does not make a man an Artist any more than a knowledge of perspective does—it is merely a refining of one's means towards representing things and one step further away from the hieroglyph by adding to the representation of a thing the conscious Will of the Medium through which one sees it.

One of these days some genius will turn it to account and make it part of the necessary equipment of an Artist.

For the present in its exact sense "impressionism" does not come within the scope of your considerations. Of course I agree with what you say, given the rough and tumble and un-Jameson like use of the word.

You can make impression stand for whatever you like but not add -sm or -ist without being challenged by the astigmatic.

Yours sincerely,   JOHN S. SARGENT.

31, TITE STREET,
CHELSEA, S.W.,
April 3rd (1911 *or* 1912).

MY DEAR JAMESON,
        Thanks for your kind letter.

I am glad you take my bit of special pleading good naturedly. I was afraid after having posted my letter that I had not made clear that I was not quarrelling with what you said about Impressionism but only defining the term.

LADY D'ABERNON.

Of course your meaning is the general accepted one and the right one in the context as long as the precise meaning is so little known—it will be years before the idea itself will have become familiar even to most painters—when it is, there will have to be a foot note in your book.

The habit of breaking up one's colour to make it brilliant dates from further back than Impressionism—Couture advocates it in a little book called "Causeries d'Atelier" written about 1860—it is part of the technique of Impressionism but used for quite a different reason.

Couture, Delacroix, Orchardson break up their colour but they are not Impressionists.   Yours sincerely,

JOHN S. SARGENT.

In these letters there are phrases not easy to interpret. For instance, the writer has spoken of the retina as though it could be watched and studied as a separable portion of the organ of vision. "Adding to the representation of a thing the conscious will of the medium through which one sees it" implies more than was meant by Sir Joshua Reynolds when he spoke of "seeing with the dilated eye." It suggests that the retina intervenes between the spectator and the scene to be observed, and that on it, as on a stained glass window through which light is transmitted, changes take place which can be studied and chronicled. The retina performs no such function. The observer cannot disintegrate the process of vision, nor will any "conscious will" enable him to analyze the office of the retina, any more than it would enable him to trace the operation of a mental perception on the substance of the brain. The phrase should perhaps be taken as suggesting no more than a heightened consciousness in the process of observation at a given moment. But, however that may be, the deep interest and the true interest of the letters lie in the revelation they afford of Sargent's attitude to the quality of Impressionism as shown in the work of Monet. He recognizes that here is an epoch in the history of painting, a point of departure, and the disclosure of a new possibility in pictorial art. Not, it should be noted, so much through the discovery of a new technical process, as by the rendering in paint of phenomena which had hitherto eluded the vision of painters.

Was he at all affected by the novel vision of which he was so keenly aware?

Can it be traced in his own work?

To answer the question we must estimate these influences and their novelty more exactly. What did they, in effect, consist of, and what was the novelty they imported? The introduction of light into a picture had been an aim of many schools of painting, notably of the Dutch; but what no school had hitherto adequately apprehended was the relation between colour and light. Colour had been regarded as an attribute of the object, and not the product of scintillant vibrations transmitted to the eye. In the painting of Monet there was revealed the truth which science had already established, that colour varies with light, and differs from moment to moment as the scale of light alters. It was in order to arrest this fugitive quality of colour and its flickering inconstancy that Monet would multiply his representations of the same object, as when he painted fifty canvases of one haystack and reiterated his studies of Rouen Cathedral. Sargent used to say that when he visited Monet at the Savoy Hotel, he found him surrounded by some ninety canvases—each one the record of a momentary effect of light over the Thames. When the effect was repeated and an opportunity occurred for finishing the picture, the effect had generally passed away before the particular canvas could be found.

It was no permanent attribute of the scene that Monet tried to express, but its momentary colour aspect under various degrees of illumination. He set out on his career as a painter without any preconceived idea or scientific theory, but gifted with an exceptional power of vision he painted what he saw, the visible world drenched in light and ceaselessly changing in colour as the light ebbed or strengthened. Gradually and *pari passu*, with his apprehension of the scientific truth, he developed a technique which enabled him to catch and render this elusive quality. Mr. MacColl, in an illuminating article* on the subject, has referred to the method of the Impressionists as "a new handling

* See "Encyclopædia Britannica," article "Impressionism and Modern Art," by the same author.

of colour by small broken touches in place of the large flowing touches characteristic of Monet," and, summarizing the characteristics of these painters, he goes on to say that the ideas dominating the school were: (1) Abolition of conventional brown tonality. But all browns, in the fervour of this revolt, went the way of conventional brown, and all ready-made mixtures like the umbers, orchres, siennas, were banished from the palette. Black itself was condemned. (2) The idea of the spectrum, which, as exhibiting the series of primary or pure colours, directed the reformed palette. (3) These colours being laid on the canvas with as little previous mixture on the palette as possible to maintain a maximum of luminosity, and being fused by touch on the canvas as little as possible for the same reason.* Here we have a terse statement of the Impressionist method as practised by Monet.

Thus it would appear that Monet has gone further than his predecessors in a certain visual discernment, and that his genius has enabled him to evolve a technique which will render on canvas this field of luminous notation. Broad sweeps of the brush and large areas of colour varying only in tone have been replaced by lesser touches of less mixed colour, producing on the canvas a closer adherence to the colour sensations experienced when contemplating the object which gave rise to them. As a result of this there certainly entered into pictorial art a new freshness and vitality. Every object being rendered on the canvas under the magic influence of light, there resulted a greater unity of impression. Light and shade were brought closer together in tone, the violent contrasts of the old chiaroscuro were dispensed with. Definition gave place to mystery, scintillation and iridescence were added to the rendering of colour. Tactile values, it is true, tended as a consequence to be relegated to a secondary position; but the gain to art, as Sargent points out, was a lasting one, permanently enriching the resources at the command of the painter. Mr. Harold Speed has defined

---

* It will be observed that Mr. MacColl has not included *broken colour* as an essential part of the Impressionist technique. At the same time, the fact must not be lost sight of that *broken colour* was made use of from time to time, and would still in some quarters be regarded as even essential to a true Impressionist picture.

the extent to which the Impressionists have varied the technique of Turner, who profoundly influenced Monet and Pissarro when they visited London in 1871. "Turner's method," he writes, "had been to lay on with large masses of pure colour, and when dry work over them thinly with other pure colours, one showing through the other. The method of putting colours down side by side and letting them blend* as they came to the eye was the invention of the Impressionists, and added greatly to the vividness of the mixtures and wonderfully extended the capacity of pigments to represent light effects."

I wished to obtain, if possible, some indication of M. Monet's own views on Sargent's letter to Mr. Jameson and on the Impressionist position generally. I had the good fortune to find Claude Monet at home on an afternoon in May, 1926. I made the pilgrimage to Giverny, supported by a letter of introduction from M. Helleu. It was an afternoon of broad sunshine. The garden which the painter had cultivated and watched with parental fondness for forty years was rich with the colour of spring flowers. A broad path led down from the house to a gateway opening on to a road. On the other side of the road, surrounded by high poplars, lay the stretch of water in which Monet cultivated every species of lily. Spanning the water was the bridge which has figured so often on his canvases. Beyond this again lay the meadowland bordering the wide waters of the Seine. At the moment Monet was conversing in his garden with two devout visitors from Japan, who presently took their leave with reverential obeisances. He was now free to peruse the letter from M. Helleu, and shortly turned to me with a cordial invitation to enter the house. We sat in the long room on whose walls hung four tiers of unframed canvases, dating from the earliest to the latest years of the master's work. The room was simply furnished, the walls of pine; green blinds tempered the strength of the sun, but through the open window came the scent from the garden, and the hum of bees. At this date Monet, born in 1840, was eighty-five years of age, but the activity of his compact frame, the vigour of his voice and the

---

* This in effect constitutes *broken colour*.

alertness of his mind pointed to an astonishing discrepancy between constitution and age. He struck a visitor as at once gay and kindly, keen in his wit, and emphatic in his prejudices, wholly simple and unaffected, with something rustic in his bearing. None could have failed to notice the touch of dandyism visible in the cuffs of ruffled lawn, which projected from the sleeves of his rough summer clothes, nor the fineness of his hands, nor the curious quality of his eye, which, magnified behind the lens of powerful spectacles, seemed to possess some of the properties of a searchlight and be ready to seize on the innermost secrets of a visible world. When Sargent's letter, of which an accurate translation had been made, was read to him he seemed frankly nonplussed, and he asked that it might be read again. A second reading found him obviously flattered by the references to himself,* but at a loss to recognize what was said as descriptive of his work. He went on to say:

L'Impressionisme ce n'est que la sensation immédiate. Tous les grands peintres étaient plus ou moins impressionistes. C'est surtout une question d'instinct. Tout celà est plus simple que ne le croit Sargent. Le mot Impressionisme a été inventé par les journaux satyriques comme raillerie, à la grande colère de Manet. J'ai fait beaucoup de mal, car j'ai été un bien mauvais exemple† . . . ce qu'il faut c'est la fraicheur de sensation. Oui il-y-a la Décoloration des tons et dans de passage d'un ton à un antre il-y-a une nuance. Par exemple entre le bleu et le jaune il-y-a quelque chose qui se passe qu'on peut exprimer dans la peinture. Il est exact que le soleil décompose tout; ainsi les fleurs sont plus jolies par temps, gris,

(this á propos of the passage in Sargent's letter to Mr. Jameson, in which he refers to the effect of an excess of light). M. Monet said that formerly painters had used one tube of paint for the shadow and another for the light, that was over and done with.

* In a previous letter to me, Monet had said: "Je vous envoie deux lettres de Sargent qui vous confirmeront l'admiration qu'il avait pour moi, ce dont je reste très fier."

† This was a consideration very present to his mind; in a letter of August 25, 1926, Madame Monet (his daughter-in-law), writing at his instance, when he was too ill to write, said: "Il est du reste plus en plus désolé, d'avoir été la cause involontaire de son nom d'Impressionisme."

He then turned to recollections of Sargent:

J'ai recontré pour la première fois Sargent et Helleu chez Durand
Ruel Rue de la Paix vers 1876. Sargent s'est precipité sur moi en me
disant. Est ce vraiment vous-vous-Claude Monet? Puis il m'a
invité a diner, rendez vous au Café de la Paix, il avait plusieurs amis
avec lui. Je leur ai indiqué lé Café du Helder, et là nous avons
demandé un salon particulier. Malheureusement il y avait plusieurs
tableaux de moi—j'étais confus en entrant, ayant honte que Sargent
etles autres pussent penser que c'était a cause de mes tableaux que
j'avais indiqué le Café Helder.

After that they remained friends till Sargent's death; in
later years meeting seldom; their lines of life diverging, but
their interest in one another suffering no eclipse.

Quand j'allais voir Sargent a Londres (M. Monet continued)
il retournait beaucoup de ses toiles les jugleant mauvaises. Non—
Sargent n'aimait pas le fleurs. Il disait ce que je n'aime pas dans les
fleurs c'est qu'elle ne sont pas en harmonie avec les feuilles—Il n'était
pas un Impressioniste, au sens où nous employons ce mot, il était
trop sous l'influence de Carolus Duran.

Monet had been suffering from his eyesight for several
months, but pointing to some pictures standing on the floor he
said: "Dernièrement un matin en sortant je me suis aperçu que
j'avais retrouvé l'usage de la vue et la perception des tons et des
teintes comme autrefois, alors j'ai fait ces tableaux." That
brought our interview to an end. The "temps gris" was
approaching. The colours of his garden were growing in intensity, and with a gesture calling my attention to the delicacy
of tint which the irises had assumed, he said good-bye.

Some days later, anxious to obtain confirmation of his view
of Sargent's letter, I sent him a copy and received the following
reply:

GIVERNY PAR VERNON, EURE,
le 21 Juin, '26.

CHER MONSIEUR,
Excusez moi de ne pas vous avoir répondu plus tôt mais
toujours un peu souffrant je ne puis encore vous écrire moi même.
Je ne puis du reste que vous confirmer ce que vous ai dit dans

notre dernière intervue. Après avoir relu attentivement votre lettre et celle copiée de Sargent je vous avoue que si la traduction de la lettre de Sargent est exacte je ne puis l'approuver d'abord parceque Sargent me fait plus grand que je ne suis, que j'ai toujours en horreur des théories enfin que je n'ai que le merite d'avoir peint directement devant la nature en cherchant à rendre mes impressions devant les effets les plus fugitifs, et je reste desolé d'avoir été la cause du nom donné à un groupe dont la plus part n'avait rien d'impressionisme.

Avec tous mes regrets de ne pouvoir vous donner entière satisfaction recevez mes sentiments les meillures.

CLAUDE MONET.

Subsequently Monet sent me a review by Paul Landormy, which he had underlined, of a book by Maurice Emmanuel on the music of Debussy. The passages that follow certainly bear out some of M. Monet's views on his own art. Writing of Debussy the reviewer says:

On se rappelle qu' à un de ses maitres, effaré de la liberté de son langage harmonique et qui lui demandé Mais quelle règle suivez-vous donc? Il repondit. "Mon plaisir." . . . Quand il s'agit de discerner le beau, de decider ce qu'il lui conviendra d'écrire, il oublie tous les principes, toutes les regles et ne prend parti que sur les impressions de son oreille. . . . Au lieu d'amalgamer les timbres pour des effets de masse, il dégage l'une de l'autre leurs personalités, ou il les marie delicatement sans alterer leur nature propre. Comme les peintres impressionistes de ce temps, il peint par couleurs pures, mais avec une sobriété délicate, que toute rudesse rebute, comme un laideur. . . . Mais un impressioniste ne l'est jamais que de tendance, de volonté, d'intention. Il ne peut aller jus qu'au bout de son système, si du moins il-y-a, système. . . . L'impressionisme n'est donc, dans son fond, qu'une apparence. Mais il est au moins une methode. . . .

If Monet disclaimed some of the theory and practice which Sargent had seen in his work, we must not too readily assume that justification for the views which Sargent expressed is wanting. Creators are not necessarily the best analysts of their own methods. Critics have deduced from Shakespeare or Velasquez principles which they would probably assert had never been present to their minds. In the case of Monet, too, humility would have made him hesitate to claim any great importance as a painter. But in any case it remains interesting that Sargent should have seen in the work of Monet these qualities, and that he regarded them as playing a real part in the development of art.

One further point remains to be noticed. In his letter to Mr. Jameson, Sargent relates that Monet had suffered from astigmatism and was therefore chronically in the state of a person with normal sight when "in a blinding light or in the dusk or dark." He thought the story amusingly significant that Monet, having been provided by an oculist with glasses, hurled them away after realizing their effect, saying: "If the world really looks like that I will paint no more!" The curious thing is that Sargent himself suffered from astigmatism and was therefore, though in a less degree than Monet, peculiarly equipped for studying the phenomena he discusses in these letters. He could speak from personal experience. The precise effect of astigmatism is, in proportion to its acuteness, to blur and confuse. The colour sense is otherwise not affected. We might have expected, therefore, to find in his work strong traces of the Impressionism which he admired so enthusiastically in Monet. It is a point on which opinions will differ. If we take Mr. MacColl's three tests,* it would probably be agreed that in Sargent's work it is generally true that brown tonality plays a very small part. On the other hand, in the use of primary colours, and in the application of colour by broken touches, there is very much less reason for reckoning him as an Impressionist. In his rendering of landscape he probably goes as near to producing the quality of dazzle in a scene as any painter has yet succeeded in doing—but that particular atmospheric iridescence associated with Monet rarely appears in the work of Sargent. That fusion of colours which takes place "under the federating power of real light" is not a common characteristic of his art. He relies too much on contrast, on the opposition of values, on emphasis and accent, on vigour of colouring, and explicit form. His painting is characterized by too much force and directness; the objects are insistent and vivid, their substance and texture are at once perceived. He is a painter essentially

* See *ante*, p. 127.

in three dimensions; in a flash he gives the weight and volume of what he sees. The light falls across the scene he paints, but it intervenes in a less degree between the scene and the spectator. The splendours are seldom veiled. He registers another order of beauty than that attained by Monet. Here and there, it is true, a water-colour of Venice (notably one in the possession of Professor Tonks) will give the aerial effects aimed at by the Impressionists, but they are attained by another technique, and the effects are more quiescent and less impermanent. On the other hand, the nuance of which Monet speaks is often noticeable in his painting* the optic occurrence, if the phrase may be allowed, at the point of juncture between two colours. In many cases he will indicate the outline of an object with a colour which is more nearly akin to the colour with which the object is juxtaposed.

For example, in the picture called *Oxen Resting* the roof is not outlined with the ruddy colour reflected from the tiles, but by the blue of the sky, which has the effect of intensifying the sense of light, heat and the vibration in the air. Pointing to this picture, and indicating this feature, he said: "That is how I see it, astigmatism gives that effect." Indeed, he used to say half in fun that the French school of Impressionism was due to the astigmatism of a man of genius (Monet). In 1888-89, as has been already stated, he was making experiments in Impressionism, and seeing how far he could incorporate into his art the lessons to be learnt from it. At Fladbury he was continually making quick studies of reflections of what Mr. Frank Rutter has described as "our vision of things seen momentarily in the duration of a flash of lightning," and the four pictures, *St. Martin's Summer, Lady Fishing, Claude Monet Sketching* (painted at Giverny in 1888) and *Paul Helleu and His Wife,* in which he makes use of broken colour, belong to these years. As has been pointed out, they are outside the main current of his art.

We must agree with Claude Monet, that Sargent was never an Impressionist in the Parisian sense of the word. When he began portrait painting in London, he had inherited, through

* See *ante*, p. 129.

Carolus Duran, certain influences from Velasquez, the relations of values, the handling of contrasts of shadow and light, and that degree of relief in modelling which is consistent with reticence of statement and simplification. But the influence of which he was pre-eminently aware was that of Franz Hals. This will be more apparent when his methods of teaching are examined.

Whether the revolution in painting brought about by the Impressionists will hereafter appear as decisive as many critics would have us believe, is doubtful. What cannot be doubted, however, is the change in taste which they effected in England. Whereas in the eighties pictures showing traces of French influence were looked on by the public and the critics* with disfavour, by 1920 a picture which failed to show French affinities had comparatively little chance of success among the fastidious. Sudden as the changes in fashion and taste are apt to be, the history of art might be searched in vain for a swing over so complete and abrupt as the last thirty years have witnessed. A corresponding change has occurred in æsthetic theory. A new school of criticism has grown up, whose business it has been to formulate fresh canons of appreciation. There is no doubt the nerves of dogmatic critics have had a bad shake, and after having been forced to eat their words about the Impressionists they are now even over-inclined to welcome developments in art which startle and surprise. Science and metaphysics have been called in to aid. Resemblance, representation, interpretation of fact, have had to give way before "significant form," abstract relation, "psychological volumes," pattern and the "emotional elements of design." The critics have, indeed, kept pace with the successors of the Impressionists. The representative quality in a work of art is now judged to be of less importance than other more pressing considerations. One of the leading critics of the new school has said: "The representative element in a work of art may or may not be harmful, always it is irrelevant." Obviously if that dogma is sound and is applied to the art of Sargent, his work must be considered as mainly

* Mr. George Moore, one of the first to open the eyes of the English art world to the French school, was an enlightened exception to this general statement.

irrelevant. No wonder they treat Sargent's art as so much material in which to flesh their spears. It is, however, impossible to ignore that an active section of advanced and cultured opinion fails to find in his work many of the qualities that certain critics claim to be essential to the highest art. Such must be the fate, for the present, of all art which has representation as its primary purpose.

Chapter XVIII

OVER Sargent in the nineties, what Henry James calls "the wand of evocation" is weak, calling up only a few echoes, which give faint occasion for conjecture. At a moment when the recollections of living men should be enlightening, they add, with one happy exception, singularly little to our knowledge. When the keenness of Sargent's early contacts with English life might have been expected to furnish correspondence, only a few notes hastily written have survived to flutter down the intervening years. As at all times he is, of course, immersed in his work. He is absorbed by the claims of his Boston contract; Moloch, Astarte, Osiris and Horus are the company of his imagination, and sitters now begin to clamour at his door. The story of his life must be read in his output. His days are strenuous with work, his recreations are music and the theatre and the company of his friends. His personality and his striking appearance are impressing themselves on a constantly widening circle of London life. Four months of the year, into which, owing to the English climate, he averred it was necessary to crowd the painting of portraits, were invariably spent in London; the late autumn and winter down to the year 1895 at Morgan Hall. In 1892 no work of his was exhibited in London. In 1893 his only picture at Burlington House was the portrait of Lady Agnew now in the National Gallery of Scotland. Painted in a high key it has a quality of prettiness which he seldom affected; it is carefully finished. Mauve, light blue and white and the method of their combination give the picture a claim of apostolic succession to the walls of the Academy. It is a careful portrait, free of any fine frenzy, sedately handled, and rather lacking in the force and fire of his dazzling technique. It was applauded by the critics, but the tide carrying Sargent forward was now breast high, and henceforward, though he was to receive plenty of criticism, he

STUDY OF ARAB WOMEN.

had rarely during the remainder of his lifetime to experience disparagement. At the New Gallery he was represented by his full-length portrait of Mrs. Hugh Hammersley and Mrs. George Lewis. To this year also belongs a very brilliant study of Mrs. Hammersley exhibited at the Royal Academy (1925). For sheer animation and vivacity, and as a character study, it ranks with the vivid sketch of Vernon Lee.

About the portrait of Mrs. Hammersley he wrote to his friend Edwin Abbey:

> I have begun the routine of portrait painting with anxious relatives hanging on my brush. Mrs. Hammersley has a mother and I am handicapped by a vexatious accident (I have no luck). The other day at the Café Royal where I collapsed after seeing the R.A. and the New Gallery I was reviving over a chop and a glass of beer when I felt a frightful sting on my thigh, dropped my hands on it, struggled with hissing flames and smoke, was taken for an unsuccessful anarchist and at last extinguished a box of Swedish safety matches, that blazed in my pocket. The remains of the box were handed round to reassure the Café and I went to the nearest apothecary where they buttered me up—I have a Turner sunset on my thigh and certain blisters on my hands—but I go about and can work in an inferior style—The exhibitions are vile. There is a remarkable portrait of a man on ship board by Gregory at the R.A. Watts' head of Walter Crane is fine and so is his Eve at the Academy very fine.
>
> Yours in adamant,
> JOHN S. SARGENT.

While these pictures were being discussed in London Sargent himself was again in America. It was the year of the Columbian Exhibition in Chicago, in the art section of which nine of his pictures were shown, including *Ellen Terry as Lady Macbeth*, *Mrs. Davis and her son*, *Life Study of Egyptian Girl*, *Miss Dunham*, *Miss Pratt*, *Mrs. Inches*, and *Homer St. Gaudens with his Mother*. Homer St. Gaudens, then about ten years old, is one of the painter's most successful studies of boyhood—naïve, ingenuous and charming, thinking the thoughts of his age without a flicker of self-consciousness. It is one of the pictures—many were to follow—in which the sitter's hands are as important as expressions of character as they are in the decorative scheme. Few artist have shown an equal ingenuity in the disposition of hands, in using them as elements in portraiture, and in varying their function in the composition. In his hundreds of portraits he rarely repeats himself. The hands he paints carry character to their finger-tips, they are vehicles of the spirit, pliant media of expression, conveying age and youth, nervous energy, resolution, delicate sensibility, or as plainly the dull opposites of these qualities. But in every case they are made to play a part as important as the eye or any feature of the face. It is only necessary to refer to the portraits of Theodore Roosevelt, John D. Rockefeller, Joseph Choate, Lord Wemyss, Mrs. Augustus Hemenway, Lady Sassoon, Mrs. Henry White, Miss Helen Dunham. In each of these portraits the hands *tell*; in some cases they are barely more than indicated, in some perhaps the drawing may be criticized, but in one and all they are alive with meaning. They are never formal, never conventional; they are inseparable from the character of the sitter.

About this time Miss J. H. Heyneman arrived as an art-student from America with a letter of introduction which she forwarded to Tite Street. In response Sargent wrote:

> I am delighted to have the prospect of making your acquaintance and wish I were able to begin correctly by calling upon you at once. My morning and afternoon daily sittings leave me little hope of being able to do so, and it would be kind of you to waive ceremony and pay a visit instead to my studio. Any day next week, after half past five, you would be sure to find me, and I will be glad to show you what few things are in my studio.

Miss Heyneman called the following week.

> In my mind's eye (she writes) I can still see Mr. Sargent come forward to meet me with a cordial simplicity that put me at once at my ease. My first impression deepened but never changed. In any company he seemed to tower over every one else in the room, as much by reason of his personality as through the accident of his height. At that time his close cut beard was dark brown and his thick hair and sharply marked eyebrows were almost black. On his broad shoulders his head looked small, and was chiefly remarkable for the

beauty of the brow, which was splendidly broad and full. His eyes were large, somewhat prominent and greenish grey in colour (they had lost the blueness which they had in early youth). His quiet humorous gaze was essentially kind rather than sharp but he missed nothing of what went on around him. In repose his glance was often half veiled and brooding, but when he became interested his eyes lit up and he fixed them, full and sparkling, upon the speaker who, inspired by that intent gaze, would often surpass himself, or tell far more than he intended.

Shortly afterwards he called at the hotel where Miss Heyne-man was staying, and insisted on seeing, not only the sketches which she had been prepared to show him, but all those she had brought to England with her. His criticisms, as he sat on the floor where the sketches were laid out, were at once friendly and drastic; he urged the necessity of self-discipline, of never being satisfied with easy conclusions, of always trying to do the thing just *beyond* one's capacity. He told her that she was too ignorant to be so clever in her drawing, that any success arrived at by chance was of little value, that the education of a painter was chiefly a matter of training eye, hand and mind to work swiftly and in unison, and that what she acquired herself would always be of more interest than what she acquired through his or any other teaching. He went on:

> Never leave "empty spaces," every stroke of pencil or brush should have significance and not merely fill in, . . . copy one of the heads by Franz Hals in the National Gallery, then you will get an idea of what I mean by leaving no empty spaces in modelling a head, work at the fine head of the old woman rather than the superficial one of the man, I will come there and give you a criticism and haul you over the coals.

Sure enough a few days later he appeared at the National Gallery. After looking at what she had done he said: "Don't concentrate so much on the features . . . they are only like spots on an apple . . . paint the head . . . now you have only nose, mouth and eyes."

Later on he advised her to go to Haarlem, and on her return wrote:

I'll come with pleasure on Tuesday. . . . I hope you'll have some copies of Franz Hals to show me. Jacomb Hood tells me that you have come back charged with enthusiasm and the spirit of knowledge. There is certainly no place like Haarlem to key one up.

His criticisms were often trenchant. "That's not a head," he would say, "that's a collection of features." "That's not a shadow, that's a hole, there is light in the darkest shadow." But though often severe, he never discouraged. No one sought his advice, whether in painting or writing or music, without gaining some new stimulus to effort. He could disapprove without wounding, and condemn without disheartening. The self-indulgence which takes the form of telling home truths was unknown to him; he respected too much the sensibilities of others. He had the good manners which have their origin in the heart, the courtesy which springs from sympathy; and if he trod delicately it was because he had a fine instinct for what others felt. This made him an invaluable and helpful critic. He accepted people as they were, he had none of that shallow passion which desires to see them different. Where he saw an opportunity to encourage he took it.

Miss Heyneman has fortunately treasured many of his dicta in relation to the study of painting.*

Meanwhile, during these years, the nineties, it had ceased to be a question who would be painted by Sargent; the question was whom would he find time to paint. Now, whatever view we take of the nineties, it was certainly a period which produced a great variety of types, though to generalize about the characteristics which they owed in common to their times is not easy. Indeed, to find a common denominator between Carmencita and Lady Faudel Phillips, between Coventry Patmore and Sir Asher Wertheimer, between Joseph Chamberlain and Graham Robertson, or between M. Leon de la Fosse the pianist and Mr. W. M. Cazalet, might well pass the wit of man. Here we may detect a difference between the task which fell to Sargent and that which confronted some of his predecessors in England. Van Dyck was able to give with plausibility a general air of

* See *post*, p. 181.

nobility to all his sitters, Sir Peter Lely an appearance of courtli-
ness, Sir Joshua Reynolds and his contemporaries a quiet look
of security and distinction. The sitters of these artists looked
out on the world for the most part with high notions of social
pride, aware of differences of status, and with the insignia of
high descent as part of their natural equipment. They fitted
as of right into backgrounds of which colonnades and patrician
homes, parks and stately trees were the appropriate setting.
Sargent's lot was to paint a world much wider, less stable and
more complicated.

In 1894 Sargent, who that year was represented in the Academy
by a portrait of Miss Chanler, and a lunette and portion of
the ceiling for the Public Library of Boston, and in the New
English Art Club by four sketches, was elected an A.R.A. His
own art was too clearly distinct from the Academic painting of
the day for him not to experience some nervousness at finding
himself in such company. In thanking Ralph Curtis for his con-
gratulations on the honour thus conferred, he wrote:

My dear Ralph,   33, Tite Street.

Thanks for your flourish of trumpets and waving of caps—If
one lives in London, as I seem to be doing vaguely, I suppose it really
counts for something to be an A.R.A. It remains to be proved; but
I shall watch for the symptoms with interest. I have had no end of
letters of congratulation from Academicians which would point to the
fact of my having more of an affinity with old fogies than I expected.
Today I have called on about 20 of them, such is the tradition and it
is a curious revelation to find the man whose name and work one has
hated and railed at for years, is a man of the world and altogether
delightful—for instances Sant, whom one considered the Antichrist.

It is characteristic of you to have saved a sketch of mine from ob-
livion, and ——'s approval tickles me although I consider him a noxious
humbug—I came across a phrase in my pious reading that must apply
to his book which I haven't read: "ce livre cheri des begomiles de
Thrace et des cathares de l'occident." This, like another quotation
from me, that you once investigated at a tea party may be obscene so
look out.   Yours sincerely,
                                    John S. Sargent.

To the same year belongs a letter to Sir Edmund Gosse, which gives in uncompromising terms Sargent's opinion of the famous "Yellow Book."

MY DEAR GOSSE,   1894.
    I have just replied in the negative to a note from Mr. Aubrey Beardsley asking my permission to reproduce your portrait in the "Yellow Book."
    From an artistic point of view I dislike that book too much to be willing to seem an habitual contributor.
    My only regret is that it should be *à propos* of your portrait, especially if you ever were willing that it should be reproduced, which I should consider a great compliment.
                                        Yours very truly,
                                            JOHN S. SARGENT.

This was written in the first year of the "Yellow Book's" existence. Aubrey Beardsley was then the art editor, Henry Harland the literary editor. The book still lives vaguely as a symbol of "fin de siècle," decadence and revolutionary movements in art and literature. The justification for such a view is not very apparent. Possibly it depended on where Volume I. was opened, and what the reader lighted on. Support for one view might have been found in the title-page of Aubrey Beardsley, the "Stella Maris" of Arthur Symons, and a "Defence of Cosmetics" by Max Beerbohm, in which occurred the ominous passage beginning: "For behold! the Victorian era comes to its end and the day of *sancta simplicitas* is quite ended. The old signs are here and the portents to warn the seer of life that we are ripe for a new era of artifice." On the other hand, the reader might have been reassured by finding contributions from Henry James, Edmund Gosse, Arthur Benson and Sir Frederick Leighton, P.R.A.

    But, however that may be, we must not infer from Sargent's letter that he condemned the art of Aubrey Beardsley; on the contrary, I have seen him linger delightedly over Beardsley's illustrations, commending their rhythm and line and the invention of their composition.

    The reception given to the first instalment of his Boston

work shown in public was tentative but favourable. The *Saturday Review* wrote: "It is enough to say that of their originality and solemn impressiveness there can be no question." That, at any rate, is true. The lunette which was exhibited at the Academy represents the children of Israel under their oppressors, Pharaoh and the King of Assyria. It now fills the vault at the north end of the Sargent Hall above the frieze of the prophets. It is a daring composition. Figures and symbols are crowded into the design, but the artist has maintained an astonishing coherence and mastery in the handling of his highly complex scheme. A fine solemnity is apparent in the design, and the figures, oppressors and oppressed alike, are keyed up to a pitch of dramatic intensity. As mural decoration it has been criticized for its want of repose, for its deficiency in that high degree of tranquillity in pattern or colour requisite where painting is to fulfil its appropriate function in the ornament of a building. But its 'originality and impressiveness' are undeniable. With the lunette were exhibited the decorations for the vaulting of the ceiling. These comprise symbolical representations of Astarte, Moloch and Nut, the Egyptian goddess and Mother of the Universe. Here, again, the originality is striking. The complicated symbolism has been woven into a satisfying design. The colouring, in which a bluish ground predominates, is delicate and sensitive in quality; the pattern created is geometric in character, but within its encompassing form it is free, light and varied. These decorations and the lunette were installed in the library in 1895. They were the result of four years of work and many years of study, and marked the first stage in that long task which in 1890 he had taken upon his shoulders. Hundreds of drawings and studies had preceded the final accomplishment. As evidence of his thoroughness we may note that in the early part of the year (1894) he spent many days at the Zoological Gardens making studies of snakes in the reptile house.

The Academy public were very puzzled as to what it all meant. The lunette was hung in the cove of the ceiling so as nearly as possible to catch the same light that it would receive in the Boston Library. This of itself provided a conundrum.

By some it was regarded as part of a new scheme of decoration for Burlington House, while others were heard to declare that it had always been there. Even those who knew better were mystified; there was no one to explain, and it certainly did not explain itself. Of this Sargent was well aware, and he wrote to Lady Lewis:

> You seem to me really to like my decoration and not to look upon it as a hopeless conundrum as most people do. I was delighted to find that you got some pleasure out of it through your eyes and were not fidgetting about the obscurity of those old symbols. What a tiresome thing a perfectly clear symbol would be.

But where a work is not only finely painted but is in addition incomprehensible, it is well qualified to attract the multitude, and so the lunette and decorations came to be the wonder of the exhibition.

STUDY FOR "THE ARCHERS."
Boston Decorations.

Chapter XIX

I MET Sargent for the first time in May, 1894, at a party given by Mrs. Henry White at Loseley. I have found a record of my first impression in a letter written at the time. After giving a list of the party it runs: "Also Sargent, who is interesting round and about his own subject, though he talks slower and with more difficulty in finding words than anyone I ever met. When he can't finish a sentence he waves his fingers before his face as a sort of signal for the conversation to go on without him—at least, that is the impression I came to after staying in the house with him." That impression was modified as time went on, though he always talked slowly. He gave the idea of one grasping at words which danced elusively in his brain; his conversation was never fluent, but, like his painting, it could be immensely descriptive. He wasted no words—it may even be doubted if he had any to waste—but those he used were like strokes of his brush, significant and suggestive; indeed, he could convey a weight of meaning by a gesture or a truncated phrase. He could transpose scenes and experiences into words with more character and tang in his rendering than many more accomplished masters of phrase. When he talked of matters relating to art, or when he was with intimates, he found words with comparative ease. Even then there was hesitation, as though he was at his easel determining the next stroke of his brush. But his hesitation was itself often expressive and in any case so characteristic that certainly no friend of his would have had it otherwise. So much lay at the back of it: such authority, such anxious sincerity, and at the same time, so much humour and finesse. No man had more entirely home-made opinions, opinions so wholly the unadulterated product of his own reflection or experience. His wit was true and direct, free of paradox, an overflow of his personality. He resembled Henry James, in that nothing would

induce him to make a speech. More than once at a dinner in
early days the shouts of the diners got him to his feet, when
he would stand struggling with his nervousness, apparently
unable to utter. On one occasion blurting out, "It's a damned
shame," he subsided into his seat amid a tempest of applause.

In the nineties he moved about in the world of London more
than in subsequent years, dining out frequently. And neither
then nor later did he consider that his fame exempted him from
making social efforts. His courtesy never failed. But he was
undoubtedly fastidious; and by no means were all people grist
to his mill. Later he became more reluctant to dine out, and in
his last years he narrowed his social ambit to very small dimensions. Even so, a considerable portion of the large correspondence he conscientiously transacted consisted of refusals to
invitations. Evenings with music were those to which his tastes
most inclined him. One such is described by Miss Heyneman,
who writes:

> In 1809 I was back again in London. My sister had a house at
> 39, Palace Court which Mr. Sargent called "The Great Good Place"
> a reference to Henry James' short story of that name. It had a large
> music room and he enjoyed evenings of music there, with two or three
> other people. I recall one occasion which could hardly be called
> quiet. It was a very hot night in July and Madame Blanche Marchesi
> and Denis O'Sullivan worked through the whole of Tristan, taking all
> the parts—tenor—bass—baritone—contralto or soprano in turn, even
> singing the chorus parts together. The windows were wide open and
> a great crowd collected outside, for both Madame Marchesi and Denis
> O'Sullivan were plainly visible, and both in wild spirits accompanied
> their singing by very dramatic gestures. Mr. O'Sullivan had taken
> off his coat and was wearing a Japanese kimono, Blanche Marchesi was
> of course in evening dress, but Mr. Sargent had not succumbed to
> the temptation of divesting himself of anything. They were all too
> absorbed to be conscious of heat, or any other discomfort, but when
> they had come to the end, the unhappy pianist rose with his shirt and
> collar wilted and feeling and looking as he expressed it like "claret
> frappé." None the less he wrote the next day "What a good time
> we had last night."

He was a great playgoer and as ready to be entertained by a
"revue" as by serious drama or the Russian ballet. His musical

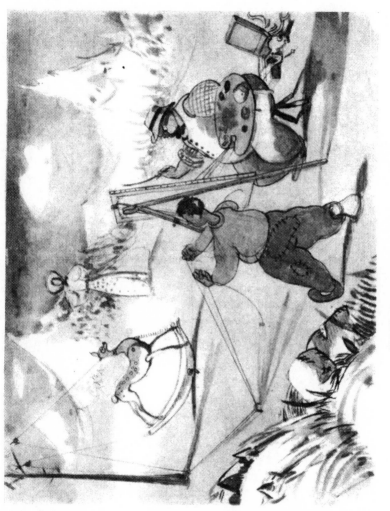

SARGENT SKETCHING IN THE ALPS.
By Professor H. V. Tonks.

gifts have been mentioned, and the question is often asked, "What did they amount to?" Joachim is credited with the remark that "had Sargent taken to music instead of painting he would have been as great a musician as he was a painter." Two eminent living musicians, however, have kindly contributed their views on this aspect of his genius. Mr. Loeffler writes:

MEADOWMERE FARM,
MEDFIELD,
MASSACHUSETTS,
January 30, 1926.

DEAR SIR,

In answer to your question about Sargent's "musicalness" permit me to jot down in a loose way the various impressions I received of this in the course of many years of my enjoying the privilege of his delightful and generous friendship. I met Mr. Sargent some 35 years ago after a Symphony Concert in Boston where I had played Lalo's "Symphonie Espagnole," a delightful work of which Sargent was very fond. He came to the Artists room that evening and with that irresistible charm of his said a few words which made one rise in one's self esteem and then arranged for our meeting a few days later at dinner in a mutual friends house. On this delightful occasion Sargent played with me "en petit Comité" the *Symphonie Espagnole* in which he revealed himself as the admirable musician which he innately was. He was quite amazing in accompanying The 3rd Movement ("Intermède") a quite splendid piece of music with rather complicated rhythms in ⅝ time, which he played with complete musical and rhythmical understanding, verve and spirit. In his luminously intelligent manner he spoke of the various characteristics of Spanish rhythms in music, quite in the manner in which M. Edouard Lalo had expounded these intricacies to me in prior years. That same evening we also played the first Sonata by Gabriel Fauré for whose music Sargent had a strong predilection which I ever sincerely shared. Sargent had the insinuating and consummate art of initiating music lovers and musicians as well, to the hidden charms, harmonic innovations and the felicitous melodic lessons (?) in the works of this unassuming composer of genius. To come back once more to our playing Fauré's perplexingly "Swift" Sonata, Sargent sailed through his part in those early days. Not by any means that he always played all the notes, but better than that, when cornered by a surprise difficulty, he revealed his genuine talent for music by playing all that which was and is most essential. In other words he was in music as in all things "frightfully" intelligent, not merely glib or clever. He knew Wagner's scores much more intimately than many musicians and in bygone years played through the better part of them with complete comprehension, deep interest and genuine love for all the beauties in them. He discriminated amazingly well. Of Richard Strauss he said: "He is often discouragingly common place, but he has a virility of saying things which is unusual and convincing, often quite in the grand manner." What he liked in Strauss' works was "the organic power, the structural design. The 'charpente,' is there; one feels the lungs, the heart, the liver, all are functioning!" Of Debussy's works he liked best, "The afternoon of a faune," and many of his Piano pieces. Strange to say "Pellias and Melisande" he thought rather "anæmic." On the whole he did not care much for "Le precieux" in any art. His ear was strangely sensitive for unusual harmonic progressions, in fact he had an unusually fine memory for them. I have known him to be haunted by certain ones, after one hearing he would not rest there until he had solved the harmonic riddle. Without the music, he would do this at the Piano by sheer tenacity of oral memory. His musical training must have been from the start unusually good, for I have heard him *solfegise* like a musician difficult passages, that he had not played well at first sight reading. His unusually great intelligence helped him in music as in everything else that he ever undertook. In the latter years S. had somewhat lost his cunning in playing the Piano. This was due no doubt to lack of practice and his failing eyesight, by which I mean that glasses interfered much with his sense of accommodation while playing. I do not know whether Sargent ever tried himself in musical composition yet there is no doubt in my mind, that had he chosen to become a musician he would have risen to eminence in our art in one way or another.

It is unusual to meet so marvellously endowed a man possessing such simplicity of manner, such goodness of heart, such genuine human kindness in his nature. He had the innate bearing and dignity of a noble man. His life was to my mind the fullest imaginable, for he was ever alert, in his joy over the petal of a flower, over a feather of a small bird, the mystery of the propelling power of a little snake in the grass. He knew a great deal about natural history. He knew a great deal because he usually remembered everything he had read. He was the most voracious and discriminating reader I have ever met. He belied the French saying "Pour devenir un grand artiste il faut être, il faut rester fruste." Fruste de connaisances they meant, *i. e.* not know too many things, not know too much. He just was a glorious exception as genius always is, and just could not help being almost omniscient with so exceptional a memory as was his. To have known

THE STUDIO, 31. TITE STREET.

so great, so lovable, so delightful a man has been one of the greatest privileges of my life. To have appreciated the honor of enjoying also his friendship may explain to you the profound affection in which I hold today his memory.

Yours sincerely,

C. M. LOEFFLER.

Mr. Percy Grainger has also been good enough to send me his impressions.

May 6th, 1926.

SARGENT'S CONTRIBUTIONS TO MUSIC.

John Singer Sargent was one of the most outstanding musicians I have ever met; for although his musical technic was not as developed as his painting technic, he had that rarest of all esthetic gifts—individualistic, balanced, critical judgment. His musical judgments, sympathies and activities welled up instinctively out of his rich musical inner nature, and were not (as are the musical doings of many a gifted amateur musician) influenced by the opinions of professional musicians, or indeed by any ascertainable outside factors whatever. To hear Sargent play the piano was indeed a treat, for his pianism had the manliness and richness of his painting, though, naturally, it lacked that polished skillfulness that comes only with many-hourly daily practice spread over many years. He delighted especially in playing his favourite, Fauré, and in struggling with the fantastic difficulties of Albeniz's "Iberia," which latter he had mastered to the point of making it a musical joy to listen to under his hands; a task that might stagger many a well-equipped concert pianist.

However, remarkable as his playing was, intense as his delight in active music-making was, I consider his greatest contribution to music lay in the wondrously beneficent influence he exerted on musical life in England. It is probable that he exerted this same influence in other lands, but I happened to witness it in England only.

In the benevolent paternal quality of his musical influence, Sargent was not only the ideal artist, but also the ideal American; for there is probably no people, today, that bring such a beautiful reverence and generosity to the support of music as do the Americans—possibly a modern manifestation of their original Puritan background. Sargent always seemed to me a typical Puritan, a typical New-Englander in his musical life. Music seemed to be less a recreation to him than a sacred duty, the duty of aiding especial musical talent wherever he found it. While he was nowise deaf to the appeal of the gifts of reproductive musicians, it was primarily the creative musicians (composers) to whom he was most powerfully drawn, and whom he aided most extensively. Out of those many musicians for whom the warmth of his musical enthusiasm was especially kindled, I recall particularly the following ones: Gabriel Fauré, Charles Martin Loeffler, Ethel Smyth, Korbay, Leon Delafosse, Debussy, Cyril Scott, Albeniz and myself.

Sargent was not content to enjoy his musical enthusiasms as merely personal pleasures; he never rested until his enthusiasms had taken practical tangible shapes beneficial to the musicians that had aroused them, and to the art of music in general. For many years (longer than I knew him) he had been the apostle of Gabriel Fauré in England, bringing over that great composer to London for public and private performances of his compositions, arranging performances of Fauré's works by the Cappe Quartet, Leon Delafosse, and other exquisite artists and the like. In my opinion Sargent is chiefly responsible for the fine understanding of Fauré's music that obtains in England. He was likewise one of the first (if not the very first) to proclaim the beauty and the importance of Loeffler's muse.

Sargent used his great prestige as a unique social as well as artistic "lion" in London, to benefit those musicians he considered worthy of help and fame. He had only to announce his approval of any musician for hostesses to spring up ready to engage these proteges, hoping that the performance of these musicians at their "At Homes" would guarantee them Sargent's coveted presence—which it usually did, for Sargent was untiring and self-effacing in all that pertained to the support of those he considered true artists. To have Sargent's approval and support was a wonderful boon to any struggling artist; highly beneficial from a practical, mundane standpoint, and deeply comforting on purely artistic grounds—for Sargent's musical mind worked like a composer's rather than like a mere music-lover's.

The things he especially enjoyed in music, the things he emphasized in his musical comments, the details his musical memory retained, were all highly specialized points, rare sparks of genius, high-lights of original workmanship that the average musician (professional or amateur) usually misses entirely, and that, as a rule, only great composers can be expected to appreciate consciously. But even great composers are seldom as balanced, as fair, as clear-eyed in their musical criticisms as Sargent was and I repeat what I asserted earlier—that esthetical judgment such as his is the rarest of all musical gifts.

The fact that he bestowed upon the music of Gabriel Fauré, the greatest depth and intensity of his musical admiration and devotion is a convincing example of the rightness of Sargent's artistic vision, of his ability to penetrate to musical essentials, of his unsusceptibility to shallow surface appeals, of his freedom from the "isms" and vogues of his day. For Fauré is one of those quietly great masters (like Bach, Cesar Franck and Frederick Delius) who, in the main, work hidden from the outer world of their own era, to emerge undyingly resplendant to future generations. But Sargent had in all musical matters the magically penetrating eye of genius. In addition he had the comforting touch of a warmly human heart, of a compassionate seer—which, by the way, explains to me, his natural sympathy with such a subject as that so illuminatingly disclosed in his painting *The Hermit*.

In all the years in which I was privileged to know him, and on all the many, many occasions on which I was made happy in meeting him, I never discovered in Sargent one act, one thought, one gesture, one opinion, judgment or sympathy that did not proclaim the true genius, the great man, the innate aristocrat. Few men were funnier than he, consciously or unconsciously. Probably his artistic dislikes were as strong as his likings but his disapprovals were buried in obscure grunts, in indecipherably broken sentences, while his approvals were always clearly and unmistakably conveyed; for he was, above all things, a *constructive* personality, and never oblivious to the actual effect of all he did and said. Two things stand out in my memory of him— his unfailing benevolence where the welfare of art was concerned, and his inscrutability in all that touched his purely personal life. He was strong in all things; always giving sympathy, never evoking it, always helpful to others, and always self-contained— a strange mixture of a compassionate Christian and a stoical Red Indian Warrior!

I cannot close this short account of my impressions of Sargent without mentioning what I, in my innermost artist's heart, owe esthetically to him and his friend, William Gare Rathbone. These two, both so individualistic and uninfluenceable in their musical perceptions, were yet united in many musical sympathies and enthusiasms. They were alike in this—that they were the finest musical amateurs that I, personally, have ever seen; that their musicality was essentially that of the composer type, that their natural attitude towards music and musicians was constructive and benevolent. Some of my years in London were, artistically speaking, dreary and hopeless enough. But into the darkness of those times, Sargent and Rathbone unfailingly shed light. To meet either of them, anywhere, was to drink a great draught of artistic and human encouragement, to feel enboldened towards further compositional experimentation, to sense an intuitive championing of all artistic genuineness and originality. For all these nobilities, which were revealed to me in moments when I was poor and desperate enough to measure their true and rare value, I shall be unforgettingly thankful as long as I have my memory.

The layman who reads these appreciations of Mr. Loeffler and Mr. Grainger will probably conclude that Joachim was not exaggerating when he spoke of Sargent as a musician. As such, Sargent entertained a deep admiration for the musical gifts of Ethel Smyth. Her singing found in him an enchanted listener, and it is in the act of singing that the drew her. Before that he had been asked to paint her. In reference to the request he wrote: "Brewster, for some time, has wanted me to do a head of her, a painting, and they say he wants her in a calm mood. Miss Smyth in a calm mood! It reminds me of Mr. Dooley's description of a fiery American general: after describing his tremendous and furious rages he says: 'He was a man who could be calm when there was anything to be calm about.'"

Chapter XX

AMONG the pictures which Sargent exhibited at the Academy in 1895 were two portraits of Coventry Patmore. One of these is now in the National Portrait Gallery; the other, a sketch of the poet's head, is one of Sargent's most brilliant achievements; as in more than one of his successful portraits the head is in profile. The sketch is not by any means the Patmore of *The Angel in the House*, but the Patmore of whom Sir Edmund Gosse* wrote: "Defiance was not a burden to him; he was 'ever a fighter' requiring for complete mental health the salubrious sensation of antagonism." His face is rugged with battle, leonine with combativeness, but illuminated with an inward and spiritual grace. It is an intimate and revealing study of character. Sir Edmund, discussing these pictures, wrote: "It is necessary to insist that he (Patmore) was not always thus ragged and vulturine, not always such a miraculous portent of gnarled mandible and shaken plumage." At the date of the picture (September, 1894), however, Patmore was seventy-one years of age and considerably older in appearance, a Fighting Téméraire drawing within sight of harbour. Those who hold that Sargent failed in the rendering of spiritual qualities, may hesitate before this sketch. Here is old age with the fires of youth still glowing within; the eyes undimmed by time; the spirit victorious over the accidents of mortality. The easy and decisive modelling of the head, the quality of the flesh scored and thinned with age, and the truth of tone, all declare it one of the artist's most noteworthy efforts. Before the sittings Patmore had written of Sargent: "He seems to me to be the greatest, not only of living English portrait painters, but of all English portrait painters." Patmore was delighted with the sketch, and when a friend told him that anyone might suppose that the unseen hand

* Edmund Gosse, "Coventry Patmore," p. 178.

153

held a whip, and that it might have been the portrait of a Southern planter on the point of thrashing his slaves and exclaiming, "You damned niggers!" the poet exclaimed: "Is not that what I have been doing all my life?" Not content with the two portraits, Sargent insisted on a third; that is how Patmore comes to figure in the frieze in the Boston Library as the prophet Ezekiel.

Another portrait of the same year is that of Mr. W. W. Graham Robertson, author of "Pinkie and the Fairies." He is painted as a slight young dandy standing on a polished floor; the figure in the long fashionable overcoat, the jade-handled cane, the carefully groomed poodle with a coloured ribbon tying up its curls, and the delicate intellectual countenance of the model, pale with weariness of thought or with dawns that have found him bandying paradox and repartee, might be taken as a symbol of the nineties. The picture speaks of the "Beardsley period," of the "Yellow Book," of the aspiration to startle and the cultivation of disillusioned detachment. Sargent has been engrossed by the significance of the problem to be solved. He has painted an individual, but he has defined a period, a type, an attitude of mind; he has put on record a date. That is an achievement to be compared with the portrait of the youth, Johan Koeymans, painted by Hals. All the mastery of tone and value he had acquired is displayed on the canvas and shown in the gradations of colour that give life and beauty to the picture. The painting is less free than in the Patmore sketch, but the modelling of the head is no less skilful. A palette more limited than usual has been employed. The introduction of the dandified poodle has given interest and vivacity to the picture and adroitly provided a half-tone between the high light of face, hands and collar and the sombre background. Other portraits shown were Mrs. Ernest Hills and Mrs. Russell Cooke, while at the New Gallery, he exhibited the portrait of Miss Ada Rehan.

At the end of 1895, finding the calls on his time in London had grown so pressing, he determined to take another studio in which to continue his Boston decorations. Accordingly, he

W. GRAHAM ROBERTSON.

gave up residing at Morgan Hall with the Abbeys and took a twenty-one years' lease of 12 and 14, The Avenue, Fulham Road. For the rest of his life when in London the greater part of his time was spent in the large studio, which, with an adjoining room where he worked at the architectural part of his decorations, comprised the new premises. They lay removed from the thoroughfare with an unwelcoming approach through a back-yard. Here he could withdraw from the world, like a bandit to his fastness, and admit visitors or not as he liked. An un-answered rap on the door was no proof that Sargent was not within. If he answered, it was invariably in his shirt-sleeves, generally with a cigarette in his mouth, and always with a robust welcome. Scores of pencil studies lay about and vast canvases were in position against the wall, and with regard to these he was always curious to hear the views of a layman, and ready to discuss his criticism and approval. The contents of his workshop next door, where he worked out problems of lighting and calculations of architectural proportion and geometrical relations, were much more recondite; here the amateur could only display a totally unintelligent interest. His famous picture *Gassed* was painted at Fulham Road, also the Generals of the War and the decorations of Boston. Some years later, when sated with painting portraits, he wrote to Ralph Curtis:

> No more paughtraits* whether refreshed or not. I abhor and abjure them and hope never to do another especially of the Upper Classes. I have weakly compromised and lately done a lot of mugs in coke and charcoal and am sick of that too, although occasionally the brief operation has been painless. I am winding up my worldly affairs in that line and now I shall be able to paint nothing but Jehovah in Fulham Road. His friends all call Him Jah, Whereas may you and the Dogaressa (Mrs. Ralph Curtis) and the children merit and receive his fatherly attention and flourish under his care.
>
> Yrs.,
> J. S. S.

It was about the same time that Sargent said to someone who lamented that in his painting he had veiled, and not revealed,

* He used this spelling in later years as a sort of signal of satiety.

the face of Jehovah: "You forget I have given up painting portraits."

One picture exhibited at the Academy in 1896 may be especially mentioned because it elicited the warm admiration of Mr. George Moore, who was far from being enthusiastic about Sargent. Mr. Moore wrote of this portrait (Miss Priestley):

> Gradually a pale-faced woman with arched eyebrows, draws our eyes and fixes our thoughts. It is a portrait by Mr. Sargent one of the best he has painted. By the side of a Franz Hals it might look small and thin, but nothing short of a fine Hals would affect its real beauty. My admiration for Mr. Sargent has often hesitated, but this picture completely wins me. . . . The rendering is full of the beauty of incomparable skill. . . . The portrait tells us that he has learned the last and most difficult lesson—how to omit. . . . A beautiful work certainly: I should call it a perfect work were it not that the drawing is a little too obvious in places we can detect the manner: it does not *coule de source* like the drawing of the very great Masters.

Thenceforward a steady stream of portraits issued from the studio in Tite Street. Max Beerbohm's caricature reproduced on p. 160, represents Sargent, with dilated eye and a countenance slightly bucolic, at his window like a farmer taking stock of his cattle, and surveying the row of applicants drawn up in the street below. Among the fashionable ladies waiting their turn may be seen boy messengers sent on in advance to keep places in the ranks, where Lady Faudel Phillips and the Duchess of Sutherland are conspicuous. One of his sitters, a famous personage, asked if she could invite some of her friends to be present at a sitting. He reluctantly assented. At three o'clock the door bell rang, and during the next half-hour the friends continued to arrive, all strangers to Sargent, most of them curiously dressed representatives of the æsthetic movement then at its height. By three-thirty the studio was thronged with an excited concourse; every moment the hubbub increased. By degrees he was pressed against his easel, and the area in which he used to step back to get a better view of his sitter was blocked. The sitting had to be abandoned.

In his early days when painting in Paris he used to relate
that Mrs. Moore, who was then sitting to him in her own house,
and who enjoyed a European fame for malaprop use of French,
took exception to a glass of flowers standing between her and the
painter. She rang the bell and when the footman appeared said,
pointing in the direction of Sargent, "Otez-moi *ce salaud*" (*sale
eau*). The embarrassed footman was at a loss what to do.

Such things appear trivial in print, but Sargent gave them
life. Any account of him which ignored this side, or failed to
show his receptivity to the humblest sources of amusement, would
be misleading. It is unnecessary, however, to draw further on
the store of such episodes with which his memory was peopled.
It was a common experience for him, as probably for all portrait
painters, to be asked to alter some feature in a face, generally
the mouth; indeed, this happened so often that he used to define
a portrait as "a likeness in which there was something wrong
about the mouth." He rarely acceded, and then only when he
was already convinced that it was wrong. In the case of Francis
Jenkinson, the Cambridge Librarian, it was pointed out that he
had omitted many lines and wrinkles which ought to be shown
on the model's face. He refused to make, as he said, "a railway
system of him." His refusal more than once led to scenes. On
one occasion the lady who had taken exception to the rendering
of her mouth became hysterical and fainted. Sargent was the
last man in the world to cope with such a situation. A friend
who happened to call found him helplessly contemplating the
scene. The model was restored to sense, but the mouth remained
as it was. To another lady who complained of the drawing of her
nose he said: "Oh, you can alter a little thing like that when
you get it home." To Lady Cholmondeley, of whom he did
two portraits, he always called the planes of the nostrils "the
devil's own."

A sitter has given me an account of being painted by Sargent
in 1902:

> At one of my sittings during which Mr. Sargent painted my hands
> I sat motionless for two hours. A certain way in which I had un-
> consciously put my hands together pleased him very much because the

posture, he said, was clearly natural to me. He implored me not to move. We worked very hard—he with his magical brush, I with my determination to control fidgets and the restless instincts to which sitters are prone when forced to remain still for any length of time, for the most part we were silent. Occasionally I heard him muttering to himself. Once I caught: "Gainsborough would have done it! . . . Gainsborough would have done it!"

He was working at fever heat, and it was so infectious that I felt my temples throbbing in sympathy with his efforts, the veins swelling in my brow. At one moment I thought I was going to faint with the sense of tension and my fear to spoil the pose which had enthused him.

At the end of two hours he declared that the hands were a failure, and he obliterated them.

"I must try again next time," he said in a melancholy tone. At the next sitting he painted the hands quickly as they now appear a tour de force in the opinion of some, utterly unsuccessful in the eyes of others.

My husband came several times to the sittings. On one occasion Mr. Sargent sent for him specially. He rode across the Park to Tite Street.

He found Mr. Sargent in a depressed mood. The opals baffled him. He said he couldn't paint them. They had been a nightmare to him, he declared, throughout the painting of the portrait.

That morning he was certainly in despair. . . . Presently he said to my husband: "Let's play a Fauré duet." They played, Mr. Sargent thumping out the bass with strong stumpy fingers. At the conclusion Mr. Sargent jumped up briskly, went back to the portrait and with a few quick strokes, dabbed in the opals. He called to my husband to come and look: "I've done the damned thing," he laughed under his breath.

My sister, on the occasion of her visit to the studio during my last sitting, remembers seeing Mr. Sargent paint my scarf with one sweep of his brush.

What appeared to interest him more than anything else when I arrived was to know what music I had brought with me.

To turn from colour to sound evidently refreshed him, and presumably the one art stimulated the other in his brain.

He used to tell of Duse that she consented to give one sitting. She arrived at midday and at five minutes to one rose from her chair, saying, "Je vous souhaite de vivre mille ans et d'avoir la gloire et beaucoup d'enfants, mais au revoir," and he never saw her again.

He had very decided views as to what clothes suited particular sitters best. If for some reason they preferred their own choice it was always to the detriment of the picture. For that superb group of the four American Professors now at the Johns Hopkins Institute, Baltimore, Sir William Osler proposed to wear his Doctor's gown; Sargent said at once:

No I can't paint you in that. It won't do. I know all about that red. You know they gave me a degree down there and I've got one of those robes. Musingly he went on "I've left it on the roof in the rain. I've buried it in the garden. It's no use. The red is as red as ever. The stuff is too good. It won't fade. Now if you could get a Dublin degree? The red robes are made of different stuff and if you wash them they come down to a beautiful pink. Do you think you could get a Dublin degree? No, I couldn't paint you in that Oxford red! Why, do you know, they say that the women who work on the red coats worn by the British soldiers have all sorts of troubles with their eyes.

The picture was painted in 33, Tite Street. In the background is the horseman by Greco, familiar to those who visited his studio. None of his work excels this picture for solemnity and dignity. The Academic atmosphere is there at its best; it has judicial calm and authority. He has rendered a noble conception with the utmost economy of means; for impressiveness and solidity of structure, for gradation in tone and recession, for reflection in the light and luminosity in the shade this picture will rank with his finest work. In the life of Sir William Osler we read that "Sargent worried over posing them and evidently did not think them beauties." Indeed, after seeing Osler he said he had never before painted a man with an olive-green complexion.

In later years, at any rate, Sargent took pleasure in the presence of someone besides the sitter in the studio. He liked listening to what was said, and however intense his concentration, he always seemed to follow and be able to join in the conversation. I never saw him more amused than when, about to paint a famous statesman, he received a letter from the organizer of the movement to have the portrait done, giving a list of topics suitable for discussion during the sittings. I remember the first topic was the "Irish question." Sargent and the Irish question! Max Beerbohm could not have desired a better subject for his pencil.

More than once he had occasion to be embarrassed and also amused by the subsequent fate of his pictures. Once one distinguished sitter had his hand painted out and later begged that it might be painted in again. On another occasion a husband, alarmed at his wife's decolletage, had a water-colour representation of tulle added in the name of propriety before the picture was exhibited. The following letter, written to me in 1897, shows the sort of request to which he was only too much accustomed:

> As you are going to R——do if the opportunity occurs, rather discourage the idea of my going down to do some fussy retouches to the picture that B—— fancies it requires—among others to bring the color of the hair up to date. I think it would be a great pity. There are also hopeless difficulties in the way of doing the hand any better. Every year I get in Italy, an invitation for some long past week-end to run down to R—— and catch that little golden shade that I unaccountably missed years ago. You might have a chance of suggesting that old pictures ought to be left in peace.

When invited to alter a face and "soften" an expression, he left no room for ambiguity in his answer.

> DEAR ——,
>
> I have received your kind letter and if I thought an interview was of the slightest use and would not lead to a further discussion I would of course welcome it.
>
> But the point on which we differ is one with which a long experience of portrait painting has made me perfectly familiar—I have very often been reproached with giving a hard expression to ladies portraits, especially when I have retained some look of intelligence in a face, besides amiability, as I consider myself forced to do in this case.
>
> The expression of ⸻'s face in the portrait is kind and indulgent, with over and above this, a hint at a sense of humour. If I take this out, it will become as soft as anyone can desire. But as a matter of fact nothing will make me, much as I regret not meeting your wishes.
>
> Yours truly,
> JOHN S. SARGENT.

31. TITE STREET.

By Max Beerbohm.

Many will remember the injuries done at the Adademy to Sargent's portrait of Henry James by a suffragette on May 4, 1914. The moment the outrage was discovered Sargent was telegraphed for. What followed is described by Mr. Lamb, the Secretary to the Royal Academy:

> Just as I returned to the Academy (he had accompanied the woman to the police station) and found some of the Council already arrived, Sargent came into the room, and, although he must have seen out of the corner of his eye the horrid ruin of his portrait gaping there on the settee, he came straight over to me, with real anguish breaking out over his whole big person and exclaimed "My dear Lamb, what a dreadful business for you, I *am* so sorry." On my telling him I had got the criminal locked up he went on "A mad-woman and a police-court! How awful for you!" And it was only when I led him to the picture that he thought of examining the real disaster. I have no doubt that other friends can quote similar instances of his quick self-forgetting sympathy.

That illustrates very well a certain definite kind of magnanimity characteristic of him. It is true that given good cause he was capable of bearing resentment, but when such cause was absent, it was the feelings of others which were uppermost in his mind. His benevolence welled up spontaneously. He did not suffer his personal stake to weigh in the balance. There was no ostentation, the benefit was conferred, the altruistic thing done, without his thinking twice about it.

It was rare for him to speak of his portraits or comment on his sitters, still rarer for him to write about either. The following letter about his portrait of President Wilson, addressed to his friend Mrs. Hale, is one of the few instances to the contrary:

THE NEW WILLARD,
WASHINGTON,
D. C.
Oct. 20, 1917.

MY DEAR MARY,
I recognized your handwriting on the ottawa poem.
Here I am well under weigh. Have had two sittings already and hope to have one every afternoon. My sitter is interesting looking, not at all like the Kodaks of him in the papers, and very suave and

reposeful. The White House is empty, the habitation of the lynx
and the bittern. How different from the days of Roosevelt who posed
or rather didn't pose, in a crowd. . . .

My soul longs for the Pope Building, and if the President behaves
himself I hope to be back there in two weeks.

Yours ever,

JOHN S. SARGENT.

To Mrs. Gardner he wrote at about the same time that the
President "was interesting to do, very agreeable to be with, and
the conditions are perfect, as he allows no interruptions and does
not hold levees as Roosevelt used to do."

He was never complacent. That would have been inconsistent with his humility, which was proof against applause.
Few can have heard him express himself satisfied with any work
he had done. But it was a rare pleasure to hear him exclaim
in regard to one of his latest portraits: "That will show . . . that
I can still paint." It was the nearest thing to self-contentment
that in the course of thirty years I ever heard him express.

He was adamant where the reproduction and exhibition of
pictures was concerned. He held the view that the artist, and
not the owner, was the arbiter. In the following letter to the
then secretary of the National Portrait Society he states his
position:

MADAM,

In reply to your consent for my request to exhibit a portrait,
the consent of the owner having been already obtained, I write to
point out, as I have done on similar occasions, that I consider this
to be the reverse of the order in which such consents should be applied
for when it is a question of an annual exhibition.

I make it a rule not to give my consent when that of the owner has
been obtained first.

Yours faithfully,

JOHN S. SARGENT.

Chapter XXI

ON January 14, 1897, Sargent was elected an Academician by a large majority in a ballot against B. W. Leader. In the July following he deposited temporarily a portrait of Herr Johannes Wolff as his diploma work, signed the roll and received his diploma. In 1900 he replaced the portrait by *A Venetian Interior*, exhibited in the Academy Exhibition of that year. It had been painted for his friend Mrs. Curtis, the owner of the Palazzo Barbaro, where he very often stayed when in Venice. It had failed to meet with her approval; it had offended in two ways; the portrait of herself was said to anticipate advancing years, and her son seated on a table in an attitude of nonchalance was inconsistent with the deportment observed by Mrs. and Mr. Charles P. Curtis. Thus the picture became one of the cornerstones of the Diploma Gallery.

The picture has a quality of charm, indefinable, but to as great a degree, perhaps, as any picture by Sargent. He has made use of the most abbreviated means. By the aid of a few smudges he has indicated the sumptuous Venetian decoration, the carvings round the pictures, the scrolls and cherubs on the walls, the lunettes above the doors; accuracy of eye and infallibility of touch could hardly go further, the room bathed in warm light and luminous shadows is filled with the local spirit. Mrs. Curtis, with her embattled dignity, and her husband, with his more venerable reposefulness as he looks at a volume of engravings, are seen in the foreground; further back in the room is the younger generation, Ralph the son and artist, jaunty and debonair, and beside him in a high light the graceful figure of his wife. Further away the remainder of the room in deep shadow tells of another and an older Venice, of another and a more spectacular social life.

163

In 1898 he began his series of Wertheimer portraits,* and writing to Lady Lewis shortly afterwards he described himself as being in a state of "chronic Wertheimerism." Each picture as it left the studio served to whet afresh the appetite of the great art dealer. Indeed, Mr. Asher Wertheimer's only regret was that there were not more Wertheimers for Sargent to paint. There were no bounds to his admiration for the artist, or limits to his desire for the perpetuation of his family on canvas. The series began appropriately enough with the portraits of Mr. and Mrs. Asher Wertheimer which were exhibited in the Academy of 1898. It was the year of their silver wedding, and they were to be presented to the world in a form which would long outlive any anniversaries that they or many generations of their descendants were likely to celebrate. The portrait of Mrs. Asher Wertheimer bears an aspect of great dignity, of a serene and distinguished old age. She looks out of the canvas with a gaze of kindly benevolence, and with not a little of quiet wisdom. Representation may or may not be "irrelevant"; here, by means of it, the artist has been able to move the spectator. Those whose faith in that aspect of art may have been shaken can hardly fail to find their confidence restored as they look on this impressive rendering of a fellow-creature.

As an example of skill in presenting character the portrait of Mr. Wertheimer, who peers rather than gazes at the spectator, is even more remarkable. We are aware of success rather cynically enjoyed, of assessments as acute in the case of humanity as of works of art, of antipathies lived down by sheer astuteness, of triumphant pertinacity and of commercial secrecy. But no one picture of the Wertheimer series surpasses, and it may be doubted if any equals, the portrait of the two sisters Miss Ena (now Mrs. Robert M. Mathias) and Miss Betty (now Mrs. Eustace A. Salaman). They are painted standing side by side. The elder and taller of the two, dressed in white satin, has her arm round the waist of her sister who, slighter and less tall, is in a gown of deep red velvet. The design is compact, balanced and rhythmic. The arms of the younger sister fall by her side, and

* That these pictures now belong to the nation is largely due to the diplomatic persuasion of Lord D'Abernon.

MRS. ASHER WERTHEIMER.

here Sargent has introduced a feature which has contributed not a little to the distinction of the picture. He has painted an open fan of transparent material in the right hand of the model, the spokes turned towards the spectator, and by this means he has prolonged the lines and carried on the tones of the right arm. The open fan has given life and interest to this section of the canvas and, set off against the red dress, has helped to balance the distribution of dark and light in the picture. The lines of the right arm are reminiscent of the portrait of Madame Gauthereau; they have the same fluent vertical fall, while the arm itself is turned in much the same way towards the spectator. The iridescent ivory tints of the white dress, merging into the delicate blues and greys of the Chinese vase, the flesh tones, the background, and the beautifully painted hair of the two girls show a consummate mastery of colour. This picture is one of the completest expressions of Sargent's art. No stroke of the brush is without significance; every accessory contributes to the harmonious unity of the group; there is no dull or unnecessary passage. The result is a picture full of vigour and vitality, constructed and modelled with astonishing solidity, and of great decorative quality. The subject was well suited to his brush. The two girls, in the prime of youth and splendid types of their race, form a seductive contrast: the elder glowing, opulent and triumphant; the younger slighter and less dramatic, sheltered rather than dominated by her sister; the one in full sail, the other, by comparison, gently floating on more quiet seas. Of this picture Mr. Roger Fry wrote: "This is in its way a masterpiece. The poses of the figures are full of spontaneity and verve, and the contrast between the leaning figure of the younger girl and the almost exaggerated robustness of her sister is entirely felicitous. And the arrangement once attained, in this case with such conspicuous good fortune, Mr. Sargent has recorded it as no one else could have done."

Mrs. Mathias was again seen on the walls of the Academy in 1905 in the picture known as *A Vele Gonfie*. Unfortunately this picture, one of the finest of the series, was not included in the bequest to the nation.

While engaged at Fairford on his Boston decorations Sargent had made several attempts to model in clay. Modelling thenceforward was for him a recognized means to attaining his effects in the library decorations. In 1901 he exhibited at the Academy *The Crucifix*, his most important piece of sculpture. No one who looks at it can doubt Sargent's emotional interest in these decorations.*

Here on a Byzantine cross Sargent has placed the figure of the dying Christ; Adam and Eve are stationed closely to it in a crouching attitude on either side, each holding a chalice under an arm of the Cross to receive the Blood of Christ. At the foot of the Cross is a pelican feeding its young with the blood from its breast, an ancient symbol of the Resurrection. Below the feet of the Saviour is the serpent, signifying evil partially subdued. Above the arms of the Cross are written the words: "Remissa Sunt Peccata Mundi." The Crucifix, the groundwork of which is gold, is so placed in the Sargent Hall that the foot of the Cross forms part of the frieze of the angels. The remainder of the Cross is included in the scheme of the lunette of the Trinity immediately above. The angels of the frieze, two of whom uphold the Cross, carry the instruments of the Passion. Woven on the garments of the two supporting angels are the symbols of the Eucharist, wheat and wine. The angels, eight in number, to symbolize regeneration, are clad in Byzantine draperies, their faces aglow with the beatific vision, and illumined by the sanctity of their office. The frieze, as in the case of that of the prophets, is divided from the lunette by a cornice. On this is written an inscription which Sargent found in the Cathedral of Cephalu in Sicily. "Factus Homo, Factor Hominis, Factique Redemptor. Corporeus Redimo Corpora Cordi Deus."†

The lunette contains three colossal figures. These are the Persons of the Trinity. They are bound by a single red cloak

---

* It now forms part of the "Dogma of the Redemption," at the south end of the Sargent Hall, facing the frieze of "The Prophets" and the lunette of "The Children of Israel under the hands of their oppressors," already referred to.

† Sargent substituted the word Redimo for Judico in the original—a change necessitated by the character of the decoration.

THE MISSES WERTHEIMER.

with a hem of gold. Their faces, slightly in relief, are exactly similar. Each raises a right hand in the manner of benediction common to the Greek Church. Thus is their oneness symbolized. A difference in the form of the crown worn by each figure indicates the difference of their several attributes.

The original bronze presented by Miss Sargent and Mrs. Ormond as a memorial to their brother now stands in the crypt of St. Paul's. There it can be judged as a work of art unrelated to the scheme for which it was designed and of which it now forms a part.

Throughout the composition we have the sense that he was profoundly conscious of the majesty of the subject with which he was dealing.*

Whistler, as soon as he saw *The Crucifixion* in the Academy, wrote to Sargent to say how fine he thought it,† and Whistler, as we learn from the Pennell Life, was not given to praising Sargent's art. Sargent himself considered that he had succeeded beyond his hopes. It was a work for which he had more liking than he generally allowed himself to entertain for his achievements. He gave to a few of his friends a small reproduction, and in a letter to Lady Lewis gave directions how it should be hung.

I am sending you the little bronze crucifix which I feel I rather thrust upon you, but still I know you will like it if only that it will remind you of the better big one. It ought to be hung about the level of one's eye and if possible not in too strong a side light. A top light is best but not easy to find in a house unless you can find room for it on your staircase. But to dictate where a gift horse is to go would be looking the recipient in the mouth as Solomon says. I am only too delighted that it should be in your house.

In 1902 Sargent spent the month of August in Norway. There he painted *On His Holidays*, a salmon river tumbling with agitated waters through a rocky channel with a portrait

* The idea of Adam and Eve receiving the blood of Christ on the Cross is found in a thirteenth-century window at Angers, and in another at Bourges. These are referred to in Émile Male's "Religious Art in France, Thirteenth Century," a book which was in the possession of Sargent and sold after his death. The American sculptor St. Gaudens, in a letter, described the Crucifix as a "masterpiece."

† E. R. and J. Pennell, "The Whistler Journal," p. 35.

of young McCulloch lying on one of the rocks beside the salmon he had caught. The picture has the chilling accuracy of a photograph. It is a plain unvarnished tale, told in a cold Northern light, the work of an accomplished craftsman who has for the time being doffed the rôle of artist.

In London it was becoming rarer to meet him at the houses of other people. His circle was contracting to the radius of his real preferences. He had by no means a comprehensive interest in humanity; on the contrary, his taste in people as time went on became narrowly restricted. It was, in fact, only in a chosen circle that he was completely at his ease. No man could work at such pressure and not require that his relations with his fellowmen should be free of effort and constraint and devoid of formality. The "social function" element was irksome and distasteful to him. The commerce of words was only free and unhampered in a familiar atmosphere, in places where he could be mentally in his shirt-sleeves, in all "the quotidian undress and relaxation of his mind." Friendships which he had once formed he did not change or abate. To the end of his life he continued and carried along with him those he had made in his early days. But others were formed. In 1898 he painted Mrs. Charles Hunter, the wife of Mr. Charles Hunter, a north-country coalowner, and the sister of Dame Ethel Smyth the composer. The Hunters entertained considerably in London. In the country they had a seventeenth-century house, Hill Hall, near Epping, some twenty miles by road from Hyde Park Corner. It was furnished and decorated in the Italian style and in admirable taste by Mrs. Hunter, who, herself keenly interested in the arts, had the faculty of gathering within the fold of her generous hospitality rising and risen lights of the literary and artistic world.

Sargent had paid tribute in kind to his hostess by marbling two immense columns, veritable Jackim and Boaz, in the hall, painting with the skill of the most accomplished house decorator.

Writing in 1912 from Hill Hall, Henry James says:* . . . "I have made . . . this much a dash into the world. It is the

---

* "Letters," ii., p. 241.

ALFRED WERTHEIMER.
National Gallery, Millbank.

world of the wonderful and delightful Mrs. Charles Hunter, whom you may know (long my very kind friend), and all swimming just now in a sea of music; John Sargent (as much a player as a painter), Percy Grainger, Roger Quilter, Wilfred de Glehn and others: round whose harmonious circle, however, I roam as in outer darkness, catching a vague glow through the veiled windows of the temple, but on the whole only intelligent enough to feel and rue my stupidity—which is quite the wrong condition." In this world there could often be seen on Sunday and occasionally on week-days an assembly of notables seasoned with more fashionable and less renowned members of society. Henry James, George Moore, Max Beerbohm, Sargent, Professor Tonks, Wilson Steer, D. S. MacColl, de Glehns, Ethel Smyth, Percy Grainger, Roger Quilter, Cyril Scott, were among those most often to be found there. It was in just such company Sargent was most at ease, and it was such surroundings that his friendship with Mrs. Hunter henceforward secured for him. As the years went by, work during seven whole days of the week made it difficult and physically irksome for him to leave London. He stayed, too, at Lympne, Houghton and Panshanger. But paying visits—although once he was there no one seemed more care free—entailed in his case a surprising amount of preliminary worry. His real home was the house of his sister Emily. He talked to her every morning on the telephone, and when not dining out he dined with her in her room looking over the Thames. This was hung with the red damask that he had bought for her in Venice and, like her other rooms, with the pictures he had painted for her. Most evenings they had guests. Henry James, Mrs. Curtis, Professor Tonks, Wilson Steer, de Glehns, Nelson Ward, the Harrisons, Barnards, Alfred Parsons, Joseph Farquharson, R.A., Erskine Childers, and a few Academicians formed the nucleus of their society. Professor Tonks writes: "I was introduced to his mother and sister by Steer, and was invited to Mrs. Sargent's flat (as it then was) in Carlyle Mansions to dinner, very often now it seems to me, looking back, where I spent some of the happiest evenings of my life. Sargent was generally there, and I have a feeling that those who were not fortunate enough to meet him at those dinners missed the best of him. The evenings were very informal; we generally went in our ordinary clothes, and there was a sense of freedom which encouraged everyone to speak at his best. Sargent was on these occasions decidedly a good talker. As a public speaker he was a complete failure; at a dinner given to him by the Chelsea Arts Club he could do little else than hang on to the table, but at the table in Carlyle Mansions he made an admirable host, enjoyed talking himself and listening to others. He had a very accurate memory, disconcerting at times, as he had a way of correcting careless quotations. He was a most honest and fearless expresser of his views, perhaps a little irritable on contradiction, more so as time went on."

Every autumn after his mother's death in 1905 would see him crossing the Channel, always with his sister Emily, and either with the de Glehns or Miss Eliza Wedgwood, or the Misses Barnard, or Mrs. Ormond and her children, bound for some sketching centre in Italy or Corfu, Majorca or Spain, or in the Val d'Aosta. To the latter place he and his sister went in three successive years, and it was there that he painted *Cashmere*, *The Hermit* and well-known pictures of his nieces lying in various attitudes by the clear running brook, in brilliant Oriental clothes, which he took with him from London for the purpose. One year he travelled with a stuffed gazelle, bought at Rowland Ward's, which was to figure in some landscape. Here, too, he painted the portrait of himself by fixing a mirror to the trunk of a tree. This was a task that bored him unspeakably, and after a few strokes of his brush he would dash off to the brook to do one of his sketches. The gazelle was left at the painters' chalet in the Val d'Aosta, the portrait now hangs in the Uffizi.

What scenery did Sargent prefer? We have already noticed how little he concerned himself with panorama and distance, and that he preferred "close ups"; within these limits and given bright sunshine his range was exceedingly wide. His letters contain some indications of his preferences. Writing to Ralph Curtis from the Palazzo Barbaro in 1913 he said:

The de Glehns my sister and I are off in a day or two to the Lake
of Guarda, where we have discovered a nasty little pension on a little
promontory, which is otherwise paradise—cypresses, olives, a villa, a
tiny little port, deep clear water and no tourists.

Again writing to the same correspondent he says:

ROME.
MY DEAR RALPH,
    I wish it were possible to accept your kind invitation and the
Dogaressa's (Mrs. Curtis) but it were easier for a camel to pass through
a rich man's eye. The time is getting so short. I foresee that I shall
hang on here till the train starts for Chelsea. . . . In spite of scirocco
and lots of rain we have been seeing the villas within miles round thanks
to Mrs. Hunter's motor. They are magnificent and I should like
to spend a summer at Frascati and paint from morning till night at the
Tortonia or the Falconiere, ilexes and cypresses, fountains and statues
—ainsi soit il—amen.

To Mrs. Adrian Stokes he wrote:

    Ronda is a most picturesque place with magnificent scenery. It
is on the edge of a tremendous cliff that looks across a great hollow
with fine angular rocky ranges of mountains that would just suit
Stokes. The objection to it is that the small boys are perfect devils
and throw stones at painters and worry them out of their wits.

He had no liking for trim and ordered gardens; they had to
be derelict or at any rate unkempt, and the more time had
played undisturbed with the tresses of tree and shrub the
more was his eye satisfied. Of Aranjuez he wrote:

    This place is perfectly charming, grand gardens with Caver-
nous avenues and fountains and statues, long neglected—good
natured friendly people—lunch in the open air under arbours of
roses. These Spaniards are the most amiable people in the world, they
put themselves out for you in the most extraordinary way. With the
common people it is no disadvantage being an American, for their
newspapers told them that they gave us the most tremendous licking
in Cuba. And the Artists and better people will do anything for a
stranger.

Venice, once his favourite haunt, he thought had been rather
marred for an artist by "the swarms of larky smart Londoners

whose goings on fill the *Gazette*," goings on which, however, never failed to afford him amusement.

These extracts show his fidelity in taste to the environment of his childhood and early training. But olive and ilex, fountain and statue, sunlight and shade, rocks and running water were to him just problems of form and colour, opportunities for the exercise of his supreme craftsmanship rather than settings for moods induced by association or reflection.

In the winter of 1905 he was in Palestine "getting new fuel for his decorative work"; he was disappointed with the result.

> Some new material (he wrote to Lady Lewis) I have secured but it is different from what I had in view and not abundant—no miraculous draught but I shall still fish here for a while and try to bring back some weightier stuff than lots of impossible sketches and perhaps useless studies.

In January, 1906, he was in the neighbourhood of Jerusalem when news reached him of his mother's illness and death. He was deeply affected. He telegraphed begging that the funeral should be delayed till his return. This was done. Meanwhile he spent days of agitated distress waiting at Jaffa for a boat. A strong tie had been broken. He was a devoted son.

> Everything is dreadful (he wrote) except that her friends were good and that death itself came unsuspected and unrecognized. . . .*

To these tours through Europe in his chosen company he owed some of the happiest months of his life. He was away from portraits, which by 1909 had become wearisome to him. As early as 1906 he had written to Lady Lewis: "I have now got a bomb-proof shelter into which I retire when I sniff the coming portrait or its trajectory." Abroad he could go where his eye led him, and choose his subject; life was plain sailing on a sea of summer. He would breakfast at 7.30, and then sally out to sketch, working till the light failed. His energy was inexhaustible. The hours of sunshine were treasured like gold. Sight-

* Letter to Lady Lewis.

seeing was reserved for rainy days. In the evenings he would play chess, or the piano where one was available—duets, with Mrs. de Glehn or Miss Eliza Wedgwood, from Brahms, Schumann or Albeniz. "The only pleasure," he wrote, "of coming back to one's own house is the pleasure of unpacking the *bibelots* one has got elsewhere—good wholesome sentiment."

Chapter XXII

SARGENT'S greatest portraits are not the product of any particular period, they lie scattered through his work. In the first English years we get the *Misses Vickers, Mrs. Boit, Mrs. Hemenway*, and then in 1895 *Coventry Patmore* and *Graham Robertson*. In 1897 Mrs. Carl Meyer's portrait was shown at the Academy. None of his pictures is more effectively organized and composed, none is more melodious. It strikes a note of gaiety as of silver bells. There is the optimism of spring in the running lines of the composition and the freshness of the rose and pink colour which swim through the picture. Sumptuousness in dress and furniture tells its story of opulence, but it is refined and rarefied, robbed of its insistence, and subdued to the central purpose of the design. The colour scheme is closely related; remove a ribbon, straighten a fold of the dress, release a figure from the pattern of the sofa, or dispense with an accent and the whole picture would suffer, its unity would crumble. There is nothing obvious or redundant, nothing that is not charming, even exciting, in this triumphant artistry. The Meyer picture was followed by the *Wertheimer* series, *Miss Jane Evans, Mrs. Charles Hunter, Lady Faudel Phillips* and in 1900 the *Wyndham* group.

This is one of his most purely and unmistakably English pictures, a *tour de force* in characterization, drawing and the handling of white. Three figures dressed in white, and a white sofa in the lower half of the picture presented formidable difficulties: a risk of suggesting a section of geological strata. The artist has posed the elder sister seated on the back of the sofa, in profile, her head slightly turned to the spectators; her delicate intellectual beauty dominates the scene and carries the white into the upper section of the canvas. Further relief to the mass has been obtained by the magnolias, which effect the transition

LADY SASSOON.

into the shadow of the room beyond. The beauty of the picture lies not only in the colour and drawing, but in the impression of serenity and calm. Sargent has here isolated these sisters from the world and encompassed them with their own associations. They are back once again in the surroundings that made their common bond; their mother's picture by Watts is seen on the wall beyond, the noise of life is hushed for the moment. There is a charming sentiment in the composition without a trace of sentimentality.

In the following years the Academy saw the portraits of *Mrs. Charles Russell, C. S. Lock, Mrs. Leopold Hirsch*, the *Marlborough* group, *M. Leon Delafosse* and in 1907 the portrait of *Lady Sassoon*.

In the portrait of Lady Sassoon, Sargent has conveyed a subtle impression of the individuality of his sitter. Evidently he was here confronted with a highly strung temperament, features of exceptional distinction and refinement, and a personality kindly, alert—even to the point of restlessness—and instinct with pride of race. The result is both a study of character and a work of art. It is painted with the utmost freedom and dexterity. The tumultuous crown of feathers in the hat, the movement suggested in the pose of the figure, the quick play of light and shade over the black silk cloak, the elegant and sensitive hands, all contribute to an impression bordering on flurry. Yet in spite of this a certain nobility and calm, deeper than momentary agitation, is the ultimate effect of the composition. Not infrequently Sargent is criticized for opaqueness or leatheriness in his paint, for a want of luminosity and charm in his colour; here there is no trace of these defects. The delicate ivory white of the skin has a quality of transparency, the liveliness of the black and the softness of the rose-colour, introduced to give freshness to the scheme, are delightful. All has been painted with a sure and fluent touch. If the spectator disregards the portrait and considers solely the picture, he is at once struck by the beauty of the design, its plastic structure, the crisp freshness of the colour, and the black background on which the figure has been wrought. This has a quality of range and mystery purely atmospheric, its depth appears illimitable, an effect which Sargent has equally achieved in the case of his portrait of *Lord Wemyss*. Of the latter picture Mr. Downes says: "His lordship did not like it at all and was not the least disposed to conceal his feelings in the matter." Mr. Downes has been entirely misinformed. The picture, subscribed for by friends, was painted for Lord Wemyss' ninetieth birthday. Sargent considered it one of the best portraits he had painted, a view which was fully shared by the sitter. Nothing is more remarkable in this picture than the way in which the dreariness of modern dress has been disposed of, and a frock coat and tall hat made to serve the end of art. The hat, held in the left hand, reflects a subdued accent of light; the lines of the coat barely to be distinguished from the background, lose all rigidity in the obscurity, emphasize the composition and indicate the upright carriage and dignity of the figure. The hands, which supply a half-tone in the lower section of the canvas, are a fine example of the painter's gift for modelling, and illustrate a topic to which he often referred—namely, the effect on the circulation and consequently on the tones of the hands when they are held downwards for more than a few moments.

The picture of Lord Wemyss, 1909, may be regarded as the close of Sargent's official career as a portrait painter: after that he painted only when importunity made it churlish to refuse, or his own decided inclination prompted him to accede.

It is more difficult with Sargent than with most artists to determine the approximate date of any given picture. We can see that the *Misses Vickers* is an early and *F. J. H. Jenkinson* a late work; we can safely assign to the years 1888-89 certain essays in Impressionism; and we could even feel confident that *Wineglasses* and *An Atlantic Storm* were painted in his youth; but, apart from these instances, his transitions as a portrait painter are so slight and so gradual that his pictures painted after 1884 show differences of style which are scarcely perceptible.

As time progressed and his facility grew, there may be noticed a tendency to emphasis, especially in draperies, the folds becoming deeper, the planes more complicated, while lights and accents are flicked on to the canvas with increasing skill and effect. But in the broader aspects of structure, design and colouring his style shows no variation that can be related to a year or a decade. His best pictures are those with the least definite backgrounds, his least successful those that have an out-of-door *mise en scène*. His English scenery in his full-length portraits is cold and artificial, often arbitrary as a photographer's studio. In the multitude of his works his excellence as a painter of animals is too frequently lost sight of. Yet who has painted dogs with the same characterization, whether we take the self-conscious dandyism of the poodles in the pictures of Asher Wertheimer and Graham Robertson the fussy intelligence of the Duke of Portland's collies, or the care-free repose of the terrier in the Hunter group? Or who has rendered with equal perspicacity the slow strength of oxen, the texture of their coats, their imperturbability and their gaze of patient enquiry? Whether he is painting a herd of goats on a hillside or horses picketed in their lines, he gives their distinguishing character just as he makes the utmost use of them for his design.

Although he gave up portrait painting he went on with his charcoal and pencil heads, and a census of these would produce a startling figure. It has been found impossible to arrive at even an approximate estimate of those he did in London and America. A distinguished diplomatist made a habit, when he found himself at dinner next to a lady he did not know, of saying: "How do you like your Sargent drawing?" He declared that as a conversational gambit it was successful nine times out of ten. But it is not by these drawings that Sargent will live: they are likenesses and deliberate exercises in skill; it is only in comparatively few that his genius is apparent.

Though he left a considerable fortune there is little doubt that he could have doubled or trebled it. Money was a part of the machinery of life in which he took very little interest. His charges for portraits varied considerably: for the *Vickers* group (1884) he received £400, the *Ladies Acheson* group (1901) £2,100, for the *Baltimore Doctors* (1906) £3,000, for the *Marl-*

borough group (1906) 2,500 guineas. For full-lengths he received
1,000 guineas, for lesser pictures prices varying from £500 to
£800. During the War for two pictures, one of *President
Wilson*, the other of *Mrs. Duxbury*, painted for the British Red
Cross, he received £10,000 each and to that extent enriched the
funds of the society. For oil landscapes he asked prices varying
from £100 to £500, for water-colours seldom more than £50.
For eighty-three water-colours sold to an American museum in
1909 he received £4,000. For charcoal portraits he charged at
first 21 guineas, which price was gradually increased till in 1923
he began charging 100 guineas.

With regard to his drawings he wrote to Lady Lewis: "I
never know what to ask for a mere snapshot especially, if it does
not happen to be a miraculously lucky one."

It was with the utmost reluctance that he could be induced,
for the purpose of sale, to pull out any one of the water-colours
which used to lie in their frames, jammed one against the other,
in a large rack on the floor of his studio. If in response to insistence he acquiesced, he would produce one or two, always with a
good deal of gutteral protest, pointing out what he considered
their drawbacks, and qualifying them with some derogatory
title. "Vegetables," "Dried Seaweed," "Troglodytes of the
Cordilleras," "Blokes," "Idiots of the Mountains" and "Inter-
twingles" come back to me as a few of the titles bestowed on
various renderings of woodland scenery, muleteers, figures on a
hillside, and of a portrait group on a river bank. Mrs. de Glehn
remembers a picture he painted in Corfu of three figures, including herself and Miss Wedgwood, in "keepsake" attitudes,
which he labelled with complete gusto to himself as "Triple
Bosh." This picture now figures in a South American collection
under a more official title.

On another occasion in the Simplon when he had done a
water-colour of recumbent figures, with his easel fixed in a de-
pression of the ground, he called the result "A Worm's Eye View."

Mr. Downes, in his account of Sargent's "Life and Work,"
mentions that he once asked him whether "Darnation, Silly,
Silly, Pose," an alternative title for *Carnation, Lily Lily Rose,*

JOHN S. SARGENT SKETCHING

was attributable to Whistler, and that Sargent replied that it did not sound like Whistler. The author of the quip, however, was not far to seek. These mock titles, which might be multiplied, sprang from no affectation and were due to no desire to belittle what he had done, but were shot to the surface from an undercurrent of boyishness which never left him, from a horror of pomposity and portentousness about his art, and even, one might say, to check and damp down any tendency in others to an excess of admiration. They were the play of an essentially humble spirit.

Frequently the prices he asked showed that he had no idea of the commercial value of these sketches. Dealers have been known, after getting the pictures home, to proffer a further sum in acquittal of what had all the appearance of an unconscionable bargain. Indeed, the whole process of bargain and sale was conducted on such original and topsy-turvy principles that amateurs had to employ artifice in order to force the price up to a fair level. On one occasion a friend of his, afraid that on a straight deal the artist would either make a present of the picture or charge a nominal amount, professed to be acting for a South African millionaire. A picture was chosen, but Sargent objected that he did not want it to go out of the country. It was pointed out that the millionaire had a house in London for which the picture was wanted. On that understanding the deal was concluded, but on terms which remained most inadequate for the seller. When Sargent had ascertained the true facts he wrote:

My dear ——,

Your methods give me the cold shivers, and I am filled with awe when I remember the candid face you showed when I asked you if there was any nonsense about your enquiry. If there was a sun today it would go down on my perplexity and indecision if not on my wrath. I shall have to consult a clairvoyante or the bowels of a bird as to what action I must take.

Yours as a rule,
JOHN S. SARGENT.

He was more amused than incensed. Enough has been said to show that he was the least mercenary of men. He belonged neither to those whose generosity is beyond their means nor to that larger class whose means are beyond their generosity. He gave where assistance was wanted. His disregard of money was part of the largeness of his character and outlook. It may be doubted if in later years he had the least idea what he was worth. Towards the end of his life an occasion arose when it became necessary to tell him the amount which he had standing to his credit in the United States. He could only say: "It can't be mine, they've made a mistake at the Bank, it must belong to someone else." As long as he had sufficient means wherewith to pursue his art in his own way and, above all, to assist others, he was entirely indifferent to money. He made no enquiries and left to others the conduct of his affairs.

ANTHONY ASQUITH.

Chapter XXIII

WHEN Mr. John Collier was writing his book on "The Art of Portrait Painting" he asked Sargent for an account of his methods. Sargent replied: "As to describing my procedure, I find the greatest difficulty in making it clear to pupils, even with the palette and brushes in hand and with the model before one, and to serve it up in the abstract seems to me hopeless."

With the assistance, however, of two of his former pupils, Miss Heyneman and Mr. Henry Haley, it is possible to obtain some idea of his methods.

When he first undertook to criticise Miss Heyneman's work he insisted that she should draw from models and not from friends.

"If you paint your friends, they and you are chiefly concerned about the likeness. You can't discard a canvas when you please and begin anew—you can't go on indefinitely till you have solved a problem." He disapproved (Miss Heyneman continues) of my palette and brushes. On the palette the paints had not been put out with any system. "You do not want dabs of colour," he said, "you want plenty of paint to paint with." Then the brushes came in for derision. "No wonder your painting is like feathers if you use these." Having scraped the palette clean he put out enough paint so it seemed for a dozen pictures. "Painting is quite hard enough" he said "without adding to your difficulties by keeping your tools in bad condition. You want good thick brushes that will hold the paint and that will resist in a sense the stroke on the canvas." He then with a bit of charcoal placed the head with no more than a few careful lines over which he passed a rag, so that it was on a perfectly clean greyish coloured canvas (which he preferred) faintly showing where the lines had been that he began to paint. At the start he used sparingly a little turpentine to rub in a general tone over the background and to outline the head (the real outline where the light and shadow meet, not the place where the head meets the background)—to indicate the mass of the hair and the tone of the dress. The features were not even suggested. This was a matter of a few moments. For the rest he used his colour without a medium of any kind, neither oil, turpentine or any admixture. "The thicker you paint, the more your colour flows" he explained. He had put in this general outline very rapidly hardly more than smudges, but from the moment he that began really to paint, he worked with a kind of concentrated deliberation, a slow haste so to speak holding his brush poised in the air for an instant and then putting it just where and how he intended it to fall. . . . To watch the head develop from the start was like the sudden lifting of a blind in a dark room. . . . Every stage was a revelation. For one thing he put his easel directly next to the sitter so that when he walked back from it he saw the canvas and the original in the same light, at the same distance, at the same angle of vision. . . . He aimed at once for the true general tone of the background, of the hair and for the transition tone between the two. He showed me how the light flowed over the surface of the cheek into the background itself.

At first he worked only for the middle tones, to model in large planes, as he would have done had the head been an apple. In short, he painted, as a sculptor models, for the great masses first, but with this difference that the sculptor can roughly *lump* in his head and cut it down afterwards, while the painter, by the limitations of his material, is bound to work instantly for an absolute precision of mass, in the colour and outline he intends to preserve. Economy of effort in every way, he preached, the sharpest self-control the fewest strokes possible to express a fact, the least slapping about of purposeless paint. He believed, with Carolus Duran, that painting was a science which it was necessary to acquire in order to make of it an art. "You must draw with your brush," he said, "as readily, as unconsciously almost as you draw with your pencil." He advised doing a head for a portrait slightly under life-size to counteract the tendency to paint larger than life. Even so, he laid in a head slightly larger than he intended to leave it, so that he could model the edges with and into the background.

The hills of paint vanished from the palette yet there was no heaviness on the canvas; although the shadow was painted as heavily as the light, it retained its transparency. "If you see a thing transparent, paint it transparent; don't get the effect by a thin stain showing the canvas through. That's a mere trick. *The more delicate the transition the more you must study it for the exact tone.*" The lightness and certainty of his touch was marvellous to behold. Never was there any painter who could indicate a mouth with more subtlety, with more mobility, or with keener differentiation. As he painted it, the mouth bloomed out of the face, an integral part of it, not, as in the great majority of portraits, painted on it, a separate thing. He showed how much could be expressed in painting the form of the brow, the cheekbones, and the moving muscles around the eyes and mouth, where the character betrayed itself most readily; and under his hands, a head would be an amazing likeness long before he had so much as indicated the features themselves. In fact, it seemed to me the mouth and nose just *happened* with the modelling of the cheeks, and one eye, living luminous, had been placed in the socket so carefully prepared for it (like a poached egg dropped on a plate, he described the process), when a clock in the neighbourhood struck and Mr. Sargent was suddenly reminded that he had a late appointment with a sitter. In his absorption he had quite forgotten it. He hated to leave the canvas. "If only one had oneself under perfect control," he once said to me, "one could always paint a thing, finally in one sitting." (Now and then he accomplished this.) "Not that you are to attempt this," he admonished me, "if you work on a head for a week without indicating the features you will have learnt something about the modelling of the head."

Every brush stroke while he painted had modelled the head or further simplified it. He was careful to insist that there were many roads to Rome, that beautiful painting would be the result of any method or no method, but he was convinced that by the method he advocated, and followed all his life, a freedom could be acquired, a technical mastery that left the mind at liberty to concentrate on a deeper or more subtle expression.

I had been taught to paint a head in three separate stages, each one repeating—in charcoal, in thin colour-wash and in paint—the same things. By the new method the head developed by *one* process. Till almost the end there had been no features nor accents, simply a solid shape growing out of and into a background with which it was *one*. When at last he did put them each accent was studied with an intensity that kept his brush poised in mid-air till eye and hand had steadied to one purpose, and then . . . bling! the stroke resounded almost like a note of music. It annoyed him very much if the accents were carelessly indicated without accurate consideration of their comparative importance. They were, in a way, the nails upon which the whole structure depended for solidity.

Miss Heyneman subsequently left a study she had made, at Sargent's studio with a note begging him to write, "yes" or "no," according to whether he approved or not. He wrote the next day:

"I think your study shows great progress—much better values and consequently greater breath of effect with less monotony in the detail.

I still think you ought to paint thicker—paint all the half tones and general passages quite thick—and always paint one thing into another and not side by side until they touch. There are a few hard and small places where you have not followed this rule sternly enough." . . .

A few days later he called. Miss Heyneman's usual model had failed, and she had persuaded her charwoman to sit instead; Sargent offered to paint the head of the model.

This old head was perhaps easier to indicate with its prominent forms, but the painting was more subtle. I recall my astonishment when he went into the background with a most brilliant pure blue where I had seen only unrelieved darkness. "Don't you see it?" he asked, "the way the light quivers across it?" I had not perceived it; just as, till each stroke emphasized his intention, I did not see how he managed to convey the thin hair stretched tightly back over the skull without actually painting it. He painted light or shadow, a four-cornered object with the corners worn smooth, as definite in form as it was idefinite in colour, and inexpressibly delicate in its transitions. He concentrated his whole attention upon the middle tone that carried the light into the shadow. He kept up a running commentary of explanation, as he went, appraising each stroke, often condemning it and saying: "That is how *not* to do it! . . . Keep the planes free and simple," he would suggest, drawing a full large brush down the whole contour of a cheek, obliterating apparently all the modelling underneath, but it was always further to simplify that he took these really dreadful risks, smiling at my ill-concealed perturbation and quite sympathizing with it.

This second painting taught me that the whole value of a portrait depends upon its first painting, and that no tinkering can ever rectify an initial failure. Provided every stage is correct a painter of Mr. Sargent's calibre could paint for a week on one head and never retrace his steps but he *never* attempted to correct one. He held that it was as impossible for a painter to try to repaint a head where the understructure was wrong, as for a sculptor to remodel the features of a head that has not been understood in the mass. That is why Mr. Sargent often repainted the head a dozen times, he told me that he had done no less than sixteen of Mrs. Hammersley.

When he was dissatisfied he never hesitated to destroy what he had done. He spent three weeks, for instance, painting Lady D'Abernon in a white dress. One morning, after a few minutes of what was to be the final setting, he suddenly set to work to scrape out what he had painted. The present portrait in a black dress, was done in three sittings.

He did the same with the portrait of Mrs. Wedgwood and many others. Miss Eliza Wedgwood relates that in 1896 he consented, at the instance of Alfred Parsons, to paint her mother for £250. She sat to him twelve times, but after the twelfth sitting he said they would both be the better for a rest. He then wrote to Miss Wedgwood that he was humiliated by his failure to catch the variable and fleeting charm of her mother's personality—that looked like the end of the portrait. Some weeks later he saw Mrs. Wedgwood at Broadway, and struck with a new aspect he said: "If you will come up next week we will finish that portrait." She came to Tite Street, a new canvas was produced, and in six sittings he completed the picture which was shown at the Memorial Exhibition.

Miss Heyneman continues:

"Paint a hundred studies," he would say, "keep any number of clean canvases ready, of all shapes and sizes so that you are never held back by the sudden need of one. You can't do sketches enough. Sketch everything and keep your curiosity fresh." He thought it was excellent practice to paint flowers, for the precision necessary in the study of their forms and the pure brilliancy of their colour. It refreshed the tone of one's indoor portraits, he insisted, to paint landscape or figures out of doors, as well as to change one's medium now and then. He disliked pastel, it seemed to him too artificial, or else it was made to look like oil or water colour, and in that case why not use oil or water colour. . . .

Upon one occasion, after painting for me, he saw one hard edge, and drew a brush across it, very lightly saying at the same time "This is a disgraceful thing to do, and means slovenly painting. Don't ever let me see you do it. . . ." I have also seen the assertion that he painted a head always in one sitting. He painted a head always *in one process*, but that could be carried over several sittings. He never attempted to repaint one eye or to raise or lower it, for he held that the construction of a head prepared the place for the eye, and if it was wrongly placed, the underconstruction was wrong, and he ruthlessly scraped and repainted the head from the beginning. That is one reason why his brushwork looks so fluent and easy, he took more trouble to keep the unworried look of a fresh sketch than many a painter puts upon his whole canvas.

The following extracts from Mr. Haley's account of Sargent's teaching at the Royal Academy Schools, 1897-1900, throw further light on his method:

The Significance of his teaching was not always immediately apparent; it had the virtue of revealing itself with riper experience. His hesitation was probably due to a searching out for something to grasp in the mind of the student, that achieved, he would unfold a deep earnestness, subdued but intense. He was regarded by some students as an indifferent teacher by others as a "wonder"; as a "wonder" I like to regard him.

He dealt always with the fundamentals. Many were fogged as to his aim. These fundamentals had to be constantly exercised and applied.

"When drawing from the model," he said, "never be without the plumb line in the left hand"—Every one has a bias, either to the right hand or the left of the vertical. The use of the plumb line rectifies this error and developes a keen appreciation of the vertical.

He then took up the charcoal, with arm extended to its full length, and head thrown well back; all the while intensely calculating, he slowly and deliberately mapped the proportions of the large masses of a head and shoulders, first the poise of the head upon the neck, its relation with the shoulders. Then rapidly indicate the mass of the hair, then spots locating the exact position of the features, at the same time noting their tone values and special character, finally adding any further accent or dark shadow which made up the head, the neck, the shoulders and head of the sternum.

After his departure I immediately plumbed those points before any movement took place of the model and found them very accurate.

A formula of his for drawing was "Get your spots in their right place and your lines precisely at their relative angles."

On one occasion in the evening life school I well remember Sargent complaining that no one seemed concerned about anything more than an *approximate* articulation of the head upon the neck and shoulders. The procedure was, to register carefully the whole pose at the first evening's sitting of two hours. The remainder of the sittings were devoted to making a thoroughly finished tone drawing in chalk, adhering to the original outline, working from the head downwards, thus the drawing was not affected by any chance deviation from the original pose by the model. Sargent could not reconcile himself to this, the method he tried to inculcate was to lay in the drawing afresh at every sitting getting in one combined effort a complete interpretation of the model. The skull to articulate properly upon the vertebræ.

The same with all the limbs, a keen structural easy supple, moveable machine, every figure with its own individual characteristic as like as possible, an accomplishment requiring enormous practice and experience with charcoal, but taken as a goal to aim at very desirable, a method he followed in his own painting. To the student it meant a continually altered drawing, to portray the varying moods of the model.

In reference to these drawings he would frequently say: "Draw the things seen with the keenest point and let the things unseen fuse themselves into the adjoining tones."

In connection with the painting, the same principles maintained, "Painting was an interpretation of tone. Through the medium of colour drawn with the brush." "Use yourself to a large brush." "Do not starve your palette." "Accurately place your masses with the charcoal." "Then lay in the back ground" about half an inch over the border of the adjoining tones, true as possible, then lay in the mass of hair, recovering the drawing and fusing the tones with the background, and overlapping the flesh of the forehead, then for the face lay in hold by a middle flesh tone, light on the left side and dark on the shadow side, always recovering the drawing and most carefully fusing the flesh into the background, painting flesh into background and background into flesh, until the exact quality is obtained, both in colour and tone the whole resembling a wig maker's block. Then follows the most marked and characteristic accents of the features in place and tone and drawing as accurate as possible, painting deliberately into wet ground, testing your work by repeatedly standing well back, viewing it as a whole, a very important thing. After this take up the subtler tones which express the retiring planes of the head, temples, chin, nose, and cheeks with neck, then the still more subtle drawing of mouth and eyes, fusing tone into tone all the time, till finally with deliberate touch the high lights are laid in, this occupies the first sitting and should the painting not be satisfactory the whole is ruthlessly fogged by brushing together, the object being not to allow any parts well done, to interfere with that principle of oneness, or unity of every part; the brushing together engendered an appetite to attack the problem afresh at every sitting each attempt resulting in a more complete visualization in the mind. The process is repeated until the canvas is completed.

Sargent would press home the fact, that the subtleties of paint must be controlled by continually viewing the work from a distance, "stand back—get well away—and you will realize the great danger there is of overstating a tone—keep the thing as a whole in your mind. Tones so subtle as not to be detected on close acquaintance can only be adjusted by this means."

COMPOSITION.

When we were gathered in front of our display of sketches for composition awaiting some criticism Sargent would walk along the whole collection, rapidly looking at each one, and without singling out any in particular for comment, he would merely say "Get in your mind the sculptors view of things, arrange a composition, decoratively, easy, and accidental," this would be said in a hesitating manner and then he would quietly retire. On one occasion, when the subject set for a composition was a portrait the criticism was "not one of them seriously considered," many we had thought quite good, as an indication of what might be tried while a portrait was in progress. That would not do for Sargent. A sketch must be seriously planned, tried and tried again, turned about until it satisfies every requirement, and a perfect visualization attained. A sketch must not be merely a pattern of pleasant shapes, just pleasing to the eye, just merely a fancy. It must be a very possible thing, a definite arrangement—everything fitting in a plan and in true relationship frankly standing upon a horizontal plane coinciding in their place with a pre-arranged line. As a plan is to a building, so must the sketch be to the picture.

His general remarks were: "cultivate an ever continuous power of observation. Wherever you are, be always ready to make slight notes of postures, groups and incidents. Store up in the mind without ceasing a continuous stream of observations from which to make selections later. Above all things get abroad, see the sunlight, and everything that is to be seen, the power of selection will follow. Be continually making mental notes, make them again and again, test what you remember by sketches till you have got them fixed. Do not be backward at using every device and making every experiment that ingenuity can devise, in order to attain that sense of completeness which nature so beautifully provides, always bearing in mind the limitations of the materials in which you work."

It was not only students who acknowledged their debt to Sargent. Hubert Herkomer in his reminiscences writes: "I have learnt much from Sargent in the planning of lights and darks, the balance in tonality of background in its relation to the figure, the true emphasizing of essentials."

Sargent was well aware of the pitfalls that await the painter of the fashionable world, and as sitter after sitter took his place on the dais in his Tite Street studio he seemed to become more sensible of them. He tried again and again to escape, and he often, in his letters, expressed his fatigue. He wearied of the limitations imposed by his commissioned art. Painting those who want to be painted, instead of those whom the artist wants to paint, leads inevitably to a bargain, to a compromise between the artist's individuality and the claims of the model. Mannerism becomes a way out; that which pleases becomes an aim. Artistic problems give way before personal considerations; the decorative quality of a picture takes a secondary place. Sargent's sincerity, the driving need he had to express himself in his own way, his satiety with models imposed on him by fashion, culminated in revolt. He was forced, now and then, it is true, to return to his portraits, but his Boston work absorbed him more and more. The call of his studio in Fulham Road when he was in London, and of the Alps and the south of Europe in summer, came first. In 1910 his exhibits at the Academy, instead of portraits, were *Glacier Streams, Albanian Olive Gatherers, Vespers* and *A Garden at Corfu;* at the New English Art Club, *Flannels, On the Guidecca, The Church of Santa Maria della Salute, A Florentine Nocturne, A Moraine* and *Olive Grove.*

When in 1901 Mr. J. B. Manson, then a student, wrote to Sargent for advice he received the following reply:

31, TITE STREET,
CHELSEA, S.W.,
July 30th 1901.

DEAR SIR,

In reply to your questions I fear that I can only give you the most general advice. The only school in London of which I have any personal knowledge is the Royal Academy.

If the limit of age does not prevent your entering it I should advise you to do so.

There are also very good teachers at the Slade School.

You say you are studying painting to become a portrait painter. I think you would be making a great mistake if you kept that only in view during the time you intend to work in a life class—where the object of the student should be to acquire sufficient command over his material to do whatever nature presents to him. The conventionalities of portrait painting are only tolerable in one who is a good *painter*—if he is only a good *portrait-painter* he is nobody. Try to become a painter first and then apply your knowledge to a special branch—but do not begin by learning what is required for a special branch, or you will become a mannerist.

Believe me,
Yours truly,
JOHN S. SARGENT.

He was too conscientious to take refuge in a formula, but he had drawn too largely on his resources of selection and arrangement in relation to a single aspect of an artist's calling. He had not done violence to his sincerity, but it was time to turn to subjects in which there was more scope for design and composition, invention and variety. He now became immersed in decorative work and studies from nature.

Chapter XXIV

MR. GEORGE MOORE observes in one of his essays that "the criticisms of a creative artist never amount to more than an ingenious defence of his own work." However true this may be, Sargent's sincerity gave peculiar authority to the criticisms which, at too rare intervals, he made upon other painters. For the most part he was evasive about his contemporaries. He was the least pontifical person imaginable, and fellow-feeling with craftsmen made him reluctant to give adverse criticism the stamp of his authority. He was little given to theory and took but a lukewarm interest in modern criticism. I do not know that he ever sought a formula for the excellences common to a Monet and a Peruvian vase, a Rubens and a Huang Ch'uan. But it would not have been inconsistent with his view to have defined the aim of art as essential expression, the endeavour, that is to say, to express by the most persuasive and revealing means the essential qualities of the object. Good art therefore would differ from bad art in so far as it succeeded in rendering the essential. His view would certainly, while allowing a wide latitude of selection and omission, not countenance that indifference to representation which is common to much recent art. We have seen with what admiration he regarded the work of Monet. He did not extend this in the same unqualified way to Monet's followers and successors. In 1910-11 an exhibition of Post-Impressionists and others was held at the Grafton Galleries. Through some misunderstanding Sargent had been mentioned by Mr. Roger Fry in an article in the *Nation* as a supporter of the Post-Impressionist school. On January 7, 1911, he wrote the following letter to the editor:

POST-IMPRESSIONISM

To the Editor of the "Nation"

Sir,

My attention has been called to an article by Mr. Roger Fry, called "A Postscript on Post-Impressionism" in your issue of December 24th in which he mentions me as being among the champions of the group of painters now being shown at the Grafton Gallery. I should be obliged if you would allow me space in your columns for these few words of rectification.

Mr. Fry has been entirely misinformed, and if I had been inclined to join in the controversy, he would have known that my sympathies were in the exactly opposite direction as far as the novelties are concerned, that have been most discussed and that this show has been my first opportunity of seeing. I had declined Mr. Fry's request to place my name on the initial list of promoters of the Exhibition on the ground of not knowing the work of the painters to whom the name of Post-Impressionists can be applied; it certainly does not apply to Manet or Cézanne. Mr. Fry may have been told—and have believed —that the sight of those paintings had made me a convert to his faith in them.

The fact is that I am absolutely sceptical as to their having any claim whatever to being works of art, with the exception of some of the pictures by Gauguin that strike me as admirable in color, and in color only.

But one wonders what will Mr. Fry not believe, and one is tempted to say what will he not print?

Yours, etc.,

John S. Sargent.

When in 1912 Mr. D. S. MacColl wrote an article in the *Nineteenth Century*, "A Year of Post-Impressionism," he received from Sargent the following letter:

My dear MacColl,

I have enjoyed reading your article on Post-Impressionism very much—I should think it would bring a good many people to their senses—I admire the certainty with which you have refrained from hinting at the possibility of bad faith on the part of people like Matisse or at the theory that I am inclined to believe that the sharp picture dealers invented and boomed this new article of commerce.

I think you have exactly weighed the merits of Cézanne and rather over-estimated the "realism" of Van Gogh whose things look to me like imitations made in coral or glass of objects in a vacuum. As to Gauguin, of course you had to deal with him for the sake of your argument, as if there were something in him besides rich and rare colour.

Some day if we ever meet I should like to discuss with you the meaning of the word "values" and the word Impressionism.

Yours sincerely,

JOHN S. SARGENT.

In order to appreciate the value of Sargent's concurrence with Mr. MacColl's estimate of Cézanne, the following extract from the article may be quoted:

Cézanne was not a great classic; he was an artist often clumsy, always in difficulties, very limited in his range, absurdly so in most numerous productions, but "with quite a little mood" and the haunting idea of an art built upon the early Monet, at which he could only hint. He oscillated between Monet's earlier and finer manner, that of dark contours and broadly divided colour, and a painting based on the early Monet, all colour in a high key. In this manner he produced certain landscapes tender and beautiful in colour, but the figure was too difficult for him, and from difficulties he escaped into the still lifes I have spoken of, flattened jugs, apples, and napkins like blue tin that would clank if they fell. What is fatal to the claim set up for him as a deliberate designer, creating eternal images out of the momentary lights of the Impressionists, is the fact that his technique, remains that of the Impressionists, a sketcher's technique, adapted for snatching hurriedly at effects that will not wait.

It is clear that Sargent was from the first definitely hostile to the more advanced Post-Impressionists; he receded very little, if at all, from that position. He regarded the Cubists, their followers and offshoots with uncompromising disapproval. He did not consider that either they or even the great majority of Post-Impressionists, by slighting representation, were contributing in any way whatsoever, as was claimed for them by a leading critic, "to establishing more and more firmly the fundamental laws of expressive form in its barest and most abstract elements." He held that it could be more effectually and much more emotionally attained by representing also the visual and spiritual values of the thing seen. But like Monet, he was no respecter of theories. He did not pause to discuss why he painted as he did, he worked in the idiom of an inherited tradition, refreshing it with vitality and vigour, enriching it with a modernized technique, and pushing it to what many may consider its utmost limits. All around him the pictorial and plastic arts were developing on lines divergent from his own, while criticism was being forced to find formulæ and theories to fit the new movement. In an epoch of rapid change he pursued his way undeflected. Charles Furse regarded him as one of the five great Masters of portrait painting of the world. When he died in 1924 Mr. Roger Fry concluded his review of Sargent's work by saying: "I am sure that he was no less distinguished and genuine as a man than, in my opinion, he was striking and undistinguished as an illustrator and non-existent as an artist."* These two opinions mark the limits of possible divergence on the value of Sargent's art. No doubt his fame will be subject to many oscillations in future, but it is, at any rate, inconceivable that posterity should agree with Mr. Fry.

Sir Charles Holmes in his well-known work "Notes on the Art of Rembrandt," while drawing a comparison between Rembrandt and Hals, has dealt with the method and the characteristics of the painter of the *Laughing Cavalier*. Sargent's kinship with Hals is at once apparent. It is true that as Hals progressed he simplified his palette and reduced the range of his colour, whereas Sargent tended in the opposite direction as his facility increased; but in their approach, in their outlook, in the broad features of their technique, and in their respective limitations the resemblance is unmistakable. Sir Charles Holmes calls attention to Hals' "conscious fidelity of statement," within which the painter "finds room for the exercise of those faculties of selection and arrangement that mark the artist as opposed to the hack painter"; his sense of design, adequate rather than exceptional; his "supreme faculty of representation in oil paint," the mapping out of the masses and planes, the swift touches of light and shadow at the emphatic points; the manner in which "everywhere the strokes of the brush take just the course

* See also Roger Fry, "Transformations," p. 135.

EARL OF WEMYSS.

that is needed to express the infinite varieties of surfaces and substances of which the piece is built up." Such among other characteristics establish a definite similarity between the two masters. We have already seen that Sargent extolled the technical methods of Hals, and looked on him as the portrait painter with whom he had most in common. Here it will be of interest to recall some of his estimates of other artists.

At the time of the Ingres Exhibition in Paris (1914) Sargent said to M. Helleu: "Ingres, Raphael and El Greco, these are now my admirations, these are what I like." Greco was no new admiration. He was an artist of whom Sargent had an exhaustive knowledge, and regarded with increasing appreciation. Some years before his talk with Helleu he had written to de Glehn from Aranjuez:

> Almost immediately on getting to Spain I fell in with Auguste Bréal and his wife, and we joined forces as we had a lot of letters for Toledo and Madrid for the purpose of seeing unknown Grecos. It was interesting, but after all the best Grecos are in the churches that are known, and in the Prado—there are some new ones there—he is certainly one of the very most magnificent old masters.

In 1915 a pamphlet was published by a specialist* in Madrid to prove that the peculiarities of Greco's drawing were due to advanced astigmatism. The pamphlet was sent to Sargent by the Duke of Alba, whereupon he wrote as follows:

31, TITE STREET,
CHELSEA, S.W.,
Aug. 19th, 1915.

MY DEAR DUKE OF ALBA,

Many thanks for sending the pamphlet on El Greco's astigmatism—it has interested me very much although I am not absolutely convinced. Being very astigmatic myself I am very familiar with the phenomena that result from that peculiarity of eyesight, and it seems to me very unlikely that an artist should be influenced by them in the matter of form and not at all in the matter of colour where they are much more noticeable.

The colouring of Claude Monet is an absolutely genuine document perhaps the only genuine one, of the optical phenomena of astigma-

---

* "El Astigmatismo del Greco"; G. Beritens, "Especialista en las Enfermedadas de los Ojos."

tism. The conscious study of these phenomena is called "Impression-ism" (but many so-called "Impressionists" are mere imitators of his style of execution and perhaps have perfectly normal eyes, and therefore have no right to the name). If a man painted conscientiously what he saw through a bad opera glass he would note down some of the peculiarities of astigmatic vision, the decomposing into prismatic colours, and the perturbation when a bright tone comes near a dark one.

The Greco shows no trace whatever of these influences. More-over the Greco's earlier pictures were full of rich and brilliant colour, and his later ones are almost black and white. The contrary change is what one might expect in a case of astigmatism, for this condition, which breaks up colour into its prismatic elements, increases with age.

As for the elongation of his figures, it may be partly due to astigma-tism, but the Renaissance affords so many examples of this exaggeration of elegance that it may also be accounted for as a mannerism of the time derived from the imitators of Michael Angelo. Tintoretto, the Greco's master, had a tendency that way—and Primaticcio, Parmi-gianino, Jean Goujon, and other contemporaries elongated, their figures as much as he did, for the sake of elegance and not because of astigmatism. Even the most fervent admirer of El Greco cannot deny that he had some very obvious affectations, for instance the extra-ordinary airs and graces of his hands. Why should St. Francis in ecstasy and the Magdalen in the desert be making "des effets de mains" if the Greco did not wish to be elegant quand même ?

I find that I have inflicted an interminable letter on you—if you get through it, it will be thanks to your being I dare say without many distractions in your present abode. I hope you are well and that you will be coming to London one of these days.

Yours sincerely,
JOHN S. SARGENT.

The view that astigmatism decomposes into prismatic colours is novel and would scarcely find scientific support. But coming from Sargent, himself, as we know, astigmatic, it has a peculiar interest, being based on his own experience and the close obser-vation of phenomena to which he paid much attention.

On July 16, 1923, he delivered a short address at the Royal Academy in celebration of the bicentenary birth of Sir Joshua Reynolds. This involved the two things he most dreaded, publicity and a speech. At first he said nothing would induce him to read the address himself, but he finally consented. The meeting was held in the evening in the main gallery of the Academy. When Sargent rose in his place there was a tense silence, a nervous curiosity. His record as a public speaker was known to a sympathetic audience. It was evident that he was deeply agitated, the page from which he was to read fluttered in his hands like a leaf in a breeze. His opening sentences were scarcely audible, spoken in a low conversational tone with his eyes bent low on his manuscript. As he progressed, however, his voice gained a little in strength, though still broken by nervousness. It was an ordeal both for speaker and audience. When he finished there was a burst of vehement applause which showed the affection and esteem in which he was held.

SIR JOSHUA REYNOLDS

The great Master whose bicentenary we celebrate to-day in this Institution that he founded and of which he is the greatest glory, is an instance of that law by which the period of an artist is always manifest, whether his work conforms to older standards or points to future ones. In painting Sir Joshua Reynolds follows the highest traditions of the past—it is in portraiture, and by a new tendency of portraiture that he shows as a man of his own time.

Vandyck and Franz Hals had already shown the direction of this tendency, which involved a gradual departure from the extreme gravity of characterization of the earlier Masters—The conscious dignity and inviolable reserve that mark the personages of Titian and Velasquez, had given way by degrees to a more intimate and less formal bearing. Sir Joshua's subjects and those of his contemporaries seem, without loss of dignity, to have a more human way with them, just as Rembrandt's allow one a deeper communion with their mystery. The quiet eyes of the elder portraits hold one at a distance and seem to transpose the relation of the observer and the observed.

By a slow change of fashion or of taste this barrier of severance fell away, and there entered into the art of portraiture a new quality of curiosity and analysis. Sir Joshua came long before the last stages of this evolution, and his people, through all the boldness and frankness of his vision, still hold their own and keep the distance that great portraiture always maintains.

Technically, it is well known, his methods and processes were those of the great Venetians. His discourses show him to have been extraordinarily eclectic, and alive to the aims and qualities of the other Italian Schools; but in his work he was always a Venetian, practising an indirect method that involved various preparatory stages and that is practically no longer in use to-day.

A change has come with the influence of landscape and with the study of out-of-door effects—These have revealed an unlimited range of new relations of the figure to its surroundings. Instead of the figure being, as of old, almost always made the principal centre of light, it is now-a-days given the most varying place in the scale, and the methods of painting have changed with the need of a swifter notation of passing effects and novel relations.

Perhaps, for the painter, Sir Joshua's method of lighting is one of his chief originalities. He invented what, with him and with his followers, became a formula—that peculiar play of vivid light on a face that abolishes half-tones and gives an extraordinary emphasis of accent to the features and the few small shadows. It is known that his studio, had a very small window that lit his sitter like a bull's-eye lantern, giving an effect of simplification that Sir Joshua was certainly the first to make his own. Needless to say, although this method at once became common property, his own examples of the use of it have never been surpassed.

It must be left to individual taste to choose which most to admire, the simpler portraits like, among many others, the portentous head of Dr. Johnson, so grand in character and suggestion, or those more fanciful compositions in which Sir Joshua invested a portrait with all the charm of a decorative picture. His resources in this line were unbounded, and the setting, however romantic, in which he sometimes placed his people never detracted from their interest as men and women.

Perhaps there are no greater examples of this mastery than the two portraits that are the Royal Academy's proudest possessions, pictures of dim splendour, where, over all the apparatus and pomp and insignia of Royalty, two calm faces hold us enthralled.

It is well to do homage to their author in the presence of these noble works.

Another criticism of Sir Joshua is contained in a letter which he wrote after I had asked him to look at a portrait of that Master at a dealer's shop. "I didn't like the Reynolds," he wrote. "It is too early to have any of his richness and too late for his good old early hardness. Miss Montgomery ogles you under lowered brows and displays vague hands and you are not amused." He was very much given to dividing the work of individual painters into periods, sometimes rather arbitrarily it seemed, and showing a strong preference for one period over another. As it was with Reynolds, so with Turner, whose early work as illustrated ˍby the *Wreck of an Orange Ship* he admired almost to the exclusion of his later and visionary ecstasies of coloured mists and shimmering vapour. In the same way he drew a sharp distinction between the early and late painting of Monet, considering that he never surpassed, if he ever equalled, the *Olympia.**

Equally in the case of Rodin he drew a sharp line. In 1902 he wrote to Mr. MacColl:

> DEAR MACCOLL,
> Use my name by all means on the list—I would be delighted to further the scheme of having a good example of Rodin in a London gallery. . . . In case I don't turn up let me say that Rodin's early work, either the "Age d'arain" or the St. John seems to me far finer than most of his later things.and I hope that it might be one of those that would be tried for—and I would gladly subscribe.

In later years his interest in pictures seemed to centre rather in their craftsmanship than their significance; he was more taken up with the means employed than the end achieved. Composition assumed an increasingly important place in his artistic outlook. "I find as I grow old—probably a sign of senile decay"—he said to Mr. William James, "that I care less and less about the painting of things 'just the way they look,' and get more interested in—well, something more in the nature of a Wedgwood plaque." This was a notable avowal from one whose whole talent had been devoted to the painting of things "in the way they looked." It was probably the cry of the artist sated with portraiture, and absorbed by the exercise of his imagination in the field of decoration. His views often seemed "queer" or "curious" (to use two of his favourite words) to those who heard them; as when he complained that Constable was too fond of putting fine and stormy weather on the same canvas; or when he criticized Albert Durer as a draughtsman; or expressed surprise that William Blake with such originality in his ideas should have chosen an idiom so conventional by which

* See *ante*, p. 102.

to express them. Equally his indifference to the Dutch school of landscape painters was always surprisingly comprehensive, and not a little disconcerting.

In his introductory notes for exhibitions of the works of Brabazon and Zuloaga* he shows the real enlightenment of his critical powers.

The preface to a catalogue of the works of Robert Brough is an appreciation of a younger artist who was also Sargent's friend. Brough was fatally injured in a railway accident on January 19, 1905. A telegram had brought the news late on the night of the nineteenth. The next morning some friends of Brough went to Tite Street to consult with Sargent as to what could be done for the injured man; they found that Sargent had taken the six o'clock morning train for Sheffield. He arrived at the hospital in time to see his friend before he died.

3, Tite Street,
Chelsea, S.W.

If any aid were needed for the comprehension of work whose charm is so irresistible as that of the late and much regretted Robert Brough, visitors to the present Exhibition might seek it in comparing his style with that of Charles Furse whose works were shown in the same rooms a year ago. Excepting in the sad similarity of their early and tragic deaths, the contrast between these two artistic talents is absolute and enhances their respective claims to our admiration.

Furse's rugged strength and emphasis set off the grace, the fluidity the lightness of touch that are so delightful in Brough; that very rare quality of surface that seems to make the actual paint a precious substance is also brought out by contrast with the handling of a painter who seemed too impetuous in the expression of his intentions to care to be exquisite in his method. Whereas the one struck ample themes and sounded passionate music, the other was blessed with the gift of what corresponds to a pure and melodious voice. The developing of this natural gift into a perfectly supple and practised medium seems to be the direction in which his progress can best be traced when one follows it through the interesting series of portraits that are now gathered together in tribute to his memory.

In the summer of 1911, at Munich, on his way to the Tyrol, he received a letter from Mrs. Abbey on June 28, begging him

* See Appendix.

to return at once as her husband lay dying and was in anxiety about the completion of his large canvases. He arrived at Tite Street on June 30 in time to supervise the work.

To Lady Lewis he wrote:

> I am all day long busy from morning till night every day at the White City—horrid fate in this heat—I am looking after some work there of another man's who is ill and to whose rescue I had to come.

Before he left he was able to see Edwin Abbey and assure him that the alterations had been successfully completed. When Abbey's work, in the year after his death, was severely criticized by Robert Ross in the *Morning Post*, Sargent at once intervened on behalf of his friend:

Jany. 9th.

My dear Ross,

I am very glad to see that you are answering protests on your article about Abbey, because it may give you the opportunity of removing the impression that you have chosen this moment to make a one sided attack. Surely in reviewing his life's work at this final exhibition you must recognize his particular quality of dramatic insight and invention, his endless variety of characterization, his humour, his pathos and his occasional grimness. You have hurt a good many feelings by an apparent want of feeling at a time when hats are taken off. It would be handsome of you as you are still writing on the subject to appease his ghost by a mention of his good qualities as well as those that you dislike.

Do you see no imagination and beauty in those two decorative designs of the Puritan Ships and the Miners Going Down into the Earth ?

Yours sincerely,
JOHN S. SARGENT.

Chapter XXV

COROT is reported to have said during the fighting on the barricades in 1848: "What is the matter? Are we not satisfied with the Government?" Detachment from events beyond the studio or study walls has been characteristic of many great artists. During the siege of Paris Gautier wrote:

> Pendant les guerres de l'Empire
> Goethe, au bruit du canon brutal,
> Fit le divan occidental.
>
> *   *   *   *
>
> Comme Goethe sur son divan
> A Weimar s'isolait des choses
> Et d'Hafiz effeuillait les roses.
>
> Sans prendre garde à l'ouragan
> Qui fouettait mes vitres fermées,
> Moi, j'ai fait émaux et camées.

This spirit of isolation belonged markedly to Sargent. He had, as we have seen, no business instinct whatever; he left the management of his affairs to others and was ignorant of the way they were conducted. He extended this ignorance, coupled with considerable indifference, to the administration of the world's affairs. He read no newspapers; he had the sketchiest knowledge of current movements outside art; his receptive credulity made him accept fabulous items of information without question. He would have been puzzled to answer if he were asked how nine-tenths of the population lived, he would have been dumbfoundered if asked how they were governed.

It was rather surprising in a man of reading and culture, but there it was; but while his ignorance of how the world was run was sometimes disconcerting in conversation, it **was** disarming in its simplicity.

When the War broke out he failed at first to realize its significance; he was very slow in relating himself to it. In this he differed strikingly from Henry James, who was consumed from the outset with a flame of intense and passionate sympathy for the cause of the Allies. Indeed, Henry James was so little able to understand Sargent's aloofness in the early part of the War that their friendship suffered from a temporary coolness.

August, 1914, found Sargent painting in the Dolomites with Mr. and Mrs. Adrian Stokes and Colonel Ernest Armstrong in a remote part of the mountains. When news reached them that War had been declared Sargent's sole anxiety was for the fate of his sister Emily, who was in the north of France. As soon as he heard of her safety, he began unconcernedly painting again. Towards the end of August Colonel Armstrong was carried off as a prisoner of war by the Austrians to Trieuil, a few hours' journey away. He was soon in difficulties with the authorities, but Sargent in the mountains "with the high pasturing kine" went on with his painting. The War might have been in another planet for all the impression it made on his mind. The world might rock and crumble unperceived by him in the intensity of his concentration. At the beginning of October, having been a prisoner for more than a month, Colonel Armstrong wrote an urgent appeal to Sargent to come and see him. Sargent at last descended from his fastness; he interviewed the authorities in company with an Austrian acquaintance, Karl Maldona, and as a result procured the release of his brother artist.

Now no one who knew Sargent would for a moment attribute his attitude to want of heart. All who knew him would agree that he responded on the instant to emergencies which he understood, and that his sympathies were particularly lively and generous the moment he realized that there was occasion for them. But the War was outside his ken, and so involved with consequences and questions of which he was entirely ignorant, that he seemed merely conscious of being rather isolated. It was as if his imagination had suffered a complete breakdown.

No sooner had Colonel Armstrong been released than Sargent withdrew again to the mountains and resumed his painting, remaining in the Tyrol till November, when he returned to England. His reaction to the War was as yet nothing more definite than mild boredom. However that may be, it was a frame of mind of short duration.

In 1915 he exhibited at the Academy portraits of F. J. H. Jenkinson, University Librarian at Cambridge and Earl Curzon of Kedleston. The portrait of Jenkinson is one of his most easy and fluent achievements. In the Academy it formed a sharp contrast with the picture of Lord Curzon. It is a peculiarity of Sargent's art that some of his least distinguished portraits are those of the most distinguished men. This picture of Lord Curzon deals rather harshly with outside trappings and aspect. It tells little of the character, the intellectual force, the distinguished career, and the powerful personality of the sitter. It has the relative inadequacy noticeable, in the portraits of Mr. Joseph Chamberlain and Lord Balfour, President Roosevelt and Lord Roberts. In each of these portraits it is as if the artist in his desire to be truthful had understated his case, and in his anxiety to exclude the element of prestige had missed some of the personality of his sitter.

Early in 1916 Sargent again went to America. In the late summer he went on a sketching expedition to the Rocky Mountains and the west of America. He wrote to his friend and relative Mrs. Hale:

DEAR COUSIN MARY,   *August 30th,* 1916.

At the risk of importuning you with this persistent letter writing, here I go again. As I told you in my first or my last it was raining and snowing, my tent flooded, mushrooms sprouting in my boots, porcupines taking shelter in my clothes, canned food always fried in a black frying pan getting on my nerves, and a fine waterfall which was the attraction to the place pounding and thundering all night. I stood it for three weeks and yesterday came away with a repulsive picture. Now the weather has changed for the better and I am off again to try the simple life (ach pfui) in tents at the top of another valley, this time with a gridiron instead of a frying pan and a perforated India rubber mat to stand on. It takes time to learn how to be really happy.

Life was different in the Montana National Park, with the pleasant company of the Livermores. There we toured about over new trails every day. Mrs. Livermore is perfectly delightful *and plays chess.* Alas she went back east, and struck Chicago in the heat wave. The refrigerated dining room at the Blackstone Hotel saved her life, as it did all ours two weeks before. It is worth while flying there from any part of America during a heat wave. You sit in a perfect temperature over an excellent dinner and watch the crowd dying like flies outside of the window. Nero or Caligula could not have improved on it.

Please take your courage in both hands and write me a line to this hotel. I will pounce upon it when I get back from my next plunge into canned food—thirty miles away.

Yours ever,
JOHN S. SARGENT.

In the autumn he returned to Boston and in November agreed with the Trustees of the Museum of Fine Arts to decorate the rotunda. The undertaking was completed by October, 1921, when he at once entered into another contract to decorate the main stairway and library. This latter work, finished before he died, was unveiled on November 3, 1925. He was pleased with the reception given to his decoration in the rotunda and wrote in November, 1921, to Mrs. Hale:

31, TITE STREET,
Nov. 25th, 1921.

. . . Your good news about the Museum has been corroborated by various other letters and newspaper cuttings, and the fact that it is considered a success is proved by the Museum wanting *more.* They ask me to do the staircase . . . tra la la . . . it shall be done, and I am pegging away at my generals, in a dense fog that has lasted two weeks, with that light before me.

1916, the year in which he made the contract with the Trustees of the Museum, also saw the completion of his work at the Boston Library. Meanwhile the War had long begun, slowly but surely, to affect his imagination. In December, 1915, he had suffered a great loss in the death of Henry James, whom he had known for thirty years. Henry James had communicated to him, copiously enough, his sense of "living in a nightmare of the

deepest dye," and of the War as "a huge horror of blackness."
By degrees that came to be Sargent's own point of view. He
gradually replaced the passive and balanced attitude of an
ordinary American living in Europe, by an outlook warmly
generous and deeply sympathetic. The most decisive and public
symptom of this awakening was his resignation of the Prussian
Ordre pour le Mérite, tendered through diplomatic channels as
early as 1915. Letters from America show his personal anxiety.

On June 8, 1916, he wrote to me:

> MY DEAR EVAN,
> What a world you are living in—and what a succession of tre-
> mendous events have happened. That Irish affair—then that naval
> battle and now the loss of Kitchener, sledge hammer blows that shake
> us over here.
> Please write—I would like to know how you personally feel about
> it all—my sister mentioned in one of her letters that Lord Elcho,
> and, I am told, Cynthia's husband are prisoners in Egypt—Does this
> mean that they are prisoners of Turks or Arabs on the other side of
> the Red Sea ? where else could it be—I am very sorry to hear it, if it
> is true please let me know.
> I am terribly busy here with the carrying out of the plaster work
> of my ceiling—it is progressing well but it will be a long job, and I
> have to work like a nigger at modelling things that the workmen wait to
> carry off and cast. I doubt if all this is accomplished so that I can put
> up my paintings before the midsummer heat sets in—when that comes
> in July or August I shall be off to the Rockies for mountain air and
> sketching and return to this work in September. I wonder whether
> these great blows are affecting the moral. My sister's letters are
> intentionally cheerful but they date back many weeks. Please give
> me your own news and those of mutual friends—write as soon as you
> can.
>   Yrs. ever,
>   JOHN S. SARGENT.

Later he wrote:

> MY DEAR EVAN,   *July 25, 1916.*
> Our letters must have crossed, and yours is the saddest of answers
> to my question about the prisoners—it moved me very much to learn
> this cruel blow to your family. There had indeed been a piling up
> of tragedies when you wrote and coming very close home. All the

news that has reached us over here of the great allies drive are heartening, and many people believe that the last act has begun. The "page of honour"* seems now to be "attending" the British, the French, and the Russians, God bless him.

I left Boston a week ago, the work that I personally had to do with my own hands being accomplished—now the plasterers, painters and gilders will do the rest, which will take another month or more, and, in September I will return and put my paintings up. I tried one temporarily, the big Green Devil, and he looked well as far as one can judge, from the scaffolding which is on the level of the cornice. The whole architectural and ornamental scheme seems to work out on the large scale, and it has been a great satisfaction not to have to make any changes. Whether or not it is another of the palpable signs that I am getting old, I am rather revelling in the appearance this white elephant of mine is taking on of amounting to something, after all these years.

After the heat of the last days in Boston and of the many days railway journey across the endless plains it is delicious to be here among crags and glaciers and pine woods. But I shall make my way further north to the Canadian Rockies, where the scenery is grander still. I have two pleasant companions and we take daily rides on Indian ponies.

Yrs. ever,
JOHN S. SARGENT.

Oct. 19, 1916.

MY DEAR EVAN,
Yours was a frightfully interesting letter and gave me a better idea of what war looks like than anything I have read. If the accursed is still going on, which God forbid, when I get back in two or three months, I shall feel tempted to go out and have a look at it as you seem to think it would be permitted. But would I have the nerve to look, not to speak of painting? I have never seen anything the least horrible—outside of my studio.

I am back from the Rocky Mountains—I think I wrote you from there snowed up in a tent—that was the condition of things most of the time—now I am winding up my Library and the scaffolding will soon come down. I have taken a studio for a month or more to do various mugs in charcoal and one paughtrait and then I will be thinking of returning—If I could, I would do so now, for my sisters must be dreadfully anxious. . . .

Yrs. ever,
JOHN S. SARGENT.

* Allusion to a phrase in Defoe: "Victory attended him like a page of honour."

The compass of this Memoir does not admit a detailed consideration of Sargent's decorative work. In any case it would require a treatise by an expert. A full description of it is to be found in the Guide to the Boston Library and the publications of the Museum of Fine Arts, to which is added a general description by Mr. Thomas A. Fox, the architect and friend of Sargent, who gave him loyal assistance in the structural part of the work.

NOTE

In the Rotunda alone, Sargent designed and carried out four compositions in pedimented frames, four reliefs above the pedimented frames, "Fame," "Satyr and Mænad," "Arion," and "Achilles and Chiron"; above these again, in circular frames, four paintings, "Ganymede," "Music," "Astronomy," "Prometheus"; and on the left and right, and at the two ends of the elliptical Rotunda, four large compositions, "Apollo and the Muses," figures representing the Arts, "Classic Romantic Art," "The Sphinx" and "The Chimæra," with four smaller reliefs surmounting the frames of the circular paintings.   Mr. Fox states that "all the modelling, not only of the compositions themselves, but the details as well as all the painting of the canvases, was actually done by the artist himself, without the usual and supplementary aid of assistants."   His decorations over the Main Stairway and Library of the Museum of Fine Arts, including six reliefs, comprised eighteen separate works, two of them canvases of 25 by 10 feet.   The whole scheme was begun in November, 1916, and completed before the artist's death in April, 1925. The subjects are classical and mythological.   A golden ochre or biscuit colour predominates in the painting of the figures, against a back-ground of blue, both in the Rotunda and over the Main Stairway.   A number of the paintings were done in Fulham Road.   The most successful individual work is, perhaps, the half-circular lunette of the Danaides.   The subject has been simply treated; on one side of the canvas the Danaides are seen ascending the steps with laden urns to pour water into the amphora placed in the centre of the picture, on the other side they descend, bearing their urns lightened of their load.   The design has the repose looked for in mural decoration.   The composition is superior to that of the less balanced and less harmonious canvases of "The Winds," "Orestes" and "Hercules and the Hydra."   Tranquillity has been attained by the succession of vertical lines provided by the drapery of the slow-moving figures.   Indeed, subject to such reservations that a generalization of the kind requires, it is true to say that from Madame Gautreau to the Danaides, Sargent becomes rhythmic and delicate in his lines in proportion as he approaches the vertical.   In other words, his vertical have a quality less often found in his transverse and horizontal lines.   The recumbent figures in "Atlas and the Hesperides" at once occur to the mind as an exception to the general statement, and there must of course be others in the vast range of his work; but the balance of examples will be found to favour the view here expressed.

In both sets of decorations, Library and Museum, Sargent has worked out his scheme in his own way, free of definite influence.   It is possible to suggest traces of Flaxman in "Apollo in His Chariot," of Baudry in "Phaethon and Chiron," Tiepolo in "The Winds," Michael Angelo in the figure of "Philosophy," and even Raphael in the "Unveiling of Truth"; but such ascription is at best fanciful.   Sargent owed little to any recognizable influence, closely as he had studied the decorative work of the Masters named above.

Of his two series of decorative schemes, that of the Boston Library is generally considered the finer. The working out of a single theme seems to have been responsible for a higher level of excellence. The interrelation of the paintings has led to a more harmonious effect. In quality and treatment the panels are more akin. Here the realism of his art has seldom interfered with the abstract character of the scheme. Only in the frieze of the prophets is its pronounced. There it has determined the spirit and disposition of the figures. On the other hand, the painting of *Ancilla Domini*, or *Madonna and Child*, has attained a degree of simplicity and spiritual charm that may be looked for in vain elsewhere in modern art. As he progressed, the inspiration of his subject seems to have acquired a stronger hold on his imagination. As he traced the ascent from the materialism and superstition of the beginnings of religious thought to a region of pure spirituality, he was able to express the full value of the contrast, with the poetry and distinction of a fine intellectual conception and the skill of his craftsmanship.

One alone among his paintings in the Library gave rise to religious dissension. The Jews, conceiving that in his panel of the Synagogue he had reflected on the vitality of their faith by depicting the Synagogue as abased, in contrast to the Church triumphant in a neighbouring panel, endeavoured to obtain a decree ordering the removal of the painting. An Act was passed in the State Legislature in 1922 authorizing by a manifest quibble the seizure of the picture "by right of eminent domain for educational purposes in teaching art or the history of art." The pretext was too flimsy, the purpose too transparent. The Attorney General advised that the Act was unconstitutional and in 1924 it was repealed.* In October, 1921, Sargent wrote to me as follows:

"I enclose a snapshot of the President of Ireland in corroboration of 'Politics.'†

"I am in hot water here with the Jews, who resent my 'Synagogue,' and want to have it removed—and to-morrow a prominent member of the Jewish colony is coming to bully me about it and ask me to explain myself—I can only refer him to Rheims, Notre Dame, Strasburg, and other Cathedrals, and dwell at length on the good old times. Fortunately the Library Trustees do not object, and propose to allow this painful work to stay."

* For this, as for much other information from America, I am indebted to Mr. Richard Hale of Boston.

† See next page.

Chapter XXVI

ON March 29, 1918, Sargent's niece Rose Marie, daughter of Mrs. Ormond and widow of Robert André Michel who had fallen while fighting on October 13, 1914, was killed in Paris. She was attending the Good Friday service in the church of St. Gervais. The priest had just spoken the words "Mon Père je remets mon esprit entre Vos mains," when a German shell struck the building, killing seventy people, among whom was Madame Michel. She was a person of singular loveliness and charm, and had figured in many of Sargent's works, notably in *Cashmere*, *The Pink Dress* and *The Brook*. He made many studies of her hands, which he thought the most beautiful he had ever seen, and gave two casts of them to the Slade. She had travelled with him on some of his sketching tours, and her youth and high spirits and the beauty of her character had won his devotion. Her death made a deep impression on him.

Several attempts were made to induce Sargent to visit France and paint during the War. In June, 1918, he consented, and towards the end of that month he and Professor Tonks left England. He regarded the question of his outfit very seriously, and 31, Tite Street soon became littered with boots, belts and khaki. There was a succession of tryings on, an endless packing and unpacking; buckles suddenly came to play a part in the scheme of things, straps to act with "the silent inclemency of inanimate objects going their own way." At Charing Cross on the day of departure his personal equipment showed traces of difficulties partially overcome. Little as he looked like an artist, he looked even less like a military unit returning from leave. Bearded, and with a touch of the seafarer's complexion and with his burly figure, he appeared to a "Tommy" as "a sailor gone wrong." He was excited and interested. On arrival

"POLITICS."

at Boulogne he went to G.H.Q. as the guest of Field-Marshal Haig; he was received with a welcome he never forgot, and found his friend Sir Philip Sassoon to initiate him into the mysteries of the military hierarchy.

After a few days at G.H.Q. he motored to the headquarters of Major-General Sir Geoffrey Feilding, commanding the Guards Division, then at Bavincourt, twenty-five miles south of Arras.

When the Division went into the line again on July 13 he followed General Feilding's headquarters, which were then about five miles from Berles au Bois. Sargent occupied one of the iron huts which had been built into a high bank to avoid observation and bombs. On the 16th he was joined by Professor Tonks. General Feilding writes: "Sargent messed with us: we were a mess of about fourteen with him and Tonks. Breakfast and luncheon depended as to time on our various jobs, each of us coming in as he could get away. At dinner we were all together. He was a delightful companion, and we all loved him. He used to talk the whole time, and there was always some competition to sit next to him. He took an enormous interest in everything going on, he discussed music, painting and every imaginable subject."

Professor Tonks writes:

Sargent entered completely into the spirit of his surroundings. I don't think he ever grasped much about the military campaign in actual being, which is curious as he had in his library and had read with deep interest many books on the Napoleon campaigns. I could never make him understand differences of rank, no not the most obvious, so I gave up trying. Things which seemed the commonplaces of war surprised him as when he said to General Feilding one Sunday when the Band was playing "I suppose there is no fighting on Sundays." Sometimes I used to wonder if he knew how dangerous a shell might be, as he never showed the least sign of fear, he was merely annoyed if they burst sufficiently near to shake him. Whenever he was at work a little crowd would collect and they easily found him as he invariably worked under a large white umbrella, which the British did not mind in the least but which the Americans (for he joined them later) with the thoroughness of the new broom made him camouflage. From Ballymont we went to Arras where Colonel Hastings the Town Commandant found us quarters in about the best uninjured house in the place. Here we had two or three weeks together. He did a somewhat elaborate oil painting of the ruined Cathedral and a great many water colours of surprising skill. I never could persuade him to work in the evening when the ruined town looked so enchanting; he worked systematically morning and afternoon. One day we heard that the Guards Division were advancing so we motored towards them to find material for our subjects. We knew that a number of gassed men were being taken to a dressing station on the Doullens Road, so we went there in the evening. He immediately began making sketches and a little later asked me if I would mind his making this essentially medical subject his, and I told him I did not in the least mind. He worked hard and made a number of pencil and pen sketches which formed the basis of the oil painting known as *Gassed* now in the War Museum. It is a good representation of what we saw, as it gives a sense of the surrounding peace. I regret he did not put in something I noticed, a French boy and girl of about 8 years, who watched the procession of men with a certain calm philosophy for an hour or more, it made a strange contrast.

On July 24 Sargent wrote:

> C/o Major Lee,
> G.H.Q.,
> *Thursday 24th.*
>
> My dear Evan,
> 　I got a kind note from General Elles, thanks to you, giving me the freedom of the Tanks, but I am already here with the Guards Division and rather far away South Eastwards. I had had a lively day there before, in General Elles' absence, when Major Uzzielli took Philip Sassoon and me a joy ride in a Tank up and down slopes, and over trenches and looping the loop generally. There is a row of obsolete ones somewhere about Bermicourt that made me think of the ships before Troy.
> 　I am delightfully quartered here (in an iron tube) with General Feilding who is awfully kind and nice—and there is some good company in the Mess, and many pleasant fellows within reach—Lord Lascelles, Capt. Spencer Churchill whose occupation is crawling up to the Boche lines across No Mans Land. He carries in his pocket as a mascotte a little bronze greek head of 600 B.C. and General Haldane* who insisted on putting six volumes of Marion Crawford into my motor, with the

---

* Lieut-General Sir Aylmer Haldane, commanding 6th Corps.

ARRAS.

order in which I must read them. He was scandalized at my never having read anything of that author excepting the line "and the silence clashed against the stillness," when certain lovers met by moonlight in the Pantheon.

Whereas—I meant to be interesting—and il y a de quoi.

I will write again—God bless you.
  Yrs. ever,
      JOHN S. SARGENT.

The subject which Sargent had been specially invited to paint was a scene illustrating the co-operation of British and American troops. It will be remembered that American troops took their place for the first time in the main battle-line on May 28, 1918, in the Mondidier section. On that day General Bullard's 1st American Division, forming part of the French First Army, had captured the village of Cantigny and held it against three strong counter-attacks. By the middle of July 300,000 American troops were either in the line or in reserve. Sargent's visit coincided, therefore, with the principal American activities in the field. He was in France when Ludendorff made his final attack on July 15, and when on July 18 Foch began his counter-stroke. But the subject with which he was directly concerned, "British and American troops acting together," was not easy to capture. There was the difficulty, first, of finding the occasion, and then of its not being paintable when found. It was not until the end of September that he witnessed a scene which he thought suitable and of which he did a study, *Arrival of American Troops at the Front, France*, 1918.*

On September 11 he wrote:

                      C/o MAJOR LEE,
                          G.H.Q.,
                              Sept. 11, 1918.
MY DEAR EVAN,
    I wonder if you are coming out to the Tanks—If so I hope we can meet before I go back to London. The time is drawing nearer although there are two or three weeks yet as I needn't consider my privilege here at an end until the end of September. The weather

* The property of Miss J. H. Heyneman.

is breaking and rain and mud have set in for good I fear, and I hate
to consider my campaign over before my harvest of sketches has grown
to something more presentable in quality and quantity.   The programme of "British and American troops working together," has sat
heavily upon me for though historically and sentimentally the thing
happens, the naked eye cannot catch it in the act, nor have I, so far,
forged the Vulcan's net in which the act can be imprisoned and gaily
looked upon.   How can there be anything flagrant enough for a
picture when Mars and Venus are miles apart whether in camps or
front trenches.   And the farther forward one goes the more scattered
and meagre everything is.   The nearer to danger the fewer and the
more hidden the men—the more dramatic the situation the more it
becomes an empty landscape.   The Ministry of Information expects
an epic—and how can one do an epic without masses of men ?   Excepting at night I have only seen three fine subjects with masses of
men—one a harrowing sight, a field full of gassed and blindfolded
men—another a train of trucks packed with "chair à cannon"—and
another frequent sight a big road encumbered with troops and traffic,
I daresay the latter, combining English and Americans, is the best
thing to do, if it can be prevented from looking like going to the
Derby.

I left Tonks at Arras and came on to this neighbourhood of Ypres,
to an American Division and am now with some R.G.A. but will
probably go to Cassel where the hotel is still open.   It is delightful
not to have to dodge behind hedges when you are on Kemmel—not to
speak of other sources of satisfaction, at the events of the last month !
What a pity winter is setting in when everything is going so well.

I hardly deserve a letter, having written so rarely, but I want to
know whether there is a chance of our meeting over here.   Philip
Sassoon has been awfully kind and useful.

Yrs. ever,

JOHN S. SARGENT.

The scene which he witnessed with Professor Tonks, and
chose as the subject for his war picture *Gassed*, followed
the attack of the 4th and 6th Corps on August 21.   The 6th
Corps had attacked astride of Ayette with the 99th Brigade* of
the 2nd Division on the right and the 2nd Guards Brigade on
the left.   The Germans put down a gas-shell barrage, which failed
to stop the advance.   Later in the day the heat of the sun set

* Ninety-ninth Brigade was made up of 24rd Royal Fusiliers, a battalion of the
Royal Berkshire and the 60th Rifles.

ARTILLERY ON THE MARCH.

the gas in movement, and the 99th Brigade and the 8th Brigade
of the 3rd Division, which passed through them to capture
Courcelles, were caught in it. It is the men of these units that
appear in the picture. When the picture was finished Sargent
was in doubt what to call it.

> I don't (he wrote) quite agree with your objections to the title
> "gassed." The place is merely a clearing station that they were
> brought to—the date would lead people to speculate as to what
> regiments were reduced to that pitiable condition, and I think their
> identity had better not be indicated. The word "gassed" is ugly,
> which is my own objection, but I don't feel it to be melodramatic
> only very prosaic and matter of fact.
>
> I have just come from the Canadian Exhibition, where there is a
> hideous post-impressionist picture, of which mine cannot be accused
> of being a crib. Augustus John has a canvas forty feet long done in his
> free and script style, but without beauty of composition. I was afraid
> I should be depressed by seeing something in it that would make me
> feel that my picture is conventional, academic and boring—Whereas.

Incidents of the War were not favourable for the production
of works of art. The declared purpose with which pictures were
painted implied that their first concern was documentary.
Artists were sent to France to illustrate what took place, and
provide on canvas a record for posterity of the scenes enacted.
The incident which Sargent has chosen for his subject does,
it is true, carry a great deal of sentimental significance. He
has shown some of the horror of War, much of the moral quality
of those taking part in it, and has interpreted the emotional
intensity of a scene calculated to rouse compassion in the on-
looker. The maimed and broken march of a file of men, blind-
fold and striving in their stricken state to follow the directions
of a guiding hand, has been treated with impressive simplicity.
It is executed in low relief; with the severity of a processional
frieze. There is no striving after the picturesque; dramatic
account has been entirely dispensed with. It is stated in its
starkest terms, it is more than merely descriptive. He has given
a spiritual value to realism, and dignity and solemnity to the
facts. The desultory rhythm of the figures silhouetted against the

sky, the diffused light of evening, the harmony of colour with which the scene is invested, have entered into the inspiration.

On September 24 he arrived at a camp in the neighbourhood of Peronne. Near by was the Fourth Army Prisoners of War Transit Cage, under the command of Captain H. J. E. Anstruther, 26th Royal Welsh Fusiliers, whose guest Sargent became. "I suggested to Sargent," writes Captain Anstruther, "that he might like to look round the prisoners of war cage and see the various types of prisoners taken on the previous day. The ground was ankle-deep in mud after heavy rain and the constant churning up by prisoners marching in and out and up and down— some hundreds of prisoners were standing about. Sargent was deeply interested in the scene as he stood in the centre of the cage, the largest in the Army area (100 yards square), making notes and criticisms of the men and studying the various types." It is easy to imagine Sargent feeling at first embarrassed —was it quite fair? Was it not taking advantage of fellow-men in adversity studying them in a pen and sizing them up like cattle?—then the "queerness" of it getting the better of his hesitations and stimulating his vision, and finally his being caught up by the absorbing interest of the scene. After all, the prisoners themselves were indifferent to inspection: positively one can imagine him arguing to himself there wasn't any reason not to stare and take notes. A day or two later he was struck down by influenza and taken to the 41st Casualty Clearing Station near Roisel, where he was placed under the care of Doctor Stobie of Oxford. He was a week in bed, "in a hospital tent," as he wrote to Mrs. Gardner, "with the accompaniment of groans of wounded, and the chokings and coughing of gassed men, which was a nightmare—it always seemed strange on opening one's eyes to see the level cots and the dimly-lit long tent looking so calm, when one was dozing in pandemonium." He was placed in the officers' ward, warmed by an oil stove, the tent very wet and muddy, the conditions uncomfortable, men dying round him, and the aftermath of the battlefield constantly passing before him. He read a lot of the hospital books and made a sketch of one of the flaps of the tent. He was quite

uninterested in military matters, but when well enough to join
the doctors' mess he proved a great asset, and made an admirable social element—everybody liked him. It was his habit
to regard the hazards of mortality with outward calm; his
compassion, though deep, was concealed by shyness; his eye
might kindle with sympathy, his voice change when confronted
with suffering, but he shunned expression of deep feeling. And
so, too, in France, faced with sights to which he was acutely
sensitive, and suffering in its most poignant form, he continued
to maintain his habitual reserve. By sheer necessity it was the
attitude of those most concerned; it was doubly incumbent on
those taking no active part, but thrust into this tortured world,
to maintain the same reticence and acceptance.

By the end of October he was back in England. Soon after
the Armistice Sir Abe Bailey, with fine generosity, offered to
pay for three pictures for the National Portrait Gallery, which
should include the foremost figures, political, naval and military,
of the War. Naturally Sargent was approached as to his willingness to undertake one of the three. At first he declined. Great
pressure was put upon him, and in January, 1919, he wrote:
"Yes, I have written to Lord Dillon* and said that if the Trustees
should ask me again, leaving me liberty of time, I would gladly
do the Army group—gladly is polite." When consulted, he
recommended that Sir James Guthrie and Sir Arthur Cope, R.A.,
should be asked to execute the other two groups. Each painter
was to receive £5,000. Nothing but a sense of obligation
induced Sargent to embark on this undertaking. It never
appealed to him; it had to be fitted in with his work at Boston;
from the first he presaged a failure.

In May he wrote from America:

May 12, 1920.

MY DEAR EVAN,

I am beginning to see my way clear to getting back to England
in fact I am in hopes of getting a cabin on the 3rd July. . . . The
Generals loom before me like a nightmare. I curse God and man for
having weakly said I would do them, for I have no ideas about it and
I foresee a horrible failure. My new England conscience alone forbids

* Chairman of the Board of Trustees of the National Portrait Gallery.

my (*illegible*) the very real possibility of my not being able to get a ship or striking a floating mine if I do. However it will certainly be a pleasure to be in London again and to see the half a dozen people whom I have missed during this year's absence.

. . . . Haven't you been delighted with Henry James' letters? such virtuosity, such beautiful flutters—it is like watching the evolutions of a bird of paradise in a tropical jungle. There is a letter about Roosevelt in the second volume and one to Walter Berry which are miraculous fireworks.

Yr. ever,
JOHN S. SARGENT.

P.S.—I wonder if Guthrie and Cope are getting a tremendous start of me on the accursed.

In July he was once more in Tite Street. In September he wrote, again in reference to his picture of the Generals, to Sir James Guthrie:

> I have been back a couple of months and thanks to Mr. Milner* have put salt on the tails of a certain number of generals and I find each of them individually very interesting to do and the tremendous variety of types seems to give a promise of some sort of interest. But I am still merely collecting material and have not yet evolved any scheme of the picture as a whole. I am handicapped by the idea that they never could have been altogether in any particular place—so I feel debarred from any sort of interesting background and reduced to painting them all standing up in a vacuum.

High hopes were entertained of what Sargent would produce. Unfortunately he refused to allow himself any poetic licence. These soldiers never had been in one room together during the War, therefore it would be a falsification to group them as though they had. His adherence to fact stood between him and a work of art. The background, in his view, had to be neutral, carrying no import of time or place. The Generals had, as he said, to be painted in a vacuum. The result is a group devoid of artistic interest. The Generals appear to be collected on a stage from which the curtain has just risen, and about to advance as a chorus to the footlights, a view borne out by the playhouse architecture of the background. Individual

---

* Director of the National Portrait Gallery.

heads are finely painted; but as a composition it has failed. The arrangement is forced and rigid and wanting in poise. It was probably beyond the skill of man to avoid a tendency to monotony in representing a sequence of brown boots and spurs; some artifice, at least, of lighting was required, but this has not been given. The spectator is confronted with seventeen gentlemen in khaki looking out of the picture, and gathered together for no conceivable purpose other than to stand for their portraits. On the other hand, as a series of literal resemblances of those who led British armies to victory it provides a veracious record, and this, when all is said and done, was the object when the commission was given.

With the exception of his picture *Gassed*, the war as such cannot be said to have influenced favourably Sargent's art. It is true that he painted some fine water-colours in France, but in these the war plays a small part; they are just scenes he might have chosen on any one of his sketching holidays, with here and there indications of military occurrences incidental to the setting. In the same way his commemorative panels painted for Harvard University are lacking in any quality of inspiration.

Chapter XXVII

IN the course of his career Sargent received decorations and diplomas from many countries; America, France, Italy, Germany and Belgium, each in turn paid him honour. In England in 1904 he received a D.C.L. from the University of Oxford. In 1907 he was offered a knighthood by the Prime Minister. Pleading his American citizenship, he replied as follows:

THE RT. HONBLE.
SIR HENRY CAMPBELL BANNERMAN.

31, TITE STREET,
CHELSEA.

DEAR SIR HENRY,

I deeply appreciate your willingness to propose my name for the high honour to which you refer, but I hold it as one to which I have no right to aspire as I am not one of His Majesty's Subjects but an American Citizen.

Believe me,
With very great respect,
JOHN S. SARGENT.

In 1913 he was given the degree of LL.D. by the University of Cambridge.

Gratifying as these titles of fame may have been, they were a source of great perturbation to Sargent in so far as they necessitated a public appearance. It was no light thing for him to step from the shelter of Tite Street into the applause of the Sheldonian Theatre. Even when assured that no speech would be expected he seemed afraid lest some unforeseen contingency should bring upon him the hated ordeal. And then what would be his position? He shuddered at the thought. In reply to a letter asking him to address a philosophical society of Harvard University on Art he drafted a reply which gives an idea of his invincible repugnance to speaking in public:

SCENE IN VENICE.

DEAR SIR,

. . . It is an honour that I fully appreciate and am deeply grateful for having been thought entitled to. I should be pleased to accept if I had the least right to hope that a miracle would happen in my favour. The miracle of overcoming something like panic when asked to speak has never happened to me yet, and the spectacle of panic instead of a speech is the entertainment I have afforded and long since resolved not to afford again. The annals of the society would have a disaster to chronicle that I feel bound to spare them by declining an honour that would entail the saddest consequences. . . .

This nervousness in public did not hinder him from doing public work; it did, however, prevent him, on the resignation of Sir Edward Poynter in December, 1918, from accepting the Presidency of the Royal Academy. When pressed very hard he said to his friend Sir Arthur Cope: "I would do *anything* for the Royal Academy but that, and if you press me any more, I shall flee the country." Sir Arthur adds: "There is no doubt that if he had allowed his name to stand he would have been elected, not only without dissent, but with acclamation." In the conduct of the Academy's affairs Sargent was loyal and active. Things had changed since he had paid his ceremonial calls as an A.R.A. on "the old fogeys"* of 1894. The Academy was still the Academy, but it had greater width of view; it was more alive to movements of art going on outside Burlington House.

In 1917 he resigned the Trusteeship of the Tate Gallery and in a letter to Mr. D. S. MacColl gave his reasons:

I am sorry (he wrote) you think I am leaving you in the lurch in the matter of the Trusteeship. I was not in it long enough for it to amount to that. In fact I resigned as soon as I realized that I was the only painter. To elect one painter on a board of that sort looks to me like throwing a possible sop to the body of artists, and his position would be that of the small appendix or some other survival in an organism. The fact of my being an Academician also complicates matters more than I can foresee or measure. You and others on the Board undoubtedly represent a systematic opposition to the Academy, with influential backing and I don't know what fell purposes with which a member of the Academy cannot sympathize—or be associated —Inside that body I am looked upon as a frequent and ineffectual

* See *ante*.

advocate for changes and a nonconformist to that kind of loyalty that consists in maintaining that everything is perfect. But that is a very different thing from joining those who oppose it as an institution and very likely disapprove of its system.

He was a conscientious teacher in the Academy Schools, regarded, as we have seen, by some as a "wonder" and by others as difficult to follow. He used to say of himself that he had no gift for teaching. "When I first met Brough," he told Miss Heyneman, "I often criticized his work, but though Brough always agreed and seemed struck by a suggestion he never once changed a detail in response to advice. . . ." In the same way: "When I first took up teaching work at the R.A., I painted for the students from a model during a whole day, carrying on the canvas from stage to stage, explaining as I went. They thanked me profusely, but when I arrived for my next criticism I found that not one of the class of about forty had made the smallest attempt to follow what I had shown them."

Another of the public duties Sargent undertook was in connection with the Chairmanship of the British School at Rome. On the death of Edwin Abbey he became the principal adviser of the Board of Management on matters connected with painting. In 1912, when the School was incorporated by Royal Charter, he became an original member of the Council. He twice refused the Chairmanship of the Faculty of Painting: first, on its formation, in favour of Sir Edward Poynter, and again when Sir Edward died, in favour of Mr. George Clausen. In 1921 he was persuaded to take the position when Mr. Clausen resigned. It meant going perilously close to publicity; he accepted with reluctance. A board room, and above all a chairmanship, might involve a speech—still there were calls which no one who paid regard to duty could refuse. When once he was there, his judgment and authority were of the highest value; his personality exactly the one needed. With his broad-mindedness and hostility to what was stereotyped and conventional he acted as a bulwark agains sectarian tendencies. Before this he had secured the appointment as original members of the Faculty of Painting of Wilson Steer and Henry Tonks, two artists for whose work he had a deep admiration. When Sir Edward Poynter at the time of the appointment asked who Professor Tonks was, Sargent had difficulty in controlling his indignation and jerked out vehemently, "A great teacher," with a menacing emphasis on the "great."

Few artists have been more consistently applauded in their lifetime than Sargent, few have seen their work maintain through many years greater popularity with the public. There had never been a moment since 1875 when his pictures had not found a ready market, there had never been a year when he had not more commissions than he could execute. Critics, after the first hesitations, had, with few exceptions, consistently eulogized his paintings; dealers had been resolute in their acquisition; fellow-artists had acclaimed him; and the public, the fourth estate in the formation of a painter's reputation, had made him their favourite. The prices realized by his pictures at auction rose steadily. His first picture to be sold at Christie's was *Autumn on the River*, 30 by 19 inches, which brought £52 10s. for the South African War Fund in 1900. In 1906 *Miss Ellen Terry as Lady Macbeth*, owned by Sir Henry Irving, brought £1,260. In 1910 *Expectancy: A Young Girl* 39½ by 33¼ inches, was sold for £504. In 1916 *Rehearsal of the Bas de Loup Orchestra* fetched £231. In 1924 *The Hospital at Granada*, 20 by 27½ inches, was bought on behalf of the Felton Bequest, Melbourne, for £2,205. The highest price paid for a water-colour before his death was in 1920, when £750 was paid for the *Church of the Gesuati on the Zattere, Venice*.* Appreciation of his water-colours has since then rapidly increased. The view is even entertained that they will do more than his oil paintings to maintain the level of his fame. To some, such a view will be on a par with Matthew Arnold's whimsical declaration that Shelley's prose will outlive his verse. But, however that may be, the skill and vitality with which

---

* At the sale at Christie's, July 24, 1925, Sargent's 237 oil paintings and drawings fetched £170,000. There is no parallel for such a sale. The purchasers were, I believe, without exception, either American or English. The works of Sargent are as highly prized in 1927, and in the esteem of the public have survived one of the most likely periods for reaction.

Sargent's water-colours state the realities that delight the eye, and now and then cast over those realities a vesture of imagination, suggest that it is something deeper than fashion which has given them their present renown. They have a happy air of impromptu, of the artist having come upon a scene at a particular moment and there and then translated it into paint. He set his face against anything like "picture making"; his water-colours are fragmentary—pieces of the visible world broken off because they appealed to his eye, not because they made a specially paintable subject or evoked a mood. Nearly all of them are done under Southern skies or in mountainous country. He had a preference for scenes in which the hand of man had taken a part; if he turned to natural scenery, he chose wildness rather than beauty, strange effects in mountain formation, gorges, tumbling glaciers, or rocks strewn as though they were the missiles on a Titans' battlefield. But, whatever he painted, water-colour in his hands seemed to lose something of its limitation and become a more powerful medium, giving the substances represented a solidity and volume more associated with oil-colour. His general habit was to make the lightest indications in pencil to fix the relative position of objects, and then, after wetting the paper, to paint with great rapidity. It was not his habit to use the opaque method; he trusted for his high lights to the white of the paper. From the white of the paper he would with equal facility conjure the satin of a dress, the texture of a marble, or the silky flanks of an ox. He paints as a man of muscle rather than mood. He does not, like Brabazon, transmute his scenes into melody. His power is displayed in the supremacy of his drawing, the opulence of his colour, the skill of his statement, finite as it often is, and the glowing warmth of his sunlit scenes. And in these he excels, not so much by the subtlety of his omissions as by the harmony of his assertions and his exuberant objectivity.

It was only after Sargent met Brabazon in 1886 or 1887 that he took to water-colours on a scale at all comparable to his work in oils. From then onwards, whenever other calls on his time allowed, he devoted a portion of the year to working in this medium. Here and there in his work we may fancy that the influence of Brabazon is present, especially in some of the more subdued renderings which he has given of the side canals in Venice; but these are rare. For the most part he is entirely himself, deriving from no one. He followed his own pleasure; every picture is the offspring of exultation in his facility; their spontaneity is pronounced, they flow from his hand with the turbulence of water from a mill race. If little is added to what he represents, nothing is taken away. If the scenes he paints delight us, the same delight will be found in his renderings of them. To live with Sargent's water-colours is to live with sunshine captured and held, with the lustre of a bright and legible world, "the refluent shade" and "the ambient ardours of the noon." If the modern painter of water-colours aims at slightness, and to-day shorthand is preferred to definition, that was not the aim of Sargent. He never ran the risk of emptiness. He cultivated in his compositions full measure, pressed down and running over. When Mr. James showed him a water-colour he had done Sargent said: "Very nice, but *terrifically* slight; I'd like to see you make one without any sky or water. Work out these forms" (pointing to a tangle of bushes in the foreground). Mr. James answered that he had made such attempts but always lost, in so doing, the effect of the whole. He said: "But I don't see how you can . . . *see* . . . the whole until you have made some of the parts."

Of his own water-colours he was a severe critic; rarely satisfied, deprecating praise, and always ready to point out what he regarded inadequate or mistaken. When he brought home one of his well-known sketches, *Quarry at Chocorua*, Mrs. James said to him: "How delightful it must be to know that every time you work you will bring back something fine." Sargent replied: "But I hardly EVER do! Once in a great, *great* while."

Neither in his water-colours nor his oil painting did he turn for subjects to the humbler walks of life. Destiny prescribed for him the rôle of a portrait painter of the social world. He had brought the tradition with him from Paris; he had grown up in the age of Duran, Bonnat, Dagnan Bouveret, and Boldini, when to have your portrait painted was a normal incident of fashionable life. In London he carried on the tradition. He was unaffected by the change taking place in Paris in the character of subjects which the rising artists were painting. Posterity will learn about the epoch of Sargent only what is to be gathered from a study of the eminent, the rich and the successful. He painted, in fact, the world of which Henry James wrote. His migration to England put an end to his interested outlook on peasant life and folk subjects, fisherwomen by the sea, dancers in Spanish cabarets, Parisian flâneurs in the Luxembourg Gardens, Venetian water-carriers and beggar girls. The future student of the social life of the last fifty years in France will be able to reconstruct much of it from the work of French painters. In England there has been nothing which corresponds to this dedication of the highest talent to making works of art from the life of the people, from a butcher's wife in her bath to an advocate pleading in the law courts. Conditions in England decided the direction of Sargent's genius. He was turned from his experiments in Impressionism, and his leanings towards subjects like the Spanish dancers; civilization for him became "the litter in which we forget the bearers." And as the chronicler of the *beau monde* like Van Dyck in his day, and like Reynolds, Romney, Lawrence and Gainsborough in theirs, he established within a few years a supremacy hardly disputed.

Through the munificence of Sir Joseph Duveen, those who visit the Tate Gallery now see side by side the work of Sargent and that of the French Impressionists. To pass from the French school to Sargent is to make an abrupt transition. A new idiom is exchanged for one that modern criticism would have us believe, has said its last word. But in taking stock of the situation we must recognize that Sargent's work should be compared not with the French school of to-day, but with the portrait painters of the past. And the moment we do this, strong though the influence of fashion inevitably is upon our æsthetic appreciations, we cannot doubt that he will maintain a distinguished place in the company of eminent painters.

Degas said at the graveside of Corot: "The artist will be

replaced with difficulty, the man never." That must correspond
with what is felt by many who knew Sargent.

In personal appearance he was a striking figure. Standing
over six feet in height, he maintained a remarkable uprightness
of carriage, and, though in later years decidedly a heavy man,
he was to the end of his life quick and emphatic in his movements. Advancing years had made his prominent grey-blue
eyes more noticeable, but had done nothing to lessen the keenness with which they seemed to rake the field of vision. Great
painters have usually been men of strong physique. Sargent
appeared to escape the fatigues of more normal humanity; at the
end of a long day's work his mind would be serene and cool, his
temperament buoyant; he would show no sign of fag either in
brain or limb.

His health was remarkable. Occasional attacks of influenza
and a certain liability to sore throat alone disputed his seeming
invulnerability. And as to his sore throats, he declared these
were induced by his duties on the hanging Committee of the
Royal Academy, which necessitated sitting many hours in a room
while pictures were dragged across the floor, filling the air
with particles of carpet. When asked to dinner by Sir George
Henschel after one of these attacks, he wrote from Scheveningen:

> I left London last Thursday and came to Holland because I cannot
> talk Dutch and so would hold my tongue and give my throat a chance.
> Here there is enough sea air to make it necessary to hold on to railings
> and lamp-posts, and I am regaining my voice slowly, but I know that
> if I talked for half an hour I should be dumb again for a week. If I
> came to your dinner my voice would be taken away with the fish.

His burly full-blooded aspect was deceptive: it gave no
warrant of the diffidence and gentleness that lay beneath. A
stranger would never have suspected that behind such alacrity
and power was an almost morbid shrinking from notoriety and
an invincible repulsion from public appearances. In this he
presented a continual paradox. It was an engaging trait, and
perhaps helped to preserve the freshness and delicacy of his
perception, enabling him the better to estimate the sensibilities

of others. During the War a famous musician in Paris was in straitened circumstances; Sargent, anxious to help, wrote as follows, enclosing a substantial sum:

"COPLEY-PLAZA,"
BOSTON,
ÉTATS-UNIS.

MON CHER FAURÉ,

Il y a si longtemps que nous ne nous sommes vus que je me persuaderais facilement que c'est dans quelque vie antérieure que mes atômes out fait la connaissance des vôtres et s'y sont fatalement accrochés. Sans vous en douter vous promenez avec vous un jumeau sentimental invétéré et inopérable. Votre souvenir et vos oeuvres me hantent et c'est peut-être vous que je salue d'un coup de chapeau quand chaque hiver je vois Sirius, et chaque printemps le premier amandier en fleur. Mais, comme à un négre, il me faut un fétiche, un objet matériel devant lequel faire mes prosternations, et je viens vous implorer à quatre pattes cette faveur, avez-vous le manuscript d'une de vos romances que vous voudriez bien m'envoyer à l'adresse ci dessus ? Ce serait pour moi un trésor inestimable—faites moi ce plaisir.

C'est un des attraits de Boston qu'on y entend souvent de vos oeuvres. Vous avez en Loeffler un interprète hors ligne et un admirateur passionné.

Passionné aussi votre admirateur et vieux ami.

JOHN S. SARGENT.

Time or distance made no difference to the warmth of his friendships; he never suffered their temperature to fall.

Charles Furse, doing decorations in a distant town in England, found himself in a difficulty; he wrote to Sargent explaining he was stuck and enclosing a diagram drawing to illustrate his dilemma. The next day, working on a high scaffolding, he was astonished to see Sargent's head appear at the top of the ladder: Sargent had broken every engagement to come to the assistance of his friend.

He was generous to a fault in deed and judgment. His kindness of heart was exceptional. The wife of an American painter fell ill; she was without anyone to look after her save her husband, who made a livelihood by teaching a class. Sargent came to the rescue, and during the wife's illness and after her death took the class, taught, and kept the pupils together till such time as the painter was able again to take them over.

He was always ready with personal service if that could be more effective than finance.

A few years ago he heard of a young French painter, who, as the result of an accident, was taken to a hospital with his sight seriously injured. Sargent, though he knew nothing of him, called at the hospital, and when told it was not a visiting day forced his way in, saying, "Nonsense." Next day he returned with an eminent oculist, and he continued his kindness in various ways till the youth was cured. Such illustrations could easily be multiplied.

There was a certain splendour about his personality, his dynamic energy, his largeness of outlook, his complete immunity from what was small or unworthy, as well as in the high simplicity and honour of his life. He hated pretensions and affectation, "that seal of mediocrity," whether in art or individuals. His opinions carried a weight which was derived from his sincerity and experience—a statement which he would certainly have met with "Tush, tush!" or some stronger deprecation. His taste was startling at times, but, supported as it always was by good reason, it was upsetting and often shook the most convinced. He was shy of emotion, inclined to shirk it when it came his way; this made him difficult to know: he seemed to protect himself in a network of repressions. This was noticeable in the War.

His response to some of the agitations common to mortality was never assertive or pronounced: it was, perhaps, too much involved with his artistic appreciations to be disengaged as a distinctive force. "L'art de peindre," wrote Fromentin, "est peur-être plus indiscret qu'aucun autre. C'est le témoignage indubitable de l'état moral du peintre où il tenait la brosse." Sargent would not have subscribed to such a doctrine: yet his painting suggests that it contains a truth. While his absorption in art was a passion, none the less he approached each problem with detachment, viewing its solution unemotionally and regarding his sitters with the level judgment of a man of science.

Positive truth, selected and arranged to convey the essential, was his aim; if that was attained other things would follow. He held that if mystery, charm and poetry were treated as an end in themselves, they were sure to lead to mannerism and disaster. In conversation he allowed himself plenty of latitude; he could caricature and embroider amusingly; he was a good hand at "picking mirth from off rotten walls," and was all for a leaven of nonsense. His work (and he thought nothing of seven hard days in the week) never unfitted him for enjoyment. He would arrive to the minute where he was due to dine, and no company but seemed richer for his presence; he was easy and mellow, and no one had fewer moods to air or antipathies to control. At all times he was natural, courteous and interested, droll with an edge, and ready to pursue whatever game was afoot, and keenly alive to everything that concerned his friends. The following letter to de Glehn, on his marriage, is characteristic.

LUNA-VUSSLA,
Sept. 20th.

MY DEAR PREMP,

I have just opened a packet of letters and find your, let us say, communication.

My God! what a trick to play to your sincere well wisher. I will up and marry in the attempt to be quits.

Well, troglodyte of the Cordilleras. I foresee that the time will come when, this first shock being over, I will spontaneously and sincerely congratulate you—especially when I see and like the lady which I feel I am sure to do—and the sooner the better—at this moment the cold sweat is on my brow. I feel as if a very boon companion had been carried off, probably for his good, but also probably to live in America which means to me personally a great loss. However and whereas and nevertheless.

These small and discreditable and ill-mannered whimperings must be stifled, and I will train for better sentiments by reading your letter which is very convincing that you are happy and likely to be permanently so.

All that your fussy and egotistical old friends will want to hang on to, is the chance or the power of contributing a little to your happiness.

Be as happy as you like Dear Sir, on those conditions.

Don't be a troglodyte and show this to her and spoil my chance of becoming her friend as well as yours. You may tell her that that is my hope and ambition and that I shall be extremely annoyed if she doesn't like me.

Yours ever,

J. S. S.

Sargent read widely. In English prose, which he knew less well than French, he admired particularly Sir Thomas Browne, Smollet, Sterne, Swift, Defoe, Gibbon, Pater Doughty's "Arabia Deserta," Samuel Butler. He seldom read English novels, and he could never appreciate Dickens. He preferred French poetry to English. He had read and remembered a great deal of Shakespeare and Shelley, but he cared little for Keats, still less for Pope: on the latter point he was very positive. I never heard of his reading modern English verse, with the exception of Flecker, whose "Hassan" certainly gave him pleasure.

War poetry he refused to read, with the exception of Julian Grenfell's "Into Battle," of which he wrote: "The verses are very fine and moving—there is something unusual in the sensation conveyed of *all* his perceptions and all his sympathies being keyed up to a high pitch by something enormous that is behind the scenes." As a rule, what he liked in books was travel, adventure and strange personal experience.

He loved writing that put before him definite images and portraits, such as Beckford's, Gobineau's and St. Simon's, and the wit and finish of Max Beerbohm's essays delighted him.

In April, 1925, he was once more due to start for America. He had shown no outward sign of ill-health. His friends had thought him tired, but he had been pursuing his ordinary life of unrestricted activity. For several days he had been engaged in his preparations, packing, lifting cases, and, in disregard of the protests of his friends, putting on himself a physical strain of much severity. On the evening of the 14th a few of his friends met at 10, Carlyle Mansions for a farewell dinner given by Miss Sargent: Mrs. Ormond, Lady Prothero, the two Misses Barnard, L. A. Harrison, Wilson Steer, Henry Tonks and Nelson Ward.

Sargent was in high spirits, he had dispatched to America the final instalment of his decorations for the Museum of Fine Arts and he was spending his last evening with his friends. He acted, as he always did at his sister's parties, as host. The party, as was the custom, broke up at 10.30. The guests said good-bye, with wishes for Sargent's speedy return; and then, after lingering a little with his sister, he drove away. It was his habit to read before going to sleep. When the maid knocked at his door on the morning of April 15, there was no answer: John Sargent was dead. Beside him lay an open volume of the "Dictionnaire Philosophique" of Voltaire. His glasses had been pushed up over his brow; he had the aspect of one quietly sleeping. Death had come with soundless tread, "unexpected and unrecognized," as in January, 1905, he had written of his mother.

J. S. S.

IN MEMORIAM

By VERNON LEE

(Copyright and all other rights given to Miss Sargent)

J. S. S.: *In Memoriam*

I

TALKING about John Sargent recently with his sisters, and hearing the letters he wrote as a small boy to Ben del Castillo, I recognize that, even more than in cases of other friends, the John Sargent I can write about is merely the one who has long existed in my mind, and, perchance, scarcely anywhere else. Also, that what I can write about him, when indeed it won't be writing about my own past self, must be taken as akin to a legend: a few genuine facts, but intermeshed with a good deal more which, as with other legends, is surmise, misinterpretation, confusion of times and places and persons—in short, incorrect and easily corrected by others. But not by me! Because John Sargent exists in my mind just like that; and that is the only John Sargent I know, and wish to write about. So that whatever rectifications may be made, I shall answer: "No doubt," or "Yes, of course," and return to my own view.

Take, for instance, the matter of John Sargent's heredity, and the respective parts played by his parents. Already his sisters have demurred to my view, and tell me that his special gifts must have come from his father's side, since among his paternal ancestors there was, at least, one painter of Colonial times. But to me, who see in recollection Mrs. Sargent painting, painting, painting away, always an open paint-box in front of her, through all the forty years I knew her, her whole jocund personality splashed, as it were, with the indigo of seas and the carmine of sunsets, to me the painting gift of John Sargent is all from his mother; while what he had from his father was the deep-seated character, the austere, self-denying strength which smelted and tempered that talent into genius. Since John Sargent, as I see him, is at bottom a puritan, for ever question-

235

ing and curbing the divine facility of his gifts, setting them new
tasks from a puritan's hatred of yielding to his own preferences,
a puritan's assertion of liberty against the wiles of enslaving
mannerism, that Delilah.   By this I account for his having
turned, with all his energy and infinite application, to tasks less
suited to his gifts than those which lay ready to his hand.   Moreover, persuaded as I am that the individual temperament of
every artist expresses itself with unconscious imperative far
more in *how* he paints than in *what he chooses to be painting*, I
account by this for the way he laid down his perfectly pure and
sharply contrasted colours; above all, for the rushing lines and
wilful but broadly generous angles, out of which the unerring
speed of his hand and his eye built up the likeness of men and
things.   Neither is this all: it was the puritan in John Sargent
who was perpetually dissatisfied with that spontaneous imaginative
vision of his, inclining him to the recondite and far-fetched, and
compelling him to an arduous search after the unsuspected aspects
and innermost qualities of whatever he painted.   If, as I imagine,
there is a portrait of John Sargent as a very young man among
the geologists on the glacier in Besnard's "École de Pharmacie,"
then the rapid, passionate concentration of the stroke of his
hammer on the moraine-stone may well be symbolical of the
deliberate and loving, but sometimes ruthless, laying bare of the
unsuspected structure of material things, and, however unconscious he remained of such psychological revelations, no less of
the soul of his sitters.   All this has been occasionally attributed
to the modern artist's craving to *faire nouveau*.   Whereas, if
ever there has been a great man (and I suspect all great men are
more or less alike in this matter) who disdained, or rather ignored,
the desire to pit his work against something done by others, it
was John Sargent.   But he was pursued by the fear of sliding
into what he himself had already done, of yielding and losing
himself in the deliciousness of his marvellous facility.   And that,
that something of Beethoven, in a man of Mozartian spontaneity
and variety, abundance and swiftness, was, I shall always
believe, the puritan heredity of John Sargent's New England
father.

VERNON LEE.

II

When I was a child, and John and Emily and I (eighteen months separating the youngest of us from the eldest) were children together, for two winters at Nice and one (so memorable) in Rome, I adored Mrs. Sargent and was rather afraid of Dr. Sargent. Not that he ever scolded me, or his own children in my presence. With perfect courtesy he passed over my vain little person, whereas Mrs. Sargent, bubbling with sympathies and the need for sympathy, treated everyone as an equal in the expansiveness of her unquenchable youthfulness and *joie de vivre*. When I come to think of it, Dr. Sargent could not have been so very tall, but his head seemed higher up than other people's, and his thin back (I see him clad in a sober pepper and salt) longer and stiffer. One knew whenever he spoke, not without an austere twang; and I, at all events had a childish impression that his words implied disapproval. It was certainly to him that I attributed the ban put upon novel-reading (or was it merely novel-reading of a Sunday?) at an age when I myself spent half my days over Fenimore Cooper and even the dangerous Chateaubriand. Similarly, he must have put some quite mysterious obstacle (I cannot for the life of me remember whether of the nature of words or doors) interposed between myself (and John, of course) and certain large *livraisons* of "Notre Dame de Paris," of which I can almost see the blood-curdling illustration of *Quasimodo au pilori*. These volumes were in a spare room—perhaps a box-room, but with something funereal— of the Sargents' flat at Nice, which I was allowed to frequent.

Their house was called Maison Virello, in the then outskirts of the town, with a garden of pepper-trees and those arid lilac and magenta winter flowers which I already detested. But *we* had the use of a much larger garden; the barracks of a house was called Maison Corinaldi, and . . . I have it! the street containing it and the Sargents' house was the Rue Grimaldi, all pronounced in French manner since the recent annexation by Napoleon III., then still glorious in waxed mustachios. In the garden common to all the many apartments of our Maison Corinaldi the children thereof naturally foregathered, among more pepper-trees, dwarf palms and other facilitations for (to me agonizing!) games of hide-and-seek. There was also a small pond, with a possibility of sailing for toy boats. Of course, John Sargent owned a toy sailing-boat, for was he not going into the United States Navy?

I used to hear that much about "Dr. Sargent's little boy" from sundry small Americans who played with me in that garden; and I must have seen him at the pond. But I am ashamed to say (it sounds like the beginning of an old-fashioned novel) that on our first introduction I actually mistook "Dr. Sargent's little boy" for another little boy (name, Tommy Walsh), and not without embarrassment to both of us. This, however, was dispelled by my ready "Do you like puzzles?" though I cannot remember the answer. Indeed, I cannot remember much about John Sargent's words and ways during that first winter—it was '66-'67—of our acquaintance. I have a vivid recollection of gruesome, historical charades, in our *rez-de-chausée*, whose steps into the garden were set with those dwarf rose-bushes aridly and artificially blooming at a season when I longed for ice and slides in gutters. Now, in these tragic representations there was always a boy, either decapitating Mary Queen of Scots with the fire shovel, or himself offering a bared neck on a footstool in the character of the Earl of Essex, myself figuring as Queen Elizabeth; but whether that boy was always or ever John Sargent, or some other of the small Americans of the Maison Corinaldi, I dare not affirm, though, as Gibbon remarks, I wish to believe. Similarly, I am not sure that Dr. Sargent's little boy took part (his sister was too delicate) in those expeditions to pick periwinkles among the dry reed-beds loomed over by the haunted Villa of Piol, or to pick up sun-dried and rain-soaked little figs such as would fall over remote orchard walls.

Be this as it may, and whether because I was no longer whirling in the unaccustomed childish sociabilities of the Maison Corinaldi and disoriented by all the unfamiliar southern things, or merely because I was now a self-sufficing person of eleven,

STUDY (PENCIL)

this much is certain, that "the Sargents" began to play a dominant part in my life only the following year, when we had moved into a gaunt house facing the sea and the sweep of the Promenade des Anglais. Then was established a regular coming and going between us; weekly, or more frequent, afternoons spent together in our respective abodes. Afternoons, moreover, *spent in painting.* For, to readers unaware of my skill as an artist, it is well to explain that, in default of the spelling and caligraphy wherein John Sargent's infantile letters show perfect mastery of which mine are entirely devoid, I fell back, like other primitives, upon the use of pictographs. These were of so vast and elaborate a kind as to require constant supplies of paints and drawing-books; indeed, I sold my acquiescence in the family's plans and a modicum of good behaviour in return for painter's requisites, replenished at every birthday or journey or infant ailment. I do not know whether at that time John Sargent yet possessed a paint-box of his own. He certainly used mine. And I feel sure that my perennial supplies of water-colours and porcelain palettes and albums of vario-tinted paper were what drew him to me; and that our fraternal friendship grew out of those afternoons of *painting together.* *Together*, in the sense that we consumed refreshments and paints in company, and conversed the while on elevated topics: I must have poured forth about the weekly nights in the family's box at the Nice opera, with vocal imitations, perhaps, of performers and discussion of the verisimilitudes in Verdi's and Donizetti's librettos. But never did John Sargent participate in my pictorial self-expression or show any interest therein: to him paints were not for the telling of stories. There were illustrated books and papers lying about, and a stretch of Mediterranean and perspectived houses and coast-lines looked in at the windows, and to the reproduction of all these did John Sargent apply himself. And with miraculous intuition and dexterity. I can see in my mind's eye (for I saw it with the bodily one within the last half century, and even hope to find it in some mislaid portfolio) a "picture" which he made for my album. I can see the clean juxtaposed blue and green of sky and waves, the splendid tossing lines of sea and ships, see even the bold pencil title in a clearer version of his grown-up writing, the title in a corner, "U.S. Ship (name, alas, forgotten!) Chasing the Slaver *Panther.*" His sister, on my mentioning this work, suggests that he may have copied it from some *Illustrated London News* or suchlike. Maybe, though I cannot recollect anything confirming her suggestion. But even if it was so copied, the rendering of the composition, the quality of the lines, above all, the fresh, slick colour which he had added, made it into a free translation, indeed, a transfiguration: thus did he already see, in that marvellous mind's eye of his, the things presented by Nature, or by other of her interpreters. At Nice, in 1867-68, John Sargent, in furtive use of his mother's paints, or long afternoons with my preposterous and horribly messy boxes, was already a painter. In spirit and in fact.

But in his parents' and apparently his own intentions, acquiescent expectation, he was a future U.S.A. sailor. That, I imagine (or was actually told), had been the chosen vocation of his father, and when for some reason, possibly health, that vocation was thwarted, Dr. Sargent, adopting another profession and, in expatriated wanderings, following none at all, had handed it over to his small son. The rather pale, melancholy dyspeptic (for did he not absorb a mysterious substance labelled "*Pepsina Porci*"?), that delicate, taciturn, austere—and oh so, so little of a jolly Tar!—father, was evidently fascinated by the profession from which fate had excluded him. He frequented American warships and admirals (considerably unlike himself in person), and I cannot but fancy that his nautical patriotism had been heightened by, and in turn heightened, the rancours he nurtured concerning the *Alabama* business, then recent history, and the British attitude towards what he spoke of as "The Rebels."

So John Sargent was taken to entertainments on board flagships at Villafranca, and his toy boats were the badge of his naval future. But Rome willed things otherwise.

III

For the following winter, 1868-69, determining my own life, decided, I believe, that John Sargent was to be, not a naval officer, but a painter.

Not because Rome—since '68-'69 meant Rome for both of us children—worked in him any such slow, far-reaching, passionate change of mind and heart as in myself. In him it was not needed; he was already himself. John Sargent remained, indeed, much of a small boy in appearance and manner; I can see him in his pepper-and-salt Eton jacket, bounding his way among the models and the costumed mendicants down the Spanish steps; and my mother used to describe "Johnny Sargent" as a "skippery boy." But for all that, I suspect he was already, however unconsciously, mature, from having a main interest in life and an orientation due to a supreme gift. So Rome's sights and atmosphere, even in those last papal years, were not required or able to work a change in him. In his quiet, grave way he was, of course, extremely interested in Rome, with the kind of interest displayed already in the accurate descriptions and dates and measurements of those earliest letters of his to Ben del Castillo. He read Becker's "Gallus" and chapters of Ampère's "Histoire Romaine à Rome." And together we spent hours over Murray's "Guide Book" and Smith's "Smaller Dictionary of Antiquities." But he never went mad about Rome, with that strange initial loathing which turned, as by an unpalatable philtre, into obsessing love. In our long discussion of dates of Emperors and names of places, and those joint readings (I can remember dear little Emily even copying out the article *Triton*) in the "Smaller Classical Dictionary," we were much of the same juvenile priggishness; but John's was a steady boyish priggishness, and borrowed the Dionysiac element from my already adolescent passion for all Rome meant. There was, of course, much fraternal give and take in our Roman interests and amusements: I took part in "bombarding" the pigs, then kept outside Porta del Popolo, with acorns and pebbles from the

Pincian Terrace; and in burning holes in bay-leaves with a burning glass, until we were expelled as "enfants mal élevés" by the ferocious French porter of the Medici Gardens. I stained my fingers and messed my frocks furbishing verdigrised coins and other antiquities in a corner of that sitting-room of the little house of the Trinità dei Monti. John, in return, took a part in those Sixtine Chapel performances of ours in Dr. Sargent's empty (and happily remote!) bedroom, warbling in mimicry of the famous Mustafà and Davies.

But there was no give and take, mere perfect fusion of desire and effort in our concentrated hunts for bits of antique marbles, digging them out of the pavement with out umbrella ferrules, and loitering behind our elders in the then desolate regions, between arum-fringed convent and villa walls, of the Esquiline and Viminal, until Dr. Sargent's stern "Come on, children" forced us to leave that half-dislodged scrap of porphyry or cipollino to some future walk in those classic purlieus. . . . Did I not recognize one of our cruelly abandoned pieces of green mottled serpentine in a gutter behind S. Maria Maggiore, some thirty years later, and should I not be able to show it you, or at least its place, even nowadays, fifty years after those walks? Walks there were, also, in less passionate search for groundsel to give Emily's canary, groundsel growing in the Roman Forum, still undisturbed by Boni's diggings. However, our spirits responded in complete unison to less childish appeals. There were yet other walks on which you would meet Cardinals, and sometimes even Pio Nono himself, a white sash round his portly white middle, distributing benedictions with two extended fingers among the bay hedges and mossy fountains of Villa Borghese. There were early winter morning waits, jammed up among black-veiled ladies in St. Peter's, not without secret refreshment of biscuits and chocolate during the patient hours before some pontifical mass; and later afternoons in tinsel-hung churches, where tapers shone dim through the stale incense, and the little organs scrunched out chords as prelude to the *bravuras* of fluted sopranos and cooing throaty falsettos. There were scamperings, barely restrained by responsible elders, through icy miles of Vatican galleries, to make hurried forbidden sketches of statues selected for easy portrayal. Nor any less wonderful the hours (*pifferari* already droning at the corner shrine) at the windows of our own lodgings, opposite the palace of the *Propaganda Fide*, watching the Cinderella coaches, with emblazoned hammercloth and hanging gold-braided footmen, and the various *Eminences*—was that the villain Antonelli?—alighting, draped in scarlet mantles and followed by scarlet ill-furled umbrellas of state. And such afternoons culminated in the advent (likewise watched from the windows) of the tin box of dinner, balanced on the head of the cookshop's porter, and balancing on *its* top the *Charlotte Russe*—whipped cream in a mural crown of sponge biscuits—expressly ordered to regale "the Sargents." *Their* parents did not have hot boxes from the cookshop. *They* kept a white-capped *chef* and gave dinner-parties with ices. . . . Indeed, with these dinner-parties my random reminiscences are at last converging back towards a narrative. For it would happen that when myself and protecting housemaid had clambered up the 200 steps leading from our Piazza Mignanelli to the one-storeyed and many-windowed house, hired for the winter by John and Emily's parents, I would meet cabs and *vetture di rimessa*, drawn up outside, and we children would eat downstairs while the dinner-party above sent us down its sumptuous broken victuals. Meanwhile, in the drawing-room, where the cupola of St. Peter's looked straight in at the windows for all the world like its sunset effigy on the lampshades we tried to imitate, in the drawing-room, between the marble busts of George Washington and of the Goddess Isis (since furnished lodgings in Rome never lacked gods or sibyls or stray martyrdoms), there were being entertained some of those legendary artists: Harriet Hosmer, Randolph Rogers, W. W. Story, and so forth, whose statues, each in every stage of wet-sheeted clay, pock-marked plaster, half-hewn or thoroughly sandpapered marble, were displayed on a weekly *day* by their explanatory creators, and which you can read about—and, of course, we children in 1868-69 were perpetually reading about—in Hawthorne's "Marble Faun." The "Marble Faun"! the illustrious prototypes of its Kenyon,

Hilda and the other lady—ah! her name was Miriam—some-how coupled (but children needn't ask why) with Beatrice Cenci —all these sculptors and sculptresses, as monumental as their own *Zenobias* and Libyan sibyls, were having coffee upstairs, with a due proportion of painters almost as crimson and gold as those lampshades.

And now I have worked my way to their presence, I am at last able to explain in what manner that winter in Rome deter-mined such share of John Sargent's future as had not been settled when destiny brought into the world one of the greatest of painters. For to these now long-forgotten immortals, Mrs. Sargent would occasionally display the sketches which her boy had made (using the maternal paint-box) when she sat on her camp-stool on some Roman villa terrace or before some sunset-flushed (for they always were flushed) broken arches of an aqueduct. Of course, the boy would never be more than an amateur, since he was, you know, going into the U.S. Navy. But for an amateur surely not without promise? . . .

I do not know that it was with my childish eyes of the body that I then saw what with the growing eyes of the spirit I have seen more and more clearly: namely dear, eloquent, rubicund, exuberant Mrs. Sargent, exhibiting those sketches not without wistful glances. And, on the other side, Dr. Sargent, thin, iron-grey and of iron, puritan stiffness, thinking perchance of the *Alabama* and the havoc she had wrought on the U.S. Navy; Dr. Sargent a little averted, or, at most, with some curt glance or word expressing his estimation of that small boy's futile talent; and, to anyone who could take his meaning, his repulsion from all this art, this expatriated fooling with paints and clay and all this doubtful world of marble fauns and spurious romance when *there*, out there, was the real, manly romance of the high seas.

IV

I began these notes about John Sargent by saying that they would embody not so much facts—though I am not aware of having invented anything—as the legend of John Sargent, de-

JOHN D. ROCKEFELLER.

posited by unnoticed accretions in my mind, and found there now that, of a sudden, he has ceased existing for me anywhere else.

This legend, which embodies, even if it does not exactly correspond with, the facts, is a very beautiful one, and runs as follows:

At the end of that winter in Rome, from no compliance with his delightful and insistent wife, still less owing to an expressed wish (I feel sure) on the part of that grave and docile son, so absorbed in the sights of the moment and the precocious habit of translating them into lines and colours—quite spontaneously Dr. Sargent found himself face to face with the startling possibility that God (since Dr. Sargent saw God's work everywhere) had given him a son who was a painter, and that if such proved to be the case, why his own wishes and hopes must go to the wall. I have confused remembrance of words to some such effect, words spoken before me or to my parents, or perhaps guesswork on the part, not of John and his sister, but of my more precociously world-wise self. For, as already said, John seemed too much absorbed in his gifts to be thinking of their future, or to use childish pressure and machinations (as I might have done) to secure their cultivation. I imagine (and this, of course, is the legend in my mind) that, being a puritan, Dr. Sargent hated his son becoming that morally and socially doubtful creature, a painter; and, at the same time, also because he was a puritan, felt bound to sacrifice his own prejudices when they agreed with his own preferences: this rigorous man, from whom John Sargent surely inherited his horror of all lines of least resistance, may have questioned the legitimacy of that fear of art and Bohemianism because he recognized how passionately he had counted on his son becoming the seafaring man himself had longed to be. Be this as it may, the sacrifice was made, and in the completest, wisest manner: all facilities should be granted for John to become a painter, but never an amateur, and only when he had received such education as might enable him to know his own mind and, if need be, turn to other things. But of the U.S. Navy there could, of course, be no more question.

Now, when I think that in 1868 we were barely out of the

days of Clive Newcome and of the "Scènes de la Vie de Bohême,"
and that even my own people, cosmopolitans and far less strait-
laced than John's New England parents, still spoke of artists as
vaguely undesirable; when I consider how far the normal life
of an art-student in Paris differed, at best, from Dr. Sargent's
habits, and what dangers must really have attended a transition
from the one to the other; when, especially, I see in my mind's eye
and hear in memory Dr. Sargent's figure and tone of voice, I
cannot help thinking that this legend of Dr. Sargent's sacrifice
of his wishes and fears to his son's genius is, whether or not
literally true, beautiful enough for us to hope it may contain
a core of truth. And its beauty is heightened, its truth vouched
for, by my recollection of the attitude of John Sargent when he
had long been a universally recognized great man, and his father,
after a life of empty expatriation, had become a silent and broken
old one. Shortly before that obscure life came to its end, I
chanced to stay with the Sargent family near Reading; and I can
never forget the loving tenderness with which, the day's work
over, John would lead his father from the dinner table and sit
alone with him till it was time to be put to bed.

"I am going to sit and smoke," the old man repeated evening
after evening, "with my son John."

That, and not any consideration of this great painting or that,
is what rounds off the legend of John Sargent's boyhood when
we were children together, more than fifty years ago.

V

This legend of the father and son is, properly, all I have to tell
about John Sargent. For our real intimacy did not last beyond
those years of our childhood and especially of that wonderful year,
last but one of the Temporal Power, which good fortune gave us
in each other's company in Rome. For while my people returned
there for another four or five years, the Sargents, perhaps for the
sake of a very good boys' school, settled in Florence. And when
circumstances drifted us also to Florence in 1873, Dr. and
Mrs. Sargent, with Emily and an additional little daughter,

had settled once more at Nice. And by that time Dr. Sargent's wisely and firmly carried out sacrifice of his own prejudices and wishes had already sent John by himself to study painting under Carolus in Paris. So our meetings became rare and brief. As happens (or happened in those distant more conservative times), once friends always friends; while with those who had been children together absence merely kept up the notion and the externalities of the interrupted fraternal intimacies of vanishing childhood. We corresponded more or less regularly, John and Emily and I; and on my part with a self-engrossed confidence that we were still and ever would be each other's closest friends. Indeed, I confess that my axiomatic belief that John Sargent was going to be *the* great painter of the future, a belief whose realization was later to surprise me as a wonderful coincidence, was at bottom due to a general faith, unadmitted but unchallenged, that everyone connected with myself must partake in the glory of my secret adolescent day-dreams. In these John Sargent was an unfailing figure. But the possession of a *bonafide* brother, sufficiently my elder to engross all my juvenile worship, left for John only a comradeship which, though largely a matter of the imagination, was never anything more. Never did his comings and goings (one can discuss such emotional details at near three score and ten!) occasion a heart-beat, nor bring those fine pangs which I had learned when almost a child (for I was a precocious votary of the *genius loci*) in my partings from Rome. Thus John remained merely *the* great painter and *the* comrade secretly expected to see in my vain self his equal and, so to speak, *twin*, in the sister-art of letters. In this taken-for-granted and, as remarked, mainly imaginary comradeship, our months of separation did not shake my faith. Nor—which was odder—was it shaken by the far-between brief meetings during our years of growing-up. One such, I remember, was on the Lake of Como—we were respectively fourteen and thirteen— where we picked up, not indeed antique marbles, but, as we had done at Nice, figs which had dropped over villa walls, while continuing, with Emily as a silent participator, our Roman discussion of the merits of Canova versus the Antique and Guido

Reni compared with Rafael; and to read once more the extracts from "Childe Harold" in the guide book. Then, some years later, came ten days in a hotel (alas! since profaned into a bank!) at Bologna; days of historical-romantic rapture, such as only adolescence can taste.

By this time I was a half-baked polyglot scribbler of sixteen, and John a year older: a tall, slack, growing youth with as yet no sign of his later spick-and-span man-of-the-world appearance; did he not protect his rather stooping shoulders with a grey plaid shawl? . . . He had very nearly completed his classical education in that Florence school and sundry German gymnasia, working hard, meanwhile, wherever there was an opportunity of drawing from the life or from casts: he was within a year or two of the promised initiation into Paris art-schools and entire independence. Yet so great was his, I know not whether to call it modesty or reserve, that I cannot remember his ever mentioning his future. So those ten days were lived by John and me in a present of our imagination, or, rather, a fantastic past we were making up as we went along; rambling, as we did—Mrs. Sargent, my mother, John, Emily and myself—by moonlight, through the mediæval arcades and under the leaning towers and crenellations of that enormously picturesque and still unspoilt city. While, of a morning, after threading our way among the bullocks charioting the vintage, we would spend hours over the portfolios of prints and the unreadable (for they were bristling with various clefs of Ut) scores of the music school. Nor was a word ever exchanged, save about the half imaginary sights we saw, the (I now think) wholly imaginary personages whose portraits surrounded us; and the music, which we had as yet scarcely ever heard, of those eighteenth-century composers who already fired my enthusiasm. It is characteristic of John Sargent's good-natured modesty and his willingness (as in Rome) to fall in with my fancies that, being a nearly grown-up painter, he readily set to copying some marvellously hideous portraits of the musicians ("Heard melodies are sweet, but those unheard are sweeter") I idolized. So that I still cherish a careful water-colour of a youthful portrait of Mozart—Mozart, who never appealed to

TOWER AT TURIN.

him, because lacking the exotic, far-fetched quality which always attracted John Sargent in music, literature, and, for many years, in persons. Which leads to the remark that those days at Bologna already showed that imaginative quality of his mind with which he transfigured my own priggish historical sentimentalities. The words "strange, weird, fantastic" were already on his lips— and that adjective *curious*, pronounced with a long and some- how aspirated *u*, accompanied by a particular expression half of wonder and half of self-irony. That word *curious* was to me, at least, his dominant word for many years, in our meetings in Florence, in Paris (on my way to England) and then, and when, after the Gautreau annoyance had made him change his abode, in the various studios he occupied in London.

Indeed, as time interposed longer intervals between our meetings, and filled up the intervening absences more and more with interests unshared by the other, that word *curious* be- came the keynote of John Sargent's and my conversation; the *cliché* representing a stereotyped reciprocal attitude such as alas, ? .., is often all that remains in the externally unchanged relations of once fraternal friends.

Recognizing such to have been the case, despite all John's unfailing kindness towards me, I recognize once more that all I can tell, first hand, of his life and character is contained in the legend of what his father did for him and what he came to feel for his father.

VI

However, I should like to say some more about the double nature which, as it seems to me, John Sargent had inherited from his exuberantly gifted, expressive and *lebenslustige* mother, on the one hand, and from his puritan, reserved and rather sternly dissatisfied father, on the other. For people appear to have seen only one side at a time, and failed to appreciate both his many- sidedness and the complexity of his genius: that double nature of his occasionally self-conflicting, but more often harmoniously blended, as becomes a creature of supreme facility and of restless, indomitable passion for the difficult.

But before going any further I ought to mention that the little which Sargent told me or let me gather in conversation about his attitude to his art does not extend much beyond our young days. For John Sargent had an artist's instinctive dislike, not indeed for ordinary "art-criticism," of which scraps would crop up in his own talk, but for a newfangled application to art of psychological research which I began attempting some thirty years ago. At that time he even overcame his great personal reserve to the extent of admonishing me, in a deliberate and emphatic *tête-à-tête*, to confine myself to literature and give up once for all such studies in empirical æsthetics as were later published in my volume "Beauty and Ugliness." In his eyes all this was preposterous and, I suspect, vaguely sacrilegious. Now, as I declined to yield to my dear old playfellow's dictation on this subject, and also failed to make him recognize that art could afford to other folk problems quite apart from those dealt with by the artist and the art-critic; as, moreover, Sargent did not like opposition nor I dogmatism, a tacit understanding henceforth kept us off anything which might lead to either. So our conversation turned more and more exclusively on books, music and people, about all of which John Sargent was a delightful talker and I an often delighted listener. With the result that the little I can tell about Sargent's views on painting must be referred solely to his and my earlier years. More particularly to his first stay in London in 1881, when he painted my portrait; to a meeting at Siena, in company with Mrs. Stillman; and to the month at Fladbury, near Evesham, when he did a pencil drawing of me. Moreover, generally speaking, to my brief yearly visits to Paris, where he would show me the Salon, and we sat talking in his studio near the Fortifications. There, and it seems as if for years, he was engrossed in perpetually dissatisfied (and, as regards the Parisian public, disastrous) attempts to render adequately the "strange, weird, fantastic, *curious*" beauty of that peacock-woman, Mme. Gautreau.

Those words I have just quoted, in use already before he went to Paris, expressed one whole side of John Sargent's tendencies. As a young man he was, and perhaps remained, especially attracted by the *bizarre* and outlandish: Spanish dancers (the *Jaleo* and the wonderful frontispiece to Miss Strettell's translations) posed and lit up in enigmatic fashion; Spanish Madonnas like idols, and Javanese dancers scarcely more barbarically improbable; and that *Fumée d'Ambregris*, a Moorish woman veiled in incense fumes, which was, I think, his earliest public success. Such were his individual predilections. But his student days with Carolus fell under the reign of Manet, Degas, Monnet and Renoir, whose realistic creed is set forth in Zola's "Mes Haines." And when I met him, during his Paris years, in 1881, he described himself as an impressionist and an "intransigeant," entirely given up to the faithful reproduction of "les valeurs." Indeed, for years after, and maybe to the very end of his days, I feel certain that his conscious endeavour, his self-formulated program, was to paint whatever he saw with absolute and researchful fidelity, never avoiding ugliness nor seeking after beauty. But, like most, though perhaps not all, supreme artists, John Sargent was not aware of what he was really about, nor in what manner his superficial verbal program was for ever disregarded by the unspoken, imperious synthesis of his particular temperament and gifts. Also, like other painters of those ingenuous, unpsychological days, John Sargent did not know that *seeing* is a business of the mind, the memory and the heart, quite as much as of the eye; and that the *valeurs* which the most stiff-necked impressionist could strive after were also *values* of association and preference. Now, to his constitution, ugliness and vulgarity were negative values, instinctively avoided. In theory, John Sargent would doubtless have defended Manet for cutting some of his figures in half and even decapitating them by the frame, let alone choosing to portray bounders and sots in ballet-stalls and bars. I can almost hear him taking a brief for Renoir's crowd of cads and shop-girls under umbrellas; and for Degas's magnificent lady in her bathroom, under the ministrations of the corn-cutter. But Sargent never painted such things himself. His faithfulness was to selected detail of reality, not to reality as a promiscuous whole; it did not go beyond perspective oddities of posture or improbable-looking colour and light on skin, hair and stuffs. And when he painted certain types of rapacity and vulgarity, he raised them to the same sublime intensity as did Rafael, that other cruellest of portrait-painters, in his hog Pope and fox-and-ferret Cardinals.

Even in these cases it must have been Sargent's taste for the far-fetched which made it possible to adhere to his puritanical rule of exercising no choice among intending sitters. And when left to itself Sargent's outspoken love of the exotic was but the unavowed love of rare kinds of beauty, for incredible types of elegance like his *Mme. Gautreau,* or the heavenly loveliness of transient light and evanescent youth in his *Carnation Lily.* The endless labour on that (surely his true) masterpiece would have been justified by himself on the score of "effects" of mingled twilight and lantern-light on faces and flowers and greensward; effects (he would have called them "curious" and later "amusing")—to be faithfully reproduced because such arduous conquests of "reality" were the puritan painter's excuse for his art. But the result of it all was the most poetical figure-picture of modern times, a picture, as Mary Duclaux said on its first appearance, which was really an altar-piece, those Barnard children in pinafores becoming more than Botticellian angels lighting up the shrine of an invisible Madonna, a Madonna immanent in the roses and lilies and the fading summer afternoon.

That picture, of any pictures ever painted perhaps the one giving me the same artistic happiness as the slow movement of certain Mozart quartets, that penetratingly beautiful *Carnation Lily,* makes me wish to say a few more words about the nature of Sargent's imagination, if only to express my gratitude for it. I have spoken, almost overmuch, of his love for the *bizarre.* But that, however evident, was a superficial trait, perhaps the mere reaction of an austerely fastidious nature against the crassness with which some of his greatest contemporaries accepted, indeed sought for, commonplace, ugly and ignoble subjects for their painting. It may also have been connected with the Parnassian, the Heredia and Leconte de Lisle movement in literature. I can conceive that at any other

time than the eighties or nineties, and with any other surroundings than the expensive and traditionless "tastefulness" of the
wordly people who sat for him, this *bizarre* element might have
vanished from Sargent's work. The boyish hankering after the
"curious" would have been entirely transmuted into the particular imaginative habit, poetical, yet of almost scientific insight,
which distinguishes Sargent as much as his individual quality
of line and colour. Just as his eye—or what we call *eye* for want
of a better name—took in with marvellous subtlety all the
visible relations making up the shape of objects, and his hand—
(again for want of a better name)—transferred them to canvas
or paper with prestigious swiftness and decision, so also Sargent's
imagination perceived all those other relations, relations for the
mind and the emotions, which give all objects and persons a
significance ramifying far beyond their mere present self, give
them, for instance, a past and a future. Thus I remember
Professor Geddes remarking that Sargent's Alpine sketches
showed a geologist the composition of the rocks and the manner
their shapes had been modelled by water and ice and sun and
wind. And Sargent was not a geologist. Similarly, no doubt,
with his portrayal of vegetation. So far was he from the complacent impressionist formula of representing things without
knowing what they were! Sargent may not have known what
they were *called*, but take, for instance, his Ruskinian rendering
of the planes and angles of architecture, why, every exquisite,
sharp, yet tender corner shows the four-square shape of the
building, records the certainty that cornice or capital or archway
would have revealed definite loveliness of shape if seen from
another or nearer point of view. Because Sargent had seen it,
felt it, remembered it, and, with no need for verbal expression,
had told us *what there would remain to be* seen, merely by his
intuitive choice of the most significant aspects actually visible.
Quite similarly do I explain the revelations of his portrait painting. I remember once asking whether he was aware of the
character of the people he painted; and his denial of all knowledge
of and interest in their psychology is surely confirmed by the
very fact that (as in the imaginary cases of that Five Towns

Magnate of Arnold Bennett's story) this most reserved and delicately unmercenary of artists did make certain portraits of certain sitters, and pocket the price, evidently without a suspicion of what he had told about those who paid it. That quite unverbal, intuitive imagination of his had fastened on the facial forms, the pose and gesture, sometimes even the accessories, which revealed the man or woman's character and life. To this kind of imagination I would apply Ruskin's adjective *penetrative*, for Sargent's art does penetrate to the innermost suggestion of everything he painted, but does so by following its merely visible elements. I do not think Sargent, despite the infinite ingenuity he showed in his attempts, was an imaginative painter like Watts or Besnard, imaginative in the sense of building up allegories and narrating events. His symbolism was immanent in the aspects which he painted. Who else has ever expressed the tragedy of war as he has done in his group of gassed soldiers, its horror conveyed without contortion or grimace; and war's tragedy assigned a subordinate and transitory place in the order of things by that peaceful landscape and the game of football in the middle distance. This composition is as majestically serene as some antique frieze; while for the emotions of the beholder it is terrible, like a chapter of Tolstoi.

I should have like to add that, besides significance, Sargent extracted and made visible the actual beauty of the world; and never so much as in the innumerable oil sketches and watercolours which make him one of the greatest of landscape painters. But I want to close on another note. More and more it has seemed to me that Sargent's life was absorbed in his painting; and the summing up of a would-be biographer must, I think, be: *he painted.* To some of us he seemed occasionally to paint to the exclusion of living. In latter years he seemed to be painting from morning till night, an easel, more than metaphorically, in every corner, a picture under way for every effect of changing weather. But looking over the portfolios and portfolios of sketches, thinking of all the more elaborated landscapes: Venice, Carrara Quarries, Alps, Architecture, and even such things as some divinely exquisite silvery wooden palings against a green

CARRARA QUARRIES.

Tyrolese meadow, I recognize that his life was not merely in painting, but in the more and more intimate understanding and enjoying the world around him, and which the work of his incomparable hand enables some of us, also, to understand and enjoy, if only in part.

As regards our friendship, I have sometimes regretted that, having started with such early intimacy, I did not get, or try, to know John Sargent better. But, after all, what can be better than knowing a great man, not in the details of his common personal existence, but in the impersonal feelings and thoughts special to his greatness, and which he enabled us to share with him?   VERNON LEE.

OXFORD,
August 13th, XXV.

Sargent's Pictures in Oils

A. PORTRAITS

Abbreviations as follows :—

C.H. = Copley Hall, Boston.
Cor. Gal. = Corcoran Gallery of Art, Washington.
Franco-Brit. = Franco-British Exhibition, White City, London, 1908.
G.C.A.G. = Great Central Art Gallery, New York.
G.G. = Grosvenor Gallery, London.
M.F.A. = Museum of Fine Arts, Boston.
M.M.A. = Metropolitan Museum of Art, New York.
N.A.D. = National Academy of Design, New York.
Nat. Port. Soc. = National Portrait Society, London.
N.E.A.C. = New English Art Club.
N.G. = New Gallery, London.
N.S. = New Salon, Paris.
N.Y. = New York.
Paris Univ. = The Universal Exposition of Paris, 1900.
Penn. = Pennsylvania Academy of Fine Arts.
Pitt. = Carnegie Institute, Pittsburgh.
R.A. = Royal Academy, London.
R.S.A. = Royal Society of Arts, London.
R.S.A., Edin. = Royal Scottish Academy, Edinburgh.
S. = Paris Salon.
St. Bot. C. = St. Botolph Club, Boston.

Date.	Title.	Owner.
1875.	Benjamin Kissam. 32×26. C.H., 1899; M.F.A., 1925.	Mrs. A. C. Train.
1877.	Portrait de Mlle. W. S., 1877.	—
1878.	Mrs. H. F. Hadden. 36×29. G.C.A.G., 1924; M.F.A., 1925.	Mrs. Hadden.
1879.	Robert de Civrieux (Age 6) with Dog. 33×19. M.F.A., 1925.	M.F.A., Boston.
,,	Carolus Duran. 37¾×46. S., 1879; Penn., 1921; Pitt., 1921.	Mr. R. F. Clark.
,,	Carolus Duran. 13½×10. Study, seated. Christies, 1925 (210).	—
,,	Carolus Duran. On panel, seated in armchair. 13½×10½. Christies, 1925 (211).	Miss Jane Nichols.
1880.	Edward Burckhardt. M.F.A. 22×18. S., 1881; N.Y., 1898, 1899; C.H., 1899; M.F.A., 1925.	Mrs. Harold Farquhar Hadden.
,,	Ralph Curtis on a beach at Scheveningen. 10×12.	Mrs. Ralph Curtis.
,,	Mrs. Charles Gifford Dyer. 24½×17. G.C.A.G., 1924.	Art Institution, Chicago.

Date.	Title.	Owner.
1880.	Gordon Gronough. Venice, 1880.	Mrs. Ralph Curtis.
„	Edouard Pailleron. S., 1880.	--
„	Mme. Edouard Pailleron. S., 1880.	—
„	Henry St. John Smith. 24×19½. C.H., 1889; M.F.A., 1925.	Henry St. John Smith.
1881.	Lady with the Rose. 84×44. G.C.A.G., 1924; M.F.A., 1883 and 1925; S., 1881; R.A., 1882.	Mrs. Harold Farquhar Hadden.
„	James Lawrence. 24×18. M.F.A., 1925; C.H., 1896.	Mrs. Nathaniel F. Emmons.
„	Mrs. James Lawrence. 24×18. M.F.A., 1925; M.M.A., 1926 (6); C.H., 1896.	Mrs. Nathaniel F. Emmons.
„	Dr. Pozzi. Signed and dated.	In Pozzi Sale. Paris, June, 1919.
„	Portrait of a Lady. 20×16. R.A., 1926 (361).	Miss V. Paget.
„	Portrait de M. E. P. et de Mlle. L. P. S., 1881.	—
„	Portrait de Mme. R. S. S., 1881.	—
„	Mme. R. S. S., 1881, Medal.	—
1882.	Mrs. Valle Austin. S., 1882; Cor. Gal., 1916–17; St.Louis, 1917; N.A.D.,1882.	St. Louis.
„	Daughters of Edward D. Boit. 87½× 87½. S., 1883; M.M.A., 1926.	M. F. A. Boston.
„	Mlle. L. Cagnard. 18×14. R.A., 1926 (362).	Alec Martin.
„	Mr. and Mrs. John W. Field. 44×32. G.C.A.G., 1924; M.F.A., 1925; Penn., 1905.	Penn. Academy Fine Arts. Presented by Mrs. J. W. Field, 1891.
„	Gigia.	Sir W. Orpen.
„	Thornton K. Lothrop. 28×21. St. Bot. C., 1888–89; C.H.,1899; M.F.A.,1916 and 1925.	Mrs. Thornton K. Lothrop.
„	Portrait de Mlle. XXX. S., 1882.	—
„	A Portrait. R.A., 1882.	H. McK. Twombly.
1883.	Mrs. Charles D. Barrows. 25×20½. M.F.A., 1925.	—
„	Portrait of a Young Girl. C.H., 1899; M.F.A., 1916.	Mrs. Charles J. White.
„	Portrait of a Child. M.F.A., 1883.	Mrs. Eleanor J. Chapman.
„	Portrait des Enfants. S., 1883.	—
„	Mrs. Charles J. White (Portrait of a Young Girl). C.H., 1899.	—
1884.	Mme. Errazuriz.	Kirkham V. Hall, N.Y.
„	Madame X. (Portrait of Mme.Gautreau). 1884. 82×43. S., 1889. M.M.A., 1926 (10).	Metropolitan Museum.
„	Mrs. Moore. 70×44. Signed and dated. R.A., 1926 (589).	C. S. Carstairs, Esq.

Date.	Title.	Owner.
1884.	Rafael del Castello Nunez.	Count Nunez de Castello. San Remo, Italy.
„	Portrait de Mme. XXX. S., 1884.	—
„	"Pointy" Dog. G.C.A.G., 1924.	Mrs. Hadden.
„	Edith, Lady Playfair. 59×38. Signed and dated. R.A., 1926 (337); St. Bot. C., 1887.	Edith, Lady Playfair.
„	Mrs. Thomas Wodehouse Legh (now Lady Newton). Signed and dated. G.G., 1884.	The Lord Newton.
„	The Misses Vickers. 53½×72. Signed and dated. R.A., 1886 and 1926 (8); S., 1885; Paris Univ., 1900.	Douglas Vickers.
„	Mrs. Henry White. R.A., 1884; Paris Univ., 1900; Cor. Gal., 1916–17; G.C.A.G., 1924.	Hon. Henry White.
1885.	Mrs. Burckhardt and Daughter. 79¼× 56½. S., 1886; M.M.A., 1926 (12).	Mrs. Harold Farquhar Hadden.
„	Mrs. Frederick Barnard. 40×21½. Inscr. "To Alice Barnard."	—
„	Madame Gautreau. 81×42. A Study. In black evening dress, holding a fan. Christies, 1925 (79); R.A., 1926 (451).	Tate Gallery.
„	Mrs. Mason. G.G., 1885.	Mrs. Edward Balfour.
„	Portrait de Mme. V.(Vickers?). S., 1885.	—
„	Robert Louis Stevenson. 20¼×24¼. N.E.A.C., 1887; G.C.A.G., 1924; M.M.A., 1926.	Mrs. Payne Whitney.
„	Robert Louis Stevenson. St.Bot.C.,1887; Penn., 1899; C.H., 1899.	Mrs. Charles P. Taft.
„	Mrs. Vickers (see Mme. V.). R.A., 1886.	—
1886.	Mrs. Douglas Dick of Pitkerro. 63×36. Signed and dated. R.A., 1926 (406).	Mrs. Douglas Dick of Pitkerro.
„	Edmund Gosse(nowSir). R.A.,1926(51).	Sir Edmund Gosse, C.B.
„	Head of a Girl. 18×15. R.A., 1926 (413).	V. C. Vickers.
„	Mrs. Harrison. R.A., 1886.	—
„	Portrait of a Lady. N.E.A.C., 1886.	—
„	Mrs. Wilton and Winston Phipps. London, 1886; G.C.A.G., 1924.	Mrs. Henry Phipps.
„	Portrait de Mme. et Mlle. B. S., 1886.	—
„	Edith, Lady Playfair. 26½×17½. Signed. R.A., 1926 (442).	Edith, Lady Playfair.
„	Mrs. Albert Vickers. 82×39. Signed. R.A., 1886 and 1926 (411).	V. C. Vickers.
„	Mrs. Cecil Wade. 64×53. Signed and dated. R.A., 1926 (349).	Miss Wade.
1887.	Gordon Fairchild. 20½×16¾. M.F.A., 1925 (139).	Gordon Fairchild.

Date.	Title.	Owner.
1887.	Mrs. Charles Fairchild. 19×18. M.F.A., 1925.	Gordon Fairchild.
„	Helen M. Harrison.	Mrs. R. H. C. Harrison.
„	Head of a Child. 16×14. Signed and dated. R.A., 1926 (383).	Mrs. Maurice McMillan.
„	Mrs. Charles E. Inches. 34×24. St. Bot. C., 1881–89; N.A.D., 1888; World's Fair, Chicago, 1893; C.H., 1897 and 1899; G.C.A.G., 1924; M.F.A., 1925; M.M.A., 1926 (16).	Mrs. Charles E. Inches.
„	Mrs. Henry G. Marquand. 66½×42. R.A., 1888; Penn., Pitt., C.H., 1924; M.M.A., 1926.	Mrs. Allam Marquand.
„	Lawrence Millet. 29½×20. Inscr. "To Mrs. Millet." R.A., 1926 (20).	Mrs. F. D. Millet.
„	Mrs. F. D. Millet. 35½×27½. Inscr. "To my Friend Mrs. Millet." C.H., 1899; R.A., 1926 (31).	Mrs. F. D. Millet.
„	Dr. William Playfair. 29½×22½. Signed. R.A., 1926 (391).	Nigel Playfair.
„	Mrs. William Playfair. 59×38. Signed and dated. R.A., 1887, 1926 (346); S., 1888.	Nigel Playfair.
„	Portrait of Child (Ruthie Sears Bacon). 48¾×36. M.F.A., 1925; M.M.A., 1926 (15).	Mrs. Austin Cheney.
„	Royal E. Robbins. M.F.A.	Mrs. John Caswell.
1888.	Dr. Gorham Bacon (Child). 1888. N.A.D., St. Bot. C., C.H., 1899.	Dr. Gorham Bacon.
„	Mrs. Edward D. Boit. 59×41½. Signed. R.A., 1888 and 1926 (280); St. Bot.C., 1888–89; Paris Univ., 1900.	Miss Boit.
„	Cecil, Son of Robert H. C. Harrison. 68×32. Signed. R.A., 1888, 1926 (556).	Mrs. R. H. C. Harrison.
„	Mrs. Malcolm Forbes, Sons of. St. Bot. C., 1888–89.	—
„	Gen. Lucius Fairchild. St. Bot. C., 1888–89; M.F.A., 1925.	State Historical Society, Wisconsin.
„	Mrs. Lucius Fairchild. St. Bot. C., 1888–89.	—
„	Caspar Goodrich. 26×19. M.M.A., M.F.A., St. Bot. C., 1888–89; N.Y., 1889–90; C.H., 1899; M.F.A., 1925; M.M.A., 1926.	Mrs. C. T. Davis.
„	Mrs. John L. Gardner.	Isabella Stewart Gardner Museum.
„	Mrs. Adrian Iselin. 60½×36½. G.C.A.G., 1924; M.F.A., 1925; M.M.A., 1926 (18).	Miss Georgine Iselin.

Date.	Title.	Owner.
1888.	Mrs. Dave Hennen Morris as a Child (1888). H. 20×22. M.M.A., 1926 (20).	Mrs. Dave H. Morris.
„	Claude Monet painting by the Edge of a Wood. 20½×25½. Christies, 1925 (140).	Tate Gallery.
„	Miss Violet Sargent.	Jean Louis Ormond.
„	Mrs. Elliott F. Shepard. 84×48. M.F.A., 1925; M.M.A., 1926 (17).	Mrs. William Jay Shieffelin.
„	Mrs. Jacob Wendell. 60×36. M.F.A., 1925.	Mrs. R. J. A. van der Woude.
1889.	Dennis Miller Bunker. 18×14. St.Bot.C., 1888, 1889; M.F.A., 1899, 1925.	Tavern Club, Boston.
„	Miss Dorothy Barnard (unfinished). 27×15. R.A., 1926 (595).	The Misses Barnard.
„	Mrs. Richard H. Derby. C.H., 1899.	Mrs. Richard H. Derby.
„	Girl in a White Muslin Dress (see Miss Anstruther Thompson). Cor. Gal., 1923.	—
„	The late Mrs. George Gribble. 88×45½. Signed. R.A., 1889 and 1926 (553).	G. J. Gribble, Esq., J.P.
„	Portrait of Mme. Helleu. 31⅞×39⅞.	Knoedler.
„	Mrs. L. A. Harrison by Lamplight. 26×21½. Inscr. "To my Friend Miss Strettell." R.A., 1926 (17).	Mrs. L. A. Harrison.
„	Paul Helleu sketching with his Wife. 26×32. M.F.A., 1925; M.M.A., 1926.	Brooklyn Museum.
„	George Henschel (now Sir). Inscr. "To my Friend Henschel." R.A., 1889; St. Bot. C., 1890; C.H., 1895.	Sir George Henschel.
„	Henry Irving (as Friar John).	—
„	Henry Irving. R. A., 1889.	—
„	Mrs. Ormond by a River. The Morning Walk.	J. L. Ormond.
„	Miss Priestley. 35½×24½. Signed. R.A., 1926 (40).	Miss Emily Sargent.
„	Miss Priestley and Mrs. Ormond. 22×16¼. R.A., 1926 (558).	Mrs. Francis Ormond.
„	Miss Violet Sargent (Mrs. Ormond), 1889. Inscr. "To Emily with a Merry Xmas." 23½×15. R.A., 1926 (366).	Miss Sargent.
„	Alice V. Shepard (age 14), 1889. G.C.A.G., 1924.	Mrs. Dave H. Morris.
„	Miss Violet Sargent.	Miss Emily Sargent.
„	Miss Ellen Terry as Lady Macbeth. S., 1890; N.G., 1889; World's Fair, Chicago, 1893; Dublin, 1898.	Tate Gallery.
1890.	Mrs. Walter Rathbone Bacon, 1890. 82×36. M.F.A., 1925.	Hon. Mrs. John F. A. Cecil.

Date.	Title.	Owner.
1890.	Miss Eleanor Brooks (Mrs. R. M. Salton-stall). Sketch. M.F.A., 1925.	Mrs. R. M. Saltonstall.
,,	Miss Eleanor Brooks (Mrs. Richard M. Saltonstall). 60×37. M.F.A., 1925; C.H., 1890.	Mrs. R. M. Saltonstall.
,,	Peter Chardon Brooks. 27×24. St. Bot.C., 1891; Boston, 1898; C.H., 1899; G.C.A.G., 1924; M.F.A., 1925.	Mrs. R. M. Saltonstall.
,,	Mrs. Peter C. Brooks. 50×40. St. Bot. C., 1891; C.H., 1899; M.F.A., 1925.	Mrs. R. M. Saltonstall.
,,	Edwin Booth (Sketch of). G.C.A.G., 1924.	Mrs. Willard Straight, now Mrs. Leonard Elmhurst.
,,	Edwin Booth. 87¼×61¾. M.M.A., 1926.	The Players, N.Y.
,,	Lawrence Barrett. N.A.D., 1890.	Players Club, N.Y.
,,	Edwin Booth (Sketch). C.H., 1896 and 1899; M.F.A., 1916.	Gordon Fairchild.
,,	Carmencita (Study). C.H., 1899.	—
,,	Carmencita (Sketch). 28½×19½. Christies, 1925 (119).	Mrs. Ormond.
,,	Mrs. Comyns Carr. 25¾×19⅞. Inscr. "Comyns Carr." Signed (apparently twice). N.G., 1890; Knoedler, N.Y., 1924.	Knoedler.
,,	Mrs. Francis H. Dewey. 36×31. Washington, 1912–13; Pitt., 1913; Worcester, 1914; M.F.A., 1925.	Francis H. Dewey.
,,	Gordon Fairchild seated in a Chair, 39×53. C.H., 1917.	—
,,	Mrs. James T. Fields. 32×53. M.F.A., 1925.	Boylston Beale, Esq.
,,	Beatrice Goelet. N.Y., 1891, 1895.	Robert Walton Goelet.
,,	Robert Harrison, 1890.	—
,,	Mrs. Augustus Hemenway. 32×25. C.H., 1897, 1899; G.C.A.G., 1924; M.F.A., 1925.	Augustus Hemenway.
,,	Joseph Jefferson (as Dr. Panglois in "The Heir at Law"). M.M.A., 1926 (22); N.Y., 1890; N.E.A.C., 1893.	The Players, N.Y.
,,	Joseph Jefferson (Head). M.F.A., 1890; G.C.A.G., 1924; M.F.A., 1925; M.M.A., 1926; M.F.A., 1922.	Estate of J. S. S.
,,	The late Lady Knaresborough (Lady Meysey Thompson). 63×39. Signed. R.A., 1902 and 1926 (565).	—
,,	Mrs. Kissam (Mrs.K). 20×36. M.F.A.. 1925; R.A., 1890; Penn., 1917; Cor. Gal., 1916–17.	Mrs. George Vanderbilt.

Date.	Title.	Owner.
1890.	Miss Louise Loring (Oil Sketch). 32×25. M.F.A., 1925.	Miss Katherine P. Loring.
,,	Mrs. Augustus Loring. 50×40. M.F.A., 1891, 1925; Penn., St. Bot. C., 1891; C.H., 1899; G.C.A.G., 1924; M.M.A., 1926.	Augustus P. Loring.
,,	Hon. Henry Cabot Lodge. N.Y., 1897; Penn., 1898; C.H., 1899; Cor. Gal., 1908–09.	H. C. Lodge, Estate of.
,,	Mother and Child (Mrs. Edward Livingston Davis and Son). N.Y., 1890 and 1891; M.F.A., 1891, 1895, 1916, 1919, 1924; Chicago, 1893; Penn., 1896; C.H., 1890; Cor. Gal., 1909.	
,,	Portrait Study (E. A.).	—
,,	Miss Katherine Pratt. 40×30. World's Fair, Chicago, 1893; Penn., 1894; M.F.A., 1895 and 1916; C.H., 1899; Cor. Gal., 1910–11; Worcester, 1914; G.C.A.G., 1924; M.F.A., 1925.	Frederick S. Pratt.
,,	Portrait of a Lady. R.A., 1890; N.E.A.C., 1896.	Miss Sargent.
,,	George Peabody. 34×26. C.H., 1898, 1899; M.F.A., 1925.	George A. Peabody.
,,	Portrait of a Lady. 40×50. R.A., 1890; M.M.A., 1926 (24).	Augustus P. Loring.
,,	Mrs. Richard M. Saltonstall. C.H., 1895, 1899; M.F.A., 1925.	—
,,	Miss Sargent (the artist's sister aboard ship). 10¾×7½. M.F.A., 1925.	Mrs. Frederick Eldridge.
,,	Saint Gaudens, Homer, and Mother, 56×37. N.Y., 1890; M.F.A., Chicago, 1983; C.H., 1899; M.F.A., 1899, 1900, 1925; G.C.A.G., 1924.	Homer Saint Gaudens.
,,	Miss Ellen Terry, Study for, as Lady Macbeth. R.A., 1926 (373).	Miss Edith Craig.
,,	Mrs. Hamilton McKown Twombley. 87×56. M.F.A., 1925.	Mrs. H. McK. Twombley.
,,	Study of Young Woman (Sally Fairchild). 30×25. M.F.A., 1925.	{ Mrs. Charles Fairchild. Gordon Fairchild.
,,	Mrs. Cornelius Vanderbilt. 1890.	—
1891.	La Carmencita. 90×54½. R.A., 1891 and 1926 (277); N.S., 1892.	Luxembourg Museum.
,,	Mrs. Edward Livingston Davis and Son. 86×48. C.H., 1899; M.F.A., 1922 and 1925; G.C.A.G., 1924; M.M.A., 1926.	Livingston Davis.
,,	Mrs. M. R.A., 1891.	—

Date.	Title.	Owner.
1891.	Mrs. Thomas Lincoln Manson. R.A., 1891; M.F.A., 1899; N.Y., 1913; G.C.A.G., 1924.	Mrs. Kiliaen van Rensselaer.
,,	Mrs. Thomas L. Manson, Jr. R.A., 1891; N.Y., 1899; C.H., 1899.	Thomas L. Manson, N.Y.
,,	A Portrait. N.G., 1891.	—
,,	Portrait de Jeune Garçon. S., 1891.	—
,,	Miss Palmer (Mrs. L. Meyers). 29½ × 24½. N.G., 1891; R.A., 1926 (388).	Mrs. L. Meyers.
,,	Edouard Pailleron and Mlle. L. Pailleron. S., 1891.	—
,,	Portrait of Young Lady. N.G., 1891.	—
,,	Hon. Thomas B. Reed. 32 × 26. Penn., 1889; Capitol, Washington, 1899; C.H., 1899; M.F.A., 1925.	House of Representatives, Washington.
,,	D. Vergères. Inscr. "A mon ami Vergères."	—
1892.	Miss Helen Dunham. N.E.A.C., 1892; World's Fair, Chicago, 1893; N.A.D., 1895; C.H., 1899.	James H. Dunham, N.Y.
,,	Master Skene Keith. 30 × 26. Inscr. "To my Friend Mrs. Keith." R.A., 1926 (367).	—
,,	Elizabeth, Lady Lewis (Mrs. George Lewis). 53½ × 30½. Signed and dated. N.G., 1893; R.A., 1926 (382).	Elizabeth, Lady Lewis.
,,	John Alfred Parsons Millet. 35½ × 23½. Inscr. "To my Friend Mrs. Millet."	Mrs. F. D. Millet.
,,	John Singer Sargent. 21 × 17. M.F.A., 1925; M.M.A., 1926.	Nat. Acad. of Design, N.Y.
,,	J. Sutcliffe of Bradford.	James Sutcliffe.
1893.	Lady Agnew of Lochnaw. 49½ × 39½. C.H., 1899; R.A., 1893, 1926 (25); Pitt., 1924.	Nat. Gal. of Scotland.
,,	Miss June Chanler (Mrs. John J. Chapman). R.A., 1894; C.H., 1899; G.C.A.G., 1924.	Mrs. Richard Aldrich.
,,	Mrs. Hammersley. Inscr. "To Henry Tonks." 32½ × 20½. R.A., 1926 (393).	Prof. Henry Tonks.
,,	Mrs. Hugh Hammersley (full-length). N.G., 1893; C.H., 1899; Pitt., 1923.	—
,,	William F. Hewer.	W. F. Hewer.
,,	Mrs. Frederick Mead. 32½ × 22½. Inscr. "To Mrs. Abbey, from her Friend John S. Sargent, 1893." R.A., 1926 (360).	Mrs. E. A. Abbey.
,,	Miss Elsie Wagg. 39½ × 27½. Signed top and bottom. R.A., 1926 (36).	Miss Elsie Wagg.

Date.	Title.	Owner.
1894.	Lancelot Allen (son of late Judge Wilfred Allen). Signed and dated. R.A., 1926 (35).	Miss Kate Allen.
,,	Antonio Mancini. Rome, 1924.	Nat. Gal., Modern Art, Rome.
,,	Portrait de M. H. H., N.S., Paris, 1894.	—
,,	Coventry Patmore (profile). 18½×13. R.A., 1926 (442).	Mrs. Francis Ormond.
,,	Coventry Patmore. 36×24. Signed and dated. R.A., 1895; M.F.A., 1899.	Museum of Occidental Art, Tokio.
,,	Portrait de Mme. H. H. N.S., 1894.	—
,,	Coventry Patmore. 36×24. Signed and dated. R.A., 1895 and 1926 (58).	Nat. Portrait Gal.
,,	Miss Ada Rehan. 93×50. N.G., 1895; Daly's Theatre, N.Y., 1895; M.F.A., 1895–96; Penn., 1896; C.H., 1899; Cor. Gal., 1914, 1915; Worcester, 1914; M.F.A., 1915, 1925; G.C.A.G., 1924.	Mrs. George M. Whitin.
1895.	A Countess. N.G., 1895; S., 1898.	—
,,	Mrs. Russell Cooke. 35×27. Signed. R.A., 1895, 1926 (398).	S. Russell Cooke.
,,	Mrs. George Batten singing. Inscr. "To Mrs. Batten." N.G., 1897; N.S., 1902; R.A., 1926.	Miss Radclyffe-Hall.
,,	Mrs. Ernest Hills. R.A., 1895.	Mrs. E. Hills.
,,	Richard Morris Hunt.	Mrs. George W. Vanderbilt.
,,	Gardiner Greene Hammond, Jr. 28×22. C.H., 1898, 1899; M.F.A., 1925.	Mrs. G. G. Hammond, Jr.
,,	Coventry Patmore (sketch for a prophet). Christies, 1925 (150).	—
,,	Coventry Patmore (head). 22½×15½.	K. Matsukata, Kobé, Japan.
,,	Portrait. N.A.D.	Jacob Wendell Coll.
,,	Portrait de Misses XXX. S., 1895.	—
,,	Mrs. Roller. 88×43½. Signed.	Major G. C. Roller.
,,	W. Graham Robertson. 89½×45. Signed and dated. R.A., 1895, 1926; N.S., 1898 (417).	W. Graham Robertson.
,,	Miss Helen Sears. C.H., 1894, 1899; M.F.A., 1925; M.M.A., 1926.	Mrs. Montgomery Sears.
1896.	The Countess Clary Aldrigen. N.G., 1896.	—
,,	Rt. Hon. Joseph Chamberlain. 63½×37. Signed and dated.	Mrs. Carnegie.
,,	Miss Fairchild (sketch). M.F.A., 1896, 1899, 1916.	Charles F. Coll.
,,	Mrs. Colin Hunter. 36×24. Inscr. "To my Friend Colin Hunter, John S. Sargent, 1896." R.A., 1896, 1926 (551).	Mrs. Colin Hunter.

Date.	Title.	Owner.
1896.	Mrs. Ian (now Lady) Hamilton. Signed. 50½×35½. R.A., 1896, 1926 (328); C.H., 1899; Penn., 1905.	Gen. Sir Ian Hamilton, G.C.B., G.C.M.G.
,,	Sir George Lewis, Bt. 31½×23½. Signed. R.A., 1896.	Elizabeth, Lady Lewis.
,,	Hon. Laura Lister. R.A., 1897; C.H., 1899.	—
,,	Mrs. (now Lady) Carl Meyer and Children. 79½×53½. Signed and dated. R.A., 1897, 1926 (331); C.H., 1899.	Adèle, Lady Meyer.
,,	Portrait of a Lady. R.A., 1896.	—
,,	Mrs. Montgomery Sears. 58×38. M.F.A., 1925; M.M.A., 1926 (34).	Mrs. Montgomery Sears.
,,	The Hon. Mrs. George Swinton. N.G., 1898; R.S.A., Edin., 1917; Chicago, 1922; G.C.A.G., 1924; M.F.A., 1925; M.M.A., 1926.	Art Inst. of Chicago.
,,	T. E. Vickers. Signed. 29×24.	Douglas Vickers.
1897.	Claude Monet. 16×13. N.G., 1888; C.H., 1899; M.F.A., 1925.	Nat. Gal. of Design, N.Y.
,,	Henry G. Marquand. 51×40½. M.F.A., 1925; M.M.A., 1926.	Metropolitan Mus., N.Y.
,,	Mr. and Mrs. I. N. Phelps Stokes. N.Y., Pitt., Philadelphia, G.C.A.G., 1924; M.M.A., 1926.	Mr. I. N. Phelps Stokes.
,,	Lord Watson. 90½×47. Painted for the members of the Legal Profession in Scotland. R.A., 1898, 1926 (359).	Faculty of Advocates, Edinburgh.
,,	Mrs. Harold C. Wilson. 59×37. R.A., 1898.	Harold C. Wilson.
,,	Johannes Wolff. Inscr. "A mon ami Johannes Wolff, '97." R.A., 1898.	—
1898.	Senator Calvin S. Brice. 58×38. Portrait Ex. N.Y., 1898; C.H., 1899; Boston Art Club, 1909; M.F.A., 1925; M.M.A., 1926.	Miss Helen O. Brice.
,,	Mrs. J. W. Crombie. 39×29. Signed and dated. R.A., 1926 (415)	Mrs. J. W. Crombie.
,,	Dr. C. D. (Carroll Dunham). N.Y., 1898; C.H., 1899; Penn., 1899.	Louis B. McCagg (?).
,,	Miss Jane Evans. 57×36½. Signed and dated. R.A., 1899, 1926 (339).	Eton College.
,,	The Hon. Mrs. Ernest Franklin. 48×42½. Signed. N.G., 1898; R.A., 1926 (356).	E. L. Franklin.
,,	Lady Faudel-Phillips. 57½×37½. Signed and dated. R.A., 1899, 1926 (350).	Sir Benjamin Faudel-Phillips.

Date.	Title.	Owner.
1898.	Mrs. Charles Hunter. 57×34½. Signed and dated. R.A., 1899, 1926 (303); C.H., 1899.	Mrs. Charles Hunter.
„	Jane, Lady Huntington. 92½×50. Signed. R.A., 1926 (392).	Miss Amy Huntington.
„	Sir Ian Hamilton, C.B., D.S.O. (head). Inscr. "To Mrs. Ian Hamilton." R.A., 1926 (53).	Gen. Sir Ian Hamilton, G.C.B., G.C.M.G.
„	General Sir Ian Hamilton (standing). 54×30. Signed. N.G., 1899; Venice, 1907; R.A., 1926 (21).	Gen. Sir Ian Hamilton, G.C.B., G.C.M.G.
„	Portrait of a Lady. R.A., 1898.	—
„	Mrs. Wilton Phipps. 35×25½. C.H., 1899; R.A., 1926 (572).	Mrs. Wilton Phipps.
„	Francis Cranmer Penrose. 56½×37½. Signed and dated. Pres. R.I.B.A. (1894–96); R.A., 1898, 1926 (45); C.H., 1899.	Royal Institute British Architects.
„	The Countess of Suffolk and Berkshire. 90×47. R.A., 1926 (271).	Countess of Suffolk and Berkshire.
„	Sir Thomas Sutherland, G.C.M.G., Chairman P. and O. S. N. Co. 56½×44½. R.A., 1898, 1926 (285).	P. and O. Steam Nav. Co.
„	Mrs. Anstruther Thomson. N.G., 1898.	—
„	Miss M. Carey Thomas. Pres. Emeritus of Bryn Mawr College. 58×38. S., 1900; C.H., 1901; Cor. Gal., 1907; M.F.A., 1925; M.M.A., 1926.	Bryn Mawr Coll.
„	Mrs. Thursby. N.G., 1898.	—
„	Miss Betty Wertheimer (Mrs. E. A. Salaman). 48×37. Oval. Signed.	—
„	Miss Hylda Wertheimer (Mrs. H. Wilson Young). 84×56.	Tate Gallery.
„	Mrs. Asher Wertheimer (early, in white). 62×40. R.A., 1898.	H. Wilson-Young (?).
„	Asher Wertheimer. 58×38. R.A., 1898; C.H., 1899; S., 1900.	Tate Gallery.
1899.	Mrs. Ralph Curtis. C.H., 1899.	—
„	James C. Carter. 57×38. M.F.A., 1925; M.M.A., 1926.	Harvard Club, N.Y.
„	The Hon. Joseph Hodges Choate. 58×38. M.F.A., 1925; M.M.A., 1926.	Harvard Club, N. Y.
„	M. Léon Delafosse. N.S., 1902; C.H., 1899; R.A., 1905.	—
„	Miss Octavia Hill. 39½×30½. Signed. R.A., 1899.	Nat. Port. Gal.
„	Lord Russell of Killowen (Lord Chief Justice of England). 64½×43½. R.A., 1900, 1926 (284).	The Hon. Mr. Justice Russell.

Date.	Title.	Owner.
1899.	Lady Victoria Stanley (now Lady Victoria Bullock). 77½×41½. Signed and dated.	The Earl of Derby, K.G.
1900.	Henry Irving as Philip II. N.G.	—
,,	Lady in a Boat. 20×27. M.F.A., 1900.	Mrs. Montgomery Sears.
,,	H. B. Brabazon. 22×15½. Christies, 1925 (149).	Miss M. S. Davies.
,,	Lady Elcho, Mrs. Tennant and Mrs. Adeane. 114×84. Signed. R.A., 1900, 1926 (292); Franco-Brit., 1908; R.S.A., Edin., 1911.	Capt. G. R. C. Wyndham.
,,	Sir Charles S. Loch (Sec. Charity Organization Soc., 1875–1914). 34½×25½. Signed and dated. R.A., 1901, 1926 (325).	Lady Loch.
,,	Sir David Richmond (Lord Provost of Glasgow). 95½×52½. Signed. R.A., 1900, 1926 (597).	Corporation of Glasgow.
,,	Hon. Mrs. (now Lady) Charles Russell. 41½×29½. Signed and dated. R.A., 1901, 1926 (55).	Hon. Sir Charles Russell, Bt., K.C.V.O.
,,	Lord Russell of Killowen (Lord Chief Justice of England). 33½×27½. Signed and dated. R.A., 1900, 1926 (12).	Hon. Sir Charles Russell, Bt., K.C.V.O.
,,	Earl of Dalhousie. R.A., 1900.	—
,,	H. B. Brabazon. 28×16½. Inscr. "To Mrs. Brabazon, John S. Sargent."	Charles Deering, Miami, Florida.
1901.	A Girl (Miss Edith French). 25½×21½. R.A., 1926 (401).	Miss J. H. Heyneman.
,,	Mrs. William Shakespeare. 29×24.	W. Shakespeare.
,,	Sir Charles, Lady Ida Sitwell and Family. R.A., 1901.	—
,,	Rev. Dr. Baker (Headmaster of Merchant Taylors School, 1870–1900). 37½×27. Signed and dated. R.A., 1926 (404).	G. W. M. Baker.
,,	Ingram Bywater (Reg. Prof. of Greek in Univ. of Oxford). 58×38. R.A., 1901.	Nat. Gal., Millbank.
,,	Mrs. Cazalet and Children. 100×65. Signed. R.A., 1901, 1926 (395).	W. M. Cazalet, J.P., D.L.
,,	John Ridgely Carter. 33½×26½. Signed and dated. R.A., 1926 (342).	J. Ridgely Carter.
,,	Mrs. William C. Endicott. 64½×45¼. R.A., 1902; G.C.A.G., 1924; M.F.A., 1925; M.M.A., 1926.	William C. Endicott.
,,	The Duke of Portland, K.G. 89×43½. Signed. N.G., 1901; R.A., 1926 (355).	The Duke of Portland, K.G.
,,	Sir Charles Tennant, Bart. 34×27. Signed. R.A., 1901, 1926 (400).	Mrs. Geoffrey Lubbock.

Date.	Title.	Owner.
1901.	Egerton L. Winthrop. 64×43. M.M.A., 1926 (37).	Egerton L. Winthrop, Jr.
,,	The Misses Wertheimer. 73×51½. N.S., 1902; R.A., 1901.	Nat. Gal., Millbank.
,,	Rose Marie and Reine Ormond.	Mrs. F. Ormond.
,,	George McCulloch.	George McCulloch.
,,	Miss Horner. 23½×15½.	—
1902.	The Lady Evelyn Cavendish (now Duchess of Devonshire). 57½×36. Signed and dated. R.A., 1903, 1926 (352).	The Duke of Devonshire.
,,	Mrs. Goetz. N.G., 1902.	—
,,	Mrs. Arthur Knowles and her Two Sons.	Arthur Knowles.
,,	Edward Partington, Lord Doverdale. 36×28.	Lord Doverdale.
,,	A Lady and her Two Sons.	T. Agnew and Sons.
,,	W. M. Cazalet, J.P., D.L. 100×65. Signed and dated. R.A., 1926 (399).	W. M. Cazalet, J.P., D.L.
,,	John Fyfe, J.P., D.L. 57½×38. Signed and dated. R.A., 1926 (385).	Corporation of Aberdeen.
,,	The Misses Hunter. 89½×89½. Signed and dated. R.A., 1902, 1926 (397); N.S., 1903; St. Louis, 1904; Paris, 1904; N.Y., 1904.	Nat. Gal., Millbank.
,,	Mrs. Leopold Hirsch. 57×36½. Signed. R.A., 1902, 1926 (34).	Leopold Hirsch.
,,	L. A. Harrison. 30×20½. Inscr. "To Pater Harrison, John S. Sargent." R.A., 1926 (381).	L. A. Harrison.
,,	The Duchess of Portland. 89×43½. Signed and dated. R.A., 1902, 1926 (288).	The Duke of Portland, K.G.
,,	G. F. McCorquodale. 57½×37½. Signed and dated. R.A., 1903, 1926 (330).	Mrs. J. L. Wood.
,,	Lord Ribbesdale as Master of the Buckhounds. 100×55. Signed and dated. R.A., 1902; Venice, 1907.	Tate Gallery.
,,	Madge Roller. 23½×17½. Inscr. "To my Friend Nettie, John S. Sargent." R.A., 1926 (581).	Mrs. Huxley Roller.
,,	Charles Stewart, 6th Marquess of Londonderry, K.G., carrying the Great Sword of State at the Coronation of Edward VII., August, 1902, and Mr. M. C. Beaumont, his Page on this Occasion. 113×77. R.A., 1904, 1926 (357).	Marquess of Londonderry, K.G.
,,	Edward Wertheimer (unfinished). 64×45.	Tate Gallery.

Date.	Title.	Owner.
1902.	Ferdinand, Ruby, Essie Wertheimer, Younger Children of Asher Wertheimer, with a Dog. 63×76. N.G., 1902.	Tate Gallery.
,,	Ronald Vickers as a Boy. 20×15. Inscr. "To Mrs. Vickers." R.A., 1926 (386).	Douglas Vickers.
,,	The 1st Earl of Cromer. 57½×38. Signed and dated. R.A., 1903, 1926 (341).	Earl of Cromer, G.C.I.E., C.V.O.
,,	Countess of Essex. 49×38¼. C.H., 1917; M.F.A., 1925; R.A., 1907.	M.F.A., Boston.
,,	Portrait de Deux Sœurs. N.S., 1902.	—
,,	Alfred Wertheimer. 64×45. R.A., 1902.	Tate Gallery.
,,	Almina Wertheimer (Mrs. Fachiri). 52½×38½.	Tate Gallery.
,,	Lady Meysey Thompson. R.A., 1902.	—
,,	Conway, Almina and Hylda Wertheimer (Children of Asher Wertheimer). 73½×52. N.G., 1902.	Tate Gallery.
,,	The Ladies Alexandra, Mary and Theo Acheson. 106×78. Signed and dated. R.A., 1902, 1926 (573).	The Duke of Devonshire.
,,	Mrs. Philip L. Agnew. 34½×28½. Signed and dated. R.A., 1903, 1926 (48).	Philip L. Agnew.
,,	William Brownlee, D.L. (Provost of Dundee). 60×37½. Signed and dated. R.A., 1926 (569).	Dundee Art Gal.
,,	William M. Chase. M.M.A., 1926.	M.M.A., New York.
,,	Mrs. Joseph Chamberlain (now Mrs. W. Hartley Carnegie). 45×32. R.A., 1903; G.C.A.G., 1924; M.F.A., 1925.	Mrs. W. C. Endicott.
,,	Francis and Conrad Ormond.	Mrs. Francis Ormond.
1903.	Miss Astor (now Mrs. Spender-Clay). 98×50. R.A., 1926 (283).	Lt.-Col. H. H. Spender-Clay.
,,	Mrs. Charles P. Curtis. 60×35. M.F.A., 1903, 1925.	Charles P. Curtis.
,,	Child's Portrait (Miss Kate Haven). 26×20. Inscr. "To my Friend, Mrs. Bacon." M.F.A., 1925; M.M.A., 1926.	Mrs. J. Woodward Haven.
,,	Alexander J. Cassatt.	Penn. Railroad.
,,	Mrs. William C. Endicott, Jr. 56×35. M.F.A., 1903, 1925; Cor. Gal., 1908.	W. C. Endicott, Jr.
,,	Mrs. Gardiner G. Hammond. 35×35. M.F.A., 1903, 1925.	Mrs. G. G. Hammond, Jr.
,,	Major Henry L. Higginson. 96×60. M.F.A., 1903; G.C.A.G., 1924; M.F.A., 1925; M.M.A., 1926.	Harvard Univ.

Date.	Title.	Owner.
1903.	Hon. John Hay. 30×25. G.C.A.G., 1924; M.F.A., 1925.	Clarence L. Hay.
„	Charles Martin Loeffler. M.F.A., 1903.	Mrs. John L. Gardner.
„	Hon. William Caleb Loring. 56×40. M.F.A., 1903, 1925; M.M.A., 1926.	W. C. Loring.
„	Dr. S. Weir Mitchell. M.F.A., 1903.	MutualAssce.Co.,Philadelphia.
„	Countess Nunez de Castello.	Count Nunez de Castello.
„	Col. W. Windle Pilkington, J.P., V.D., 35½×34½. Signed and dated. Walker Art Gal., Liverpool. R.A., 1926 (577).	Corporation of St. Helens.
„	Edward Robinson. 55×36. M.F.A., 1903; G.C.A.G., 1924; M.F.A., 1925; M.M.A., 1926.	Edward Robinson.
„	James Whitcomb Riley. 36×29. Boston, 1903; St. Louis, 1904; Cor. Gal., 1908–09; M.F.A., 1925.	Art Assoc. of Indianapolis.
„	Mrs. Arthur Lawrence Rotch. 56×36. M.F.A., 1903, 1925.	Mrs. Henry Parkman, Jr.
„	Millicent, Duchess of Sutherland. Christies, 1925 (91).	—
„	Mrs. Joseph E. Widener. Penn., 1903; M.F.A., 1903.	—
„	Peter A. B. Widener. Penn., 1903; M.F.A., 1903.	—
„	Mrs. J. William White. M.F.A., 1903; G.C.A.G., 1924.	Mrs. White.
„	Mrs. Fiske Warren and Daughter. 59×39. M.F.A., 1903; G.C.A.G., 1924; M.F.A., 1925; M.M.A., 1926.	Fiske Warren.
„	Mrs. Julius Wernher.	—
1904.	T. L. Devitt (afterwards Sir Thomas), President of the Shipping Federation. 57×37. Signed and dated. R.A., 1904, 1926 (49).	Sir T. G. Devitt, Bart.
„	Miss Mary Elizabeth Garrett. 58×38. G.C.A.G., 1924; M.M.A., 1926.	Johns Hopkins Univ.
„	Sir Henry W. Lucy. 28½×21½. Signed and dated. N.G., 1904; R.A., 1926. (555).	Lady Lucy.
„	Countess of Lathom. 88×66. Signed and dated. R.A., 1904, 1926 (583).	The Earl of Lathom.
„	Duchess of Sutherland (Head and Shoulders). R.A., 1904; N.S., 1905.	Scott and Fowles.
„	Sir Frank Swettenham, G.C.M.G., C.H. 67½×42½. Signed and dated. N.G., 1905; R.A., 1926 (322).	Sir Frank Swettenham.
„	Mrs. Hugh Smith. 41×32. Signed and dated. N.G., 1904; R.A., 1926 (396).	Vivian Hugh Smith.

Date.	Title.	Owner.
1904.	Mrs. John C. Tomlinson, N.Y., 1904.	—
„	Miss Tomlinson.	—
„	General Leonard Wood. R.A., 1904; G.C.A.G., 1924.	General Leonard Wood.
„	Mrs. Asher Wertheimer. 64×42. R.A., 1904; Franco-Brit., 1908.	Nat. Gal., Millbank.
„	Mrs. Wedgwood. 54×27½. N.E.A.C., 1909.	Miss E. Wedgwood.
1905.	Mrs. Garrett Anderson, M.D. 33×26. Signed. N.G., 1901; R.A., 1926 (419).	Sir Alan Anderson.
„	Señor Manuel Garica. 54×38. Centenary Portrait. R.A., 1905; M.F.A., 1925.	Rhode Island School of Design.
„	Mrs. Adolph Hirsch. N.G., 1905; Nat. Port. Soc., 1913.	—
„	Napier C. Hemy, R.A. 26½×20. Inscr. "To my Friend Napier Hemy." N.G., 1906; R.A., 1926 (347).	Mrs. Napier Hemy.
„	J. Seymour Lucas, R.A. Sketch 26×21. Inscr. "To my Friend Seymour Lucas, 1905." N.G., 1906; R.A., 1926 (42).	Mrs. Grubbe.
„	The Marlborough Family. R.A., 1905.	Duchess of Marlborough.
„	Mrs. Robert Mathias (Miss Ena Wertheimer), (A Vele Gonfie). R.A., 1905; Grafton (Fair Women), 1910.	Mr. Charles Deering.
„	Joseph Pulitzer. 38×28. G.C.A.G., 1924; M.M.A., 1926 (47); N.Y., 1908; Penn., 1910.	Mrs. Joseph Pulitzer.
„	Gen. Charles J. Paine. 34×28. M.F.A., 1922, 1925; M.M.A., 1926 (49).	John B. Paine.
„	Padre Sebastiano. 22×28. N.E.A.C., 1906; M.M.A., 1926 (48).	Metropolitan Museum, N.Y.
„	Mrs. E. G. Raphael. 63×44. Signed and dated. N.G., 1905; R.A., 1926 (375).	E. G. Raphael, Esq.
„	Theodore Roosevelt. 58×40. M.F.A., 1925.	The White House.
„	Madame la Duchesse de S. N.S., 1905.	—
„	The Lady Helen Vincent (Viscountess D'Abernon). 63×42½. R.A., 1905, 1926 (38).	Viscount D'Abernon.
„	Countess of Warwick and Son. 103×63. R.A., 1905; M.F.A., 1925.	Worcester Art Museum.
1906.	Maud, Daughter of George Coates. R.A., 1906.	—
„	Mrs. Frederick Guest. R.A., 1906; G.C.A.G., 1924.	Mrs. Phipps (?).

Date.	Title.	Owner.
1906.	Mrs. Harold Harmsworth (now Viscountess Rothermere). Signed and dated. N.G., 1906; R.A., 1926 (348).	Viscount Rothermere.
„	Sir Hugh Lane. 29½×24½. Walker Gallery, Liverpool, 1913.	Municipal Gallery of Modern Art, Dublin.
„	Miss Lewis (Lady Elizabeth). 34×28. Signed and dated. N.G., 1908; R.A., 1926 (414).	Lady Elizabeth Lewis.
„	Mrs. George Mosenthal. 35½×28½. R.A., 1926 (354).	Mrs. George Mosenthal.
„	Rev. Endicott Peabody. 38×58. Penn., 1907; M.F.A., 1925.	Mrs. Endicott Peabody.
„	Lady Weetman Pearson (now the Viscountess Cowdray). 63×39. Signed and dated. R.A., 1926 (317).	Viscountess Cowdray.
„	Mrs. William Raphael. 56×41. Signed and dated. R.A., 1926.	Mrs. Henry Tufton.
„	Field-Marshal Earl Roberts, K.G., V.C. 64×41. Signed and dated. R.A., 1906 and 1926 (42).	Countess Roberts.
„	Two Young Children. 21½×27. "To Violet Ormond, Xmas, 1906."	Mrs. Ormond.
„	Mrs. Edgar Speyer. 58×36. R.A., 1907; M.F.A., 1925.	Edgar Speyer.
„	Sir Edgar Vincent, K.C.M.G. (now Viscount D'Abernon). 37×27½. R.A., 1926 (394).	Viscount D'Abernon, G.C.B., G.C.M.G.
„	Drs. Welch, Osler, Halsted, Kelly (The Four Doctors). R.A., 1906; Pitt., 1907; Cor. Gal., 1907.	Johns Hopkins Univ.
„	Rev. Edmond Warre, C.B., C.V.O., D.D., sometime Headmaster of Eton. 93½×57½. Signed and dated. N.G., 1907; R.A., 1926 (562).	Eton College.
1907.	Boy and Girl in an Orange Grove. 55×22.	—
„	Mrs. Edward D. Brandegee. 60×30. G.C.A.G., 1924; M.F.A., 1925.	Edward D. Brandegee.
„	Miss Helen Brice. 58×34. N.Y., 1908; R.A., 1908; M.F.A., 1914, 1925.	Miss Helen Brice.
„	Rt. Hon. Arthur Cohen, K.C. 29½×25. N.G., 1908; R.A., 1926 (62).	Miss Cohen.
„	Lady Eden. 43×34½. R.A., 1907.	Penn. Museum (?).
„	William C. Endicott, Jr. 56×14. Cor. Gal., 1908; M.F.A., 1925.	Mrs. William C. Endicott, Jr.
„	Charles W. Eliot. 100×63. G.C.A.G., 1924; M.F.A., 1925.	Harvard Union.
„	Augustus A. Healey. 28½×32½. Cor. Gal., 1910-11.	Brooklyn Museum.

Date.	Title.	Owner.
1907.	Mrs. Huth Jackson. 58×39. Signed and dated. R.A., 1908, 1926 (52).	Mrs. Huth Jackson.
,,	The Hon. Mrs. A. L. Langman. 59×39½. R.A., 1907 and 1926 (319).	A. L. Langman, Esq., C.M.G.
,,	Sir Weetman Pearson, Bt. (now Viscount Cowdray). 63×39. Signed and dated. R.A., 1926 (299).	Viscount Cowdray.
,,	John Singer Sargent (Self).	Uffizi Gallery, Florence.
,,	Lady Sassoon. 63½×41½. Signed and dated. R.A., 1907 and 1926 (274).	Sir Philip Sassoon.
,,	John S. Sargent (Self).	Kepplestone Coll.
,,	William Thorne (Sketch). Cor. Gal., 1907; Pitt., 1907.	William Thorne.
,,	Miss Izmé Vickers. 57½×37½. Signed and dated. N.G., 1908; R. A., 1926 (6).	Miss Izmé Vickers.
1908.	Mrs. Astor (now Viscountess Astor, M.P.). 59×39. Signed and dated. R.A., 1909 and 1926 (308).	Viscount Astor.
,,	The Rt. Hon. A. J. Balfour, M.P. (now the Earl of Balfour, K.G., O.M.). 101×58. Signed and dated. R.A., 1908, 1926 (311).	Carlton Club.
,,	Edward D. Boit. 35×24. R.A., 1926 (345).	Misses Boit.
,,	Cora, Countess of Strafford. 62×44½. Signed and dated. R.A., 1926 (380).	Cora, Countess of Strafford.
,,	H.R.H. The Duke of Connaught. 63×42½. Signed and dated. R.A., 1908. 1926 (291); R.S.A., 1909.	H.R.H. The Duke of Connaught.
,,	H.R.H. The Duchess of Connaught. 63×42½. Signed and dated. R.A., 1908 and 1926 (293); R.S.A., 1909.	H.R.H. The Duke of Connaught.
,,	The Countess of Gosford (Miss Mildred Carter). 39½×29½. R.A., 1926 (592).	John Ridgeley Carter, Esq.
,,	Miss Sargent Sketching. R.A., 1926 (144).	Mrs. Francis Ormond.
,,	Miss Matilde Townshend. Cor. Gal., 1908; Penn., 1909.	Mrs. Mary Scott Townshend.
1909.	Madame Judith Gautier.	Madame J. Gautier.
,,	The Marchioness of Londonderry. 37½×27½. Signed and dated. R.A., 1926 (574).	Marquess of Londonderry.
,,	Alec McCulloch. 27×22. Sketch Portrait of a Young Salmon Fisher. Painted in Norway.	A. McCulloch.
,,	Mrs. Joseph Pulitzer. 58×38. Cor. Gal., 1912–13; M.F.A., 1925.	Mrs. Pulitzer.
,,	The Earl of Wemyss and March. 63×45½. R.A., 1909 and 1926 (314); Rome, 1911.	The Earl of Wemyss and March.

Date.	Title.	Owner.
1910.	His Grace the Archbishop of Canterbury (the Rev. Randall Thomas Davidson). 51½×41½. Signed and dated. R.A., 1911, 1926 (270).	His Grace the Archbishop of Canterbury.
„	Marchese Farinota. Inscr. "To Gonerli Farinota, Friendly Souvenir of J. S. Sargent."	Marchese Farinota.
„	Lord Milner. Twenty Years of British Art. Whitechapel Galleries.	—
„	Les Enfants Pailleron. Château Bagatelle, Paris.	Madame Pailleron.
„	Dr. J. William White. Penn.	University of Pennsylvania.
1911.	Mrs. Arthur Hunnewell. 35×27. Cor. Gal., 1912–13; C.H. 1914; M.F.A., 1925.	Mrs. Arthur Hunnewell.
„	Madame Michel (Nonchaloire). 26×31. M.M.A., 1926 (53).	Mrs. Charles E. Greenough.
„	Two Girls in White Dresses. 27½×21½. Signed. R.A., 1926 (88).	Sir Philip Sassoon.
1912.	Rose Marie. 31½×23. Signed and dated. R.A., 1913 and 1926 (2); San Francisco, 1915; M.F.A., 1916; Cor. Gal., 1917.	Mrs. Francis Ormond.
1913.	Henry James, O.M. 33½×26½. Signed and dated. R.A., 1914 and 1926 (23); San Francisco, 1915; M.F.A., 1916.	Nat. Port. Gal., London.
„	Robert Mathias. 39½×29½. Nat. Port. Soc., 1913; R.A., 1926 (506).	Robert Mathias, Esq.
„	The Countess of Rocksavage (now Marchioness of Cholmondeley). 34×26½. Inscr. "To Sybil, from her Friend John Sargent." N.E.A.C., 1914; R.A., 1914, 1926 (46).	Marchioness of Cholmondeley.
1914.	Mrs. Frederick Barnard. Anglo-American, London, 1914; R.A., 1926 (41).	The Misses Barnard.
„	The Earl Curzon of Kedleston, G.C.S.I., G.C.I.E., F.R.S., President of the Royal Geographical Society, 1911–14. R.A., 1915 and 1926 (29).	Royal Geographical Society.
„	Carl Maldoner (Bust).	C. Maldoner.
„	Pratt (Portrait Sketch). Worcester, 1914.	—
„	Two Girls in White Dresses (Eastman ?). Cor. Gal., 1914.	George Eastman, Rochester, N.Y.
„	Douglas Vickers. 29½×24½. Signed and dated. R.A., 1926 (407).	Douglas Vickers.
„	Miss Elizabeth Williamson. R.A., 1926 (121).	Mrs. Charles Hunter.

Date.	Title.	Owner.
1915.	Francis Jenkinson, M.A. Sometime Librarian in the University of Cambridge. 35½×27½. Signed and dated. R.A., 1915 and 1926 (344).	UniversityLibrary,Cambridge.
1916.	Gen. William Birdwood. Signed and dated.	Melbourne.
„	Carl, Sketch of Guide, Rocky Mountains.	—
„	Mrs. William Hartley Carnegie (formerly Mrs. Joseph Chamberlain). Boston, 1916; G.C.A.G., 1924.	Mrs. William C. Endicott.
„	Portrait of P. A. J. when a Child. Cor. Gal., 1916.	Augustus Jay.
„	Portrait of a Lady. Cor. Gal., 1916.	J. P. Morgan.
„	George W. Vanderbilt. Cor. Gal., 1916; Penn., 1917.	S. T. Biltmore, N.C.
1917.	George R. Fearing. C.H., 1917.	Mrs. George R. Fearing, Jr.
„	Daniel Nolan. 26×20. C.H., 1917; Worcester, 1918; M.F.A., 1919; Cor. Gal., 1923.	
„	President of the United States (Woodrow Wilson). Cor. Gal., N.Y., Penn., M.F.A., Cleveland, Detroit, Chicago, 1918; R.A., 1919.	Nat. Gal. of Dublin.
„	John D. Rockefeller. 58×46. M.F.A., 1925.	John D. Rockefeller.
„	John D. Rockefeller. 58×45. N.Y.,Penn., M.F.A., Chicago, Detroit, Buffalo, Cleveland, 1918; Cor. Gal., 1919.	John D. Rockefeller.
1918.	The Viscountess Acheson (Miss Carter). G.G., 1918.	J. R. Carter Coll.
„	Mrs. Percival Duxbury and Daughter. 56½ ×37½. Signed and dated. Red Cross Portrait. R.A., 1919 and 1926 (568).	Mrs. Percival Duxbury.
1919.	Mrs. Allhusen. Nat. Port. Soc., 1919.	—
1921.	Lt.-Gen. Sir G. H. Fowke, K.C.B., K.C.M.G., Adjutant-General in France, 1916-19. 56½×32. Signed and dated. R.A., 1921 and 1926 (389).	Lt.-Gen. Sir H. G. Fowke, K.C.B., K.C.M.G.
1922.	Some General Officers of the Great War. R.A., 1922.	Nat. Port. Gal.
„	*Studies* for "Some General Officers of the Great War":	—
„	Field-Marshal Viscount Allenby. Christies, 1925 (153).	—
„	Field-Marshal Viscount Allenby.	Leicester Art Gal.
„	Field-Marshal Viscount Allenby. Christies, 1925 (152).	—
„	General Lord Byng of Vimy. 22×15½.	Nat. Gal. of Canada, Ottawa.

Date.	Title.	Owner.
1922.	General the Earl of Cavan. Christies, 1925 (154).	—
„	General Sir. J. S. Cowans. Christies, 1925 (153).	—
„	Field-Marshal Earl Haig. Christies, 1925 (156).	—
„	General Lord Horne. Christies, 1925 (157).	—
„	General Sir G. F. Milne. Christies, 1925 (158).	—
„	General Lord Rawlinson. Christies, 1925 (159).	—
„	Field-Marshal Sir William Robertson. Christies, 1925 (160).	—
„	General Smuts. Christies, 1925 (161).	—
„	Field-Marshal Sir H. H. Wilson. R.A., 1926 (590).	Alec Martin.
„	Field-Marshal Sir H. H. Wilson. 22×16. Christies, 1925.	—
„	Field-Marshal the Earl of Ypres. Christies, 1925 (163).	—
„	Holker Abbott. 28×22. St. Bot. C., 1922; M.F.A., 1925.	Tavern Club, Boston.
„	Head of a Boy. M.F.A., 1925.	Mrs. Sullivan A. Sargent, Jr.
„	Boy in a Chair. M.F.A., 1925.	Miss Sally Fairchild.
„	The Countess of Rocksavage (now the Marchioness of Cholmondeley). 63½ × 35½. R.A., 1922, 1926 (343).	Sir Philip Sassoon.
„	Miss Anstruther Thomson. 26×32.	Knoedler.
„	Charles H. Woodbury. 28×16. Cor. Gal., 1921; M.F.A., 1925.	C. H. Woodbury.
1923.	The Artist Sketching. 22×27. M.F.A., 1923.	Mrs. R. T. Crane, Jr.
„	Sir Edward H. Busk, M.A., LL.B. Some-time Chairman of Convocation, University of London. 35½×27½. Signed and dated. R.A., 1923 and 1926 (4).	Sir Edward H. Busk.
„	Madame Paul Escudier. 23×28¼. Signed and inscr. "To Madame Escudier." Pitt., 1923.	Charles Deering.
„	A. Lawrence Lowell. President of Harvard University. G.C.A.G., 1924; M.F.A., 1925.	Harvard University.
„	Sir Philip Sassoon, Bt., M.P. 37×22. Signed and dated. R.A., 1924 and 1926; Liverpool, 1924.	Sir Philip Sassoon, Bt., G.B.E., M.P.
1925.	The Marchioness of Curzon. R.A., 1925.	—
„	George A. MacMillan. R.A., 1925.	Dilettanti Club, London.
„	Young Girl. M.F.A., 1925.	Mrs. Charles White.

UNDATED PORTRAITS

Title.	Owner.
Mrs. Charles B. Alexander.	—
Lady Beresford. 28×23. Inscr. "To Lady Charles Beresford, John S. Sargent." R.A., 1926 (371).	Municipal Gal., Dublin.
Lady Brooke. R.A., 1926 (428).	H. W. Henderson.
John Cadwallader.	—
Miss Beatrix Chapman.	Mrs. H. G. Chapman, N.Y.
Contessa Chiercati.	Ehrich Galleries.
Miss Charlotte Cram.	R. L. Fowler, Jr.
Miss Etta Daub (Marchesa di Viti).	—
Miss Grace Daub (Mrs. Theodore Luling).	Mrs. Theodore Luling.
Miss Helen Daub (Mrs. Thomas Spicer).	Mrs. Thomas Spicer.
Miss Katy Daub (Mrs. John Bennet).	Mrs. John Bennet.
Mrs. Edward Dodd.	—
Dorothy.	G. M. Williamson.
Eleanora Duse. 23×19. Christies, 1925 (137).	Scott and Fowles.
Mrs. F.	Charles Fairchild (?).
Louis Fagan.	Arts Club, London.
Rt. Hon. Robert Farquharson, M.P. 24×20½.	Joseph Farquharson, R.A.
François Flameng.	—
William J. Florence.	
M. de Fourcoult.	Luxembourg Mus.
Mrs. Peter Gerry.	Mrs. Richard Townsend.
Frau Marie von Grunelius. 38×27.	
Lady Millicent Hawes.	Pennsylvania Mus.
Head of a Child. 18×15. R.A., 1926 (578).	Miss Sargent.
Head of a Girl.	Joseph Farquharson, R.A.
Head of a Young Man. 17½×9½. R.A., 1926 (493).	C. J. Conway.
Dr. Joseph Joachim.	—
Lady behind a Candlestick.	Scott and Fowles.
Mlle. E. S. (Miss Sargent), S., 1916.	—
Mme. et Mlle. de B.	—
Mme. XXX.	—
Mme. Y.	—
Mrs. Richard Mortimer.	Mrs. R. Mortimer.
Frederic Law Olmstead.	Mrs. G. W. Vanderbilt.
Mrs. Francis Ormond.	Mrs. John L. Gardner.
Portrait. 57½×38. R.A., 1926 (326).	Mrs. Louis Raphael.
Portrait of a Dutchman. 23½×17½. R.A., 1926 (599).	Hugh Blaker.
Portrait of a Girl.	Mrs. Julia Francs (?).
Portrait of a Lady.	W. B. Paterson (?).
Portrait of a Girl.	Mrs. Julia Isaacs.

Title.	Owner.
Mrs. Pym.	Mrs. Pym.
Mrs. Whitelaw Reid.	—
Mrs. Arthur Ricketts. 48×37 (Oval). R.A., 1926 (61).	Mrs. Arthur Ricketts.
Mme. Belle Roche. 21½×17½. Christies, 1925 (147).	—
Auguste Rodin.	Luxembourg Mus.
Theodore Roosevelt.	James Parmelee.
Mrs. Mahlon Sands. 50×35½. R.A., 1926 (358).	M. H. Sands.
Capt. John E. P. Spicer. 62×38½. R.A., 1926 (335).	Capt. J. E. P. Spicer.
Lady Margaret Spicer. 105×59. Signed. R.A., 1926 (300).	Capt. J. E. P. Spicer.
Countess Szecheyni.	—
Mrs. George W. Vanderbilt.	G. W. Vanderbilt.
H. Galbraith Ward.	—
G. M. Williamson.	—
Mrs. W. L. Wyllie. 29×24½. R.A., 1926 (390).	W. L. Wyllie, R.A.

B. PICTURES OTHER THAN PORTRAITS

Date.	Title.	Owner.
1874.	A Staircase. 21½×18. Christies, 1925 (188).	Knoedler.
,,	Staircase, Study of a. 18¼×32¼. M.F.A., 1925.	Dr. George Woodward.
,,	Head of a Woman. 15¾×12¾. Study made in the Carolus Duran *atelier*.	—
,,	Wine Glasses. 18×14½. Signed and dated. R.A., 1926 (372).	Sir Philip Sassoon, Bt., G.B.E., M.P.
1875.	Octopus. 12¾×16. Signed and dated.	Frederick S. Sherman, N.Y.
1876.	Gitana. 28×24. Signed. N.Y., 1898; Penn., 1899.	Metropolitan Museum of New York.
,,	Nice, a Landscape View near. 23½×28½. Christies, 1925 (103).	—
,,	Orchard in Blossom near Nice. 23×29. Christies, 1925 (216).	Knoedler.
,,	Rehearsal of the Pas de Loup Orchestra. 21¾×18¼. M.F.A., 1925; M.M.A., 1926.	Museum of Fine Arts, Boston.
1878.	Cancale Harbour, Low Tide. 18×12. M.F.A., 1925.	Museum of Fine Arts, Boston.
,,	Mussel Gatherers. G.C.A.G., 1924.	Mrs. Carroll Beckwith.
,,	A Summer Idyll. 12¾×16. Signed and inscr. "To my Friend Walton." N.E.A.C., 1911.	Brooklyn Museum.
1879.	Capri. 30×32. M.F.A., 1925.	Mr. and Mrs. Francis Neilson.
,,	Head of Neapolitan Boy wearing a Red Cap. 18½×13½. Christies, 1925 (208).	Agnew.
,,	Luxembourg Gardens at Twilight. 68×36. Inscr. "To Charles F. McKim." M.F.A., 1925; M.M.A., 1926.	Minneapolis Institute of Arts.
,,	Luxembourg Gardens. Signed and dated.	John G. Johnson.
,,	A Neapolitan Boy. 18½×14. Christies, 1925 (205).	Agnew.
,,	Head of Neapolitan Boy wearing a Red Cap. 18×13. M.F.A., 1925.	Alvan T. Fuller.
,,	Neapolitan Children Bathing.	—
,,	Dans les Olives à Capri. C.H., 1917.	—
1880.	The Administrators of the Old Men's Hospital at Haarlem. After Franz Hals. 30×41. Christies, 1925 (227).	—

Date.	Title.	Owner.
1880.	Head of Æsop. After Velasquez. 18 × 14½. Christies, 1925 (234).	—
,,	Study for Ambergris. 31½×21. R.A., 1926 (558).	Miss Sargent.
,,	Portrait of a Buffoon of Philip IV. After Velasquez. 20×16½. Christies, 1925 (232).	—
,,	Head of Capri Girl.	American Art Assoc.
,,	Les Chênes.	Mrs. Grace Ellison.
,,	Court of Lions, Alhambra. 18¾×31. C.H., 1899; Christies, 1925 (97).	Scott and Fowles.
,,	Dwarf. After Velasquez. 55½×41½. Christies, 1925 (229).	Knoedler.
,,	Fumée d'Ambre Gris. 54×26¾. S., 1880.	Knoedler.
,,	Las Hilanderas. After Velasquez. 23 × 28. Christies, 1925 (230).	—
,,	Infanta Margareta. After Velasquez. 13½×9½. Christies, 1925 (235).	—
,,	Landscape. Signed and dated.	Knoedler.
,,	Las Meñinas. Copy of Velasquez. 43½×38½. R.A., 1926 (364).	Miss Sargent.
,,	Martinez Montanes. After Velasquez. 24½×20½.	Francis H. Clarke.
,,	Mid Winter, Mid Ocean. 12½×16½. M.F.A., 1925.	Mrs. Frederick Eldridge.
,,	Normandy Coast Fisher Folk. 9¾×12½. M.F.A., 1925.	Mrs. J. E. Jenkins.
,,	Oyster Gatherers of Cancale (En Route pour la Pêche). 30×48. M.F.A., 1925.	Cor. Gal., Washington.
,,	Oyster Gatherers. 16×22¾. Signed and inscr. "To my Friend Beckwith."	Miss Mary Appleton.
,,	The Parisian Beggar Girl. 25×17. M.F.A., 1925; M.M.A., 1926.	Paul Schulze.
,,	A. Pieta. After El Greco. 31×19. R.A., 1926 (561); Christies, 1925 (219).	Sir Philip Sassoon, Bt., G.B.E., M.P.
,,	Prince Balthazar Carlos. 17½×14. Christies, 1925 (233).	—
,,	Prince Balthazar Carlos. After Velasquez. 21½×17¾. Christies, 1925, (231).	—
,,	Saint holding a Book (Sketch Copy). 18×26½.	Knoedler.
,,	The Standard Bearer out of the Pictures of the Officers of St. Joris Doelen in Haarlem. After Franz Hals. 25×23. Christies, 1925 (228).	—

Date.	*Title.*	*Owner.*
1880.	A Spanish Beggar Girl. 17¾×25¼.	Paul Schulze.
„	Spanish Gypsy. 18¼×11¼. N.Y., 1898; Penn., 1899; C.H., 1899; M.F.A., 1925; M.M.A., 1926.	Louis B. McCagg.
„	Spanish Courtyard. 27×31. N.Y., 1898; Penn., 1899; C.H., 1899; M.F.A., 1925; M.M.A., 1926.	Louis B. McCagg.
„	A Study from the Three Graces by Rubens at Madrid. 18×12. Christies, 1925 (220).	—
„	Two Figures of the Administration of the Old Men's Hospital in Haarlem. After Franz Hals. 50×22. Christies, 1925 (225).	—
„	Two Heads out of the Repast of the Officers of St. Joris Doelen in Haarlem. After Franz Hals. 22½×25. Christies, 1925 (226).	—
1881.	El Jaleo. S., 1882.	Isabella Stewart Gardner Museum.
„	El Jaleo. 31¾×23¼.	Knoedler.
„	El Jaleo. 32×25¾.	Knoedler.
„	Venetian Glass Blowers. 22×32½. M.F.A., 1925.	Martin A. Ryerson.
1882.	Almond Blossom, Nice. 22×28. R.A., 1926 (297).	Miss Sargent.
„	A Capri Girl. 9×10. R.A., 1926 (218).	Miss Sargent.
„	Street in Venice (Canal). 24×18.	Mrs. Curtis.
„	The Sulphur Match. 23×16¼. G.C.A.G., 1924; M.F.A., 1925; M.M.A., 1926.	Mrs. Louis Curtis.
„	Venetian Water Carriers. 25¼×27. M.F.A., 1925; M.M.A., 1926.	Worcester Art Museum.
„	A Venetian Street (La Scala di San Rocca). 25¾×26.	Russell Cooke.
„	Venice. 20×27½. Inscr. "A mon Ami Flameng." R.A., 1926 (37).	Sir Philip Sassoon, Bt., G.B.E., M.P.
1883.	Orange Trees. 25×18. R.A., 1926 (39).	Mrs. Ormond.
„	Sortie d'Église en Espagne. 56×35. Signed.	—
„	Spanish Dance. 33½×35½.	Hispanic Society, N.Y.
„	Spanish Dancer. Study for Spanish Dancers.	Mrs. Curtis.
1884.	A Dinner Table at Night. 20×27. Signed.	V. C. Vickers.
„	The Toast (Portrait de Madame G.). 32×41. Signed. Fenway Court.	Mrs. John L. Gardner.
1885.	Sketch for Carnation, Lily, Lily, Rose. 23½×19½. R.A., 1926 (584).	Clement Parsons, Esq.

Date.	Title.	Owner.
1885.	Sketch for Carnation, Lily, Lily, Rose. 28×18. R.A., 1926 (418).	Mrs. F. D. Millet.
„	Sketch for Carnation, Lily, Lily, Rose. 28×18. R.A., 1926 (416).	Mrs. F. D. Millet.
„	Sketch for Carnation, Lily, Lily, Rose. 19½×15½. R.A., 1926 (376).	Mrs. Francis Ormond.
„	Sketch for Carnation, Lily, Lily, Rose. C.H., 1899.	—
„	Sketch for Carnation, Lily, Lily, Rose. 53½×35½. R.A., 1926 (580).	V. C. Vickers.
„	The Old Chair. 26½×21½. R.A., 1926(287).	Hugo Pitman, Esq.
„	The Home Fields. 28½×38. Inscr. "To my Friend Bromley."	Detroit Institute of Arts.
„	Whitby Fishing Boats. 18½×26. Inscr. "To my Friend Mrs. Vickers." R.A., 1926 (593).	V. C. Vickers.
1886.	Carnation, Lily, Lily, Rose. 67½×59. (Chantrey Bequest Purchase.) R.A., 1887 and 1926 (47).	Tate Gallery.
„	At Broadway, 1886. 17½×23½. R.A., 1926 (576).	Mrs. F. D. Millet.
„	A Girl with a Sickle. 23½×15½. Inscr. "To Lily Millet from her Old Friend John S. Sargent." R.A., 1926 (579).	Mrs. F. D. Millet.
„	House and Garden (F. D. Millet's). 27×35. R.A., 1926 (557).	Mrs. F. D. Millet.
„	Street in Venice. 17½×21. G.C.A.G., 1924; M.F.A., 1925; M.M.A., 1926.	Mrs. Stanford White.
„	Venetian Interior. 26¾×34. G.C.A.G., 1924; M.F.A., 1925.	Carnegie Institute of Fine Arts.
„	Venetian Bead Stringers. 26×30. G.C.A.G., 1924; M.F.A., 1925.	Buffalo Fine Arts Academy.
1888.	Calcot Mill near Reading. A Boating Party. 33×35. Christies, 1925 (82).	E. A. Milch.
„	Backwater, A. Calcot Mill near Reading. 20×27. Christies, 1925 (132).	E. A. Milch.
„	Backwater at Calcot near Reading. 24½×29½. Christies. 1925 (198); R.A., 1926 (566).	C. J. Conway.
„	Fishing. R.A., 1926 (96).	Mrs. Hugo Pitman.
„	A Morning Walk. N.E.A.C., 1889.	—
„	Sketch for Spanish Dancers. Night. 19×13½. R.A., 1926 (384).	Miss Sargent.
„	St. Martin's Summer. N.E.A.C., 1899; St. Bot. C., 1890; C.H., 1899.	—
„	St. Martin's Summer, Fladbury Rectory. 35×27½. N.E.A.C., 1899; St. Bot. C., 1890; C.H., 1899.	Knoedler.

Date.	Title.	Owner.
1888.	Under the Willows. 26×21.	J. C. Shepherd.
1889.	Javanese Dancer. 30½×12¼. Christies, 1925 (80); Paris, 1899.	Alvan T. Fuller.
,,	Javanese Girl at her Toilet. 25½×21. Christies, 1925 (118).	—
,,	Javanese Dancing Girl. 68×31½. R.A., 1926 (54).	Miss Sargent.
,,	Javanese Dancing Girl. 68½×30. R.A., 1926 (59).	Mrs. Francis Ormond.
,,	Lamplight Study. C.H., 1899; N.E.A.C., 1905.	—
,,	Lamplight Study of a Lady Singing. C.H., 1899.	—
,,	Lamplight Portrait. 18×12. Inscr. "To Miss Priestley." R.A., 1926(410).	Miss Sargent.
1890.	The Artist's Sister aboard Ship. 10¾×7½. M.F.A., 1924.	Mrs. Frederick Eldridge.
,,	The Brittany Boatman. M.F.A., 1925.	Mrs. Frederick Eldridge.
,,	The Cook's Boy. 10¾×7½. M.F.A., 1925.	Mrs. Frederick Eldridge.
,,	Head of a Dancing Girl. Signed. 25×19. R.A., 1926 (353).	Sir Philip Sassoon, Bt., G.B.E., M.P.
,,	Egyptian Dancing Girl.	Sir Philip Sassoon.
,,	Egyptian Girl. G.C.A.G., 1924; N.E.A.C., 1891.	Charles Deering.
,,	Egyptian Indigo Dyers. C.H., 1899.	—
,,	Studies of Egyptian Sculpture. 24×29. Christies, 1925 (180).	—
,,	Ightham Mote. 90×56. N.G., 1890.	Knoedler.
,,	A Mosque, Cairo. 17½×26. R.A., 1926 (302); Christies, 1925 (143).	Sir Philip Sassoon, Bt.. G.B.E., M.P.
,,	Interior of Santa Sophia. 31×24½. Christies, 1925 (93); R.A., 1926 (329).	C. J. Conway.
1893.	A Jersey Calf. 29×25. Inscr. "To Mrs. Mead, with a Merry Xmas." R.A., 1926 (567).	Mrs. E. A. Abbey.
1894.	Lunette and Portion of Ceiling. Part of Mural Decoration of the Public Library of Boston. R.A., 1894.	—
1897.	Sunset: Cairo. 24½×29. Christies, 1925 (100).	Knoedler.
1898.	A Study from a Ceiling Decoration at Ravenna. 14½×18½. Christies, 1925 (222).	—
,,	Sketch at Corfu. C.H., 1899.	Knoedler.
,,	Sketch of Erectheum. C.H., 1899.	—
,,	A Fellah Woman (Sketch). C.H., 1899.	—

Date.	Title.	Owner.
1898.	Five Female Saints and the Virgin in Prayer. From the Decorations at Ravenna. Christies, 1925 (223).	—
„	An Hotel Room. 24×17½. R.A., 1926 (591).	Mrs. Francis Ormond.
„	A Ravenna Mosaic. 18½×21½. R.A., 1926 (462).	Sir Philip Sassoon, Bt., G.B.E., M.P.
	A Ravenna Mosaic. 18×13½. R.A., 1926 (440).	Sir Philip Sassoon, Bt., G.B.E., M.P.
„	Sketch of Neapolitan Boy. C.H., 1899.	—
„	St. Mark's, Venice. The Pavement. 21×28½. C.H.,1899; R.A.,1926 (570).	Miss Sargent.
„	Virgin and Child and a Saint holding a Book. From the Decorations at Ravenna. 26×18. Christies, 1925 (224).	Knoedler.
„	The Virgin and Head of Christ. From the Decorations at Ravenna. 26×17½. Christies, 1925 (221).	—
„	Wargrave Backwater. 29½×24½. R.A., 1926 (594).	Clement Parsons.
„	Water Carriers on the Nile. 21×25. Christies, 1925 (131).	—
1899 ?	Astarte. Sketch for Boston Library Decoration. Fenway Court, C.H., 1899.	Mrs. J. L. Gardner.
1899.	Sketch of Neapolitan Boy. C.H., 1899.	—
„	Candle Light Study (The Glass of Claret). C.H., 1899.	—
„	Temple of Denderah. C.H., 1899.	—
„	Design for Mural Decoration. R.A., 1899.	—
1899 ?	Gondolas off the Doge's Palace, Venice. Christies, 1925 (142).	—
„	Interior of Italian Palace. Christies, 1925.	J. Lousada.
1899.	Interior in Venice. 25×31. (R.A. Diploma Work). Signed and dated. R.A., 1900 and 1926 (14).	Royal Academy.
1900.	Astarte. Design for Boston Library. R.A., 1926 (126).	Mrs. Francis Ormond.
1900 ?	Lady and Boy asleep in a Punt under a Willow. 22×27. Signed.	—
„	Lady in a Boat. 20×27. Signed. M.F.A., 1925.	Mrs. Montgomery Sears.
1900.	Marionettes. 28½×20. R.A., 1926 (273).	Miss Sargent.
„	The Simplon (Châlets in a Valley). 28×36. R.A., 1926 (7); Christies, 1925 (120).	Viscount Rothermere.

Date.	Title.	Owner.
1900.	Small Study of Titian. 17½×10½. R.A., 1926 (470).	Miss Sargent.
,,	Venetian Woman. 16½×12. R.A., 1926 (585).	C. J. Conway.
1902.	The Alhambra. 20½×19. R.A., 1926 (387); C.H., 1899.	Miss Sargent.
,,	Coming down from Mt. Blanc. 36×44½. Christies, 1925 (90).	Scott and Fowles.
1902?	Heaven and Hell (Two Lunettes for Boston Library). 33½×68. Christies, 1925 (169).	—
1902.	Hercules and the Hydra (Design for Boston Library). 27×24½. Christies, 1925 (175).	—
,,	Innocents Abroad. Penn., 1902.	—
,,	Little Boys, Naples. 10×11½. R.A., 1926 (409).	Mrs. Francis Ormond.
,,	Moloch (Design for Boston Library). 78½×35½. Christies, 1925 (165).	—
,,	Mont Blanc. 35½×38. Signed. R.A., 1926 (340).	Miss Sargent.
,,	On his Holidays. 52½×96. Signed. R.A. (Winter) 1909, 1926 (338); N.G., 1902.	Lady Lever Art Gallery.
,,	Orestes and the Furies (Design for Boston Library). 35×28. Christies, 1925 (176).	—
,,	Original Designs for Decoration of Boston Library. (Three Panels.) 22½×62. Christies, 1925 (166).	—
,,	Portico of a Church, with a Slight Study of Lord Ribblesdale. 34½×24. Christies, 1925 (92).	—
,,	The Prophets. 24×36. Christies, 1925 (181).	—
,,	A Salmon.	George McCulloch.
,,	A Spanish Christ, with Altar. 22½×15½. R.A., 1926 (368).	Miss Sargent.
1902?	St. Gerome, St. Roch, St. Sebastian. 31½×31½. Christies, 1925 (218).	—
1902.	Study of Goya (at St. Antonio, Madrid). 13×9½. R.A., 1926 (515).	Hon. Evan Charteris, K.C.
,,	Moses with the Tablets of the Law (Study). 31×23. Christies, 1925 (203).	—
,,	Moses (Study for Boston Library). 31½×12½. R.A., 1926 (461).	D. Croal Thomson.
1902?	Three Figures (with Study of a Martyr on reverse). 18½×11¾. Christies, 1925 (182).	—

Date.	Title.	Owner.
1902 ?	Torrent in Norway. 22×28. Christies, 1925 (146).	Martin.
1903.	His Studio. 21×28. G.C.A.G., 1924; M.F.A., 1924, 1925; M.M.A., 1926.	Mus. Fine Arts, Boston.
„	My Dining Room. 28½×23½. R.A., 1926 (333).	W. G. de Glehn, A.R.A.
1904.	David in Saul's Camp (Study for Decoration). 27½×25½. Christies, 1925 (214).	—
„	David playing before Saul. 21½×29½. Christies, 1925 (213).	—
1904 ?	Study for Drapery for Hosiah. Christies, 1925 (215).	—
1905.	Gethsemane. N.G., 1906.	—
1905 ?	Gondolas. M.F.A., 1925.	Robert C. Vose.
1905.	Head of a Gondolier. 23½×19½. R.A., 1926 (305).	Sir Philip Sassoon, G.B.E., M.P.
„	Interior of Ducal Palace, Venice. 20×27½. Signed. R.A., 1926 (575).	Viscount Lascelles, K.G., D.S.O.
„	Piazetta, Venice. 21½×27½. R.A., 1926 (315).	Mrs. Francis Ormond.
„	The Mosquito Net (Lady in White). 29½×24½. Christies, 1925 (99).	—
„	Bedouin Figures. 15½×18½.	D. Croal Thomson.
1906.	Bedouin. 25×18½. Signed. R.A., 1926 (306).	Sir Philip Sassoon, G.B.E., M.P.
„	Bedouin Chief. 27½×21½. Christies, 1925 (200); R.A., 1926 (441).	L. Sutra.
„	Bedouin Chief. 28×22. Christies, 1925 (196).	—
„	Study of Two Bedouins. 15½×28½. Christies, 1925 (193).	—
„	Bedouin Women. 10×13½. Christies, 1925 (187); R.A., 1926 (412).	C. J. Conway.
„	Temple of Denderah. 29×24. Christies, 1925 (101); R.A., 1926 (564).	Sir Frank Swettenham, G.C.M.G.
„	Plains of Esdraelon. 27½×43. R.A., 1926 (517).	Miss Sargent.
„	Jerusalem. 18½×23½. R.A., 1926 (276).	Mrs. Francis Ormond.
„	Jerusalem. 27½×21½. R.A., 1926 (316).	Miss Sargent.
„	Jerusalem. 21×27½. R.A., 1926 (294).	Mrs. F. Ormond.
„	Mountains of Moab. 25×43. R.A., 1926 (18).	Miss Sargent.
„	Mountains of Moab, R.A., 1906; R.S.A., Edin., 1911.	—
„	Mount of Olives. 25½×38. R.A., 1926 (272).	Miss Sargent.
„	Padre Albera. N.G., 1906.	Sir James Murray.

Date.	Title.	Owner.
1906.	Pavement, Jerusalem. 19×23. R.A., 1926 (310).	Mrs. F. Ormond.
„	Syrian Encampment. 21½×27½. Signed. R.A., 1926 (323).	Capt. R. Langton Douglas.
„	Syrian Study. N.G., 1906.	—
„	Arabs at Rest. 18¼×10½.	Knoedler.
1906?	The Dead Sea. 22×28. Christies, 1925 (125).	—
„	Franciscan Monk in the Garden of Gethsemane. 22×27. M.F.A., 1925.	Alvan T. Fuller.
„	Head of a Bedouin. 20½×16½. Christies, 1925 (190).	—
„	Valley of Mar Seba. 25×37½. Christies, 1925 (89).	Scott and Fowles.
„	Palestine (Bedouin lying in Foreground). 22×28. Christies, 1925 (126).	Scott and Fowles.
1907?	Architectural Study. N.G., 1907.	—
1907.	Church Steps, Rome. 21½×27½. R.A., 1926 (312).	Miss Sargent.
„	Bedouins. 10×17½. R.A., 1926 (552).	Mrs. Clegg.
„	Bedouin Arab Head.	Sir Philip Sassoon, Bt., G.B.E., M.P.
„	Falconieri Gardens, Frascati. 20×27½. R.A., 1926 (309).	Hon. Evan Charteris, K.C.
„	Fountain, Villa Torlonia. 26×22. G.C.A.G., 1924; M.M.A., 1926.	Art Institute of Chicago.
„	Fountain in Torlonia Gardens. 21½×27½. R.A., 1926.	Mrs. Francis Ormond.
„	Head of a Sicilian Girl. 17×12. Inscr. "To Philip." R.A., 1926 (365).	Sir Philip Sassoon, Bt., G.B.E., M.P.
„	Italian Sailor pulling a Rope. 25×18. Christies, 1925 (144).	—
„	Oxen Resting. R.A., 1926 (24).	Hon. Evan Charteris, K.C.
„	Sicilian Peasant. 22½×17. R.A., 1926 (351).	Fitzwilliam Museum, Cambridge.
1907?	Study of Architecture, Florence. 28×36. Christies, 1925 (108); M.F.A., 1925.	Fuller.
1907.	Roman Architecture. 27½×21½. Christies, 1925 (115); R.A., 1926 (44).	Sir Philip Sassoon, Bt., G.B.E., M.P.
„	Statue of Vertumnus of Frascati. 29½×22. R.A., 1926 (379).	Municipal Gallery, Dublin.
„	Study of a Balustrade. 27½×21½. Christies, 1925 (130); R.A., 1926 (50).	Sir Philip Sassoon, Bt., G.B.E., M.P.
„	Villa Torlonia. 27×34½. R.A., 1926 (9).	Miss Sargent.
„	Venetian Wine Shop. 21×27½. R.A., 1926 (278).	Miss Sargent.

Date.	Title.	Owner.
1907.	View in Sicily. 22×27½. R.A., 1926 (279).	Hon. Evan Charteris, K.C.
„	Villa Papa Giulio. 21½×27¼. R.A., 1926 (563).	Miss Sargent.
„	Window in the Vatican. 28×21½. Christies, 1925 (321); N.G., 1907; R.A., 1926 (321).	Sir Philip Sassoon, Bt., G.B.E., M.P.
1908.	The Brook. 21½×27½. R.A., 1926 (301).	Mrs. Francis Ormond.
„	Cashmere. 27½×42½. R.A., 1909, 1926 (92).	R. H. Benson.
„	Hermit. 38×38. M.F.A., 1925.	Metropolitan Museum, N.Y.
„	Majorcan Fishermen. 27½×21½. Signed and dated. R.A., 1926 (298).	Viscount Rothermere.
„	Horses at Palma. Majorca. 20½×27½. Christies, 1925 (151).	Agnew.
„	Ilex Wood. Majorca. 22×28. Christies, 1925 (110).	—
„	Pomegranates. Majorca. 27½×22. Christies, 1925 (113).	Scott and Fowles.
„	Pomegranates. Majorca. 22×28. Christies, 1925 (124).	Scott and Fowles.
„	Rocks and Torrents, Majorca. 22×28. Christies, 1925 (107).	—
„	Valdemosa, Majorca (Thistles and Herbage on a Hillside). 22×28.	Knoedler.
„	Pomegranate Trees. Valdemosa. 28×36. Christies, 1925 (83).	Knoedler.
„	The Moraine. 22×27. R.A., 1926 (560).	Viscount Rothermere.
„	Santa Maria Della Salute, Venice. 25×36. Christies, 1925 (102); R.A., 1926 (22).	Viscount Rothermere.
1909.	Albanian Olive Gatherers. 37×44½. Signed. R.A., 1910 and 1926 (56).	Corporation of Manchester.
„	The Brook (Rose, Marie and Reine Ormond). 21½×27½. R.A., 1926 (275).	Mrs. Francis Ormond.
„	Landscape in Corfu. 28×22. Signed. R.A., 1926 (313).	Sir Frank Swettenham, G.C.M.G.
„	Corfu. Two Girls reclining under Cypress Trees. 28×35½. Christies, 1925 (87).	D. Croal Thomson.
„	A Garden in Corfu. 21½×27½. Signed. R.A., 1910 and 1926 (286).	Viscount Rothermere.
„	Olives in Corfu. 35½×27½. Signed and dated. R.A., 1926 (5).	Fitzwilliam Mus., Cambridge.
„	Olive Trees at Corfu. 25×36. St. Louis, 1917; M.F.A., 1925.	Hon. Breckinridge.
„	Olive Trees at Corfu. 20×24. Christies, 1925 (136).	Knoedler.
„	Corfu.	Capt. R. Langton Douglas.

Date.	Title.	Owner.
1909.	Cypresses. R.A., 1912.	—
,,	Cypresses and Pines. 36×24.	Knoedler.
,,	Cypresses and Pines. N.E.A.C., 1910; R.A., 1914; G.C.A.G., 1924.	Copley Galleries.
,,	Dolce Far Niente. 16×29. N.E.A.C., 1909; M.F.A., 1925; M.M.A., 1926.	Brooklyn Museum.
1909?	Gipsy Encampment.	Sir James Murray.
1909.	Olives at Corfu. 21½×27½. Signed R.A., 1926 (307).	Capt. R. Langton Douglas.
,,	Vespers. R.A., 1910.	—
1910?	Alpine Pool. 30½×44. Christies, 1925 (96).	—
,,	Brenda Glacier. 46×36¼.	Johannesburg Art Gal.
1910.	Behind the Curtain. N.E.A.C., 1910.	—
,,	The Fountain at Bologna. 20×28. R.A., 1926 (320).	Sir Philip Sassoon, Bt., G.B.E., M.P.
,,	Chess Game. G.C.A.G., 1924.	Albert Sneck.
,,	Girls gathering Blossoms, Valdemosa. 28×22. Christies, 1925 (129).	Scott and Fowles.
,,	Horses at Palma. 21¾×28. Christies, 1925 (111).	Knoedler.
,,	Landscape at Simplon. 26×28.	Knoedler.
,,	The Loggia. R.A., 1911.	—
,,	Mountain Torrent, Simplon. 34×44. M.F.A., 1925; M.M.A., 1926.	Mrs. Montgomery Sears.
1910?	Olive Grove. N.E.A.C.,1910; C.H.,1917.	—
1910.	Olive Grove. 28×22.	Knoedler.
,,	Princess Nouronihar. 22½×28.	Knoedler.
,,	Church of Santa Maria Della Salute. N.E.A.C., 1910.	Johannesburg Gallery.
,,	Simplon. St. Bot. C., 1922; G.C.A.G., 1924.	Mrs. Montgomery Sears.
1910?	View in Simplon Valley. 37×45. Christies, 1925 (84).	Marshall.
,,	Simplon Pass. 28×36¼. Cor. Gal., 1914.	James P. Parmelee.
1910.	Shoeing the Ox. 21½×27½. Signed.	Aberdeen Gallery.
1910?	Thistles. 22¼×28. M.F.A., 1925.	Miss Grace Nichols.
,,	Thistles. 22×28. Christies, 1925 (198).	D. Croal Thomson.
,,	Thistles. 22×28. Christies, 1925 (202).	—
,,	Val d' Aosta (A Man Fishing). 22×28. Christies, 1925 (123).	Knoedler.
,,	Val d' Aosta (Stepping Stones). 22×28. Christies, 1926 (106).	Knoedler.
,,	Val d' Aosta (A Stream over Rocks). 22×28.	—
,,	Val d' Aosta (A Mountain Stream). 17×21.	Knoedler.

Date.	Title.	Owner.
1910.	A Waterfall. 28×44¼. R.A., 1911; Penn., 1914; N.A.D., 1914.	Samuel P. Peters.
1911.	Armageddon (Lunette: Design for Boston Library). 27½×54½. Christies, 1925 (171).	—
„	Armageddon (Lunette: Design for Boston Library). R.A., 1911.	—
„	Armageddon (Lunette: Design for Boston Library). 30×60. Christies, 1925 (170).	—
„	Breakfast in the Loggia. R.A., 1912.	Mr. and Mrs. F. Neilson.
„	Bringing down Marble from the Quarries to Carrara. R.A., 1912.	—
„	Church of the Gesuiti, Venice. 21½×27½. Christies, 1925 (128); R.A., 1926 (30).	Sir Philip Sassoon, Bt., G.B.E., M.P.
1911?	Nonchaloire (Mme. Michel). M.F.A., 1925; M.M.A., 1926.	Mrs. Hugo Risinger (Mrs. C. E. Greenough).
„	The Rialto. 21½×26. R.A., 1926 (26).	Mrs. F. Ormond.
„	Woman in a Cashmere Shawl. 28×21½. Inscr. "To my Friend George Roller." R.A., 1926 (282).	Major G. Roller.
„	Rialto.	George W. Elkins.
„	Venetian Woman. 16½×12½. Christies, 1925 (185).	—
1912.	The Entombment. 14½×17 (Copy: Fresco in a Church in Granada). Christies, 1925 (217).	—
„	Fountain at Granada. 22×28. Christies 1925 (109).	—
„	Granada: Sun Spots. 27½×21½. R.A., 1926 (324).	Miss Sargent.
„	Hospital at Granada. R.A., 1913.	Nat. Gal. of Victoria, Melbourne.
„	Pavement at Granada. 14×19½. R.A., 1926 (377).	Miss Sargent.
1912?	Spanish Landscape. 21½×27½.	Mus. of Occidental Art, Tokio (K. Matsukata).
„	The Sierra Nevada. 22×25½. Signed. R.A., 1926 (281).	H. W. Henderson.
„	On the Simplon Pass. 27½×25½. Signed and dated. R.A., 1926 (336).	Lt.-Col. E. A. Armstrong.
„	Spanish Gypsies. R.A., 1913.	—
„	Still Life Study. Goupil Gal., 1913.	—
„	Reconnoitring. 28×22. N.E.A.C., 1912; Pan Pacific Exhib., 1915; M.F.A., 1916, 1924, 1925; Cor. Gal., 1916, 1917; St. Bot. C., 1922; M.M.A., 1926.	—

Date.	Title.	Owner.
1912 ?	Resting. 8½×10½. Signed.	—
1912.	Two Girls Fishing. 22×28. Signed M.F.A., 1925; M.M.A., 1926.	Cincinnati Mus. Assoc.
,,	The Weavers. R.A., 1913.	Freer Gallery.
1913.	Corner of Church at San Stäe, Venice. 22×28. Signed.	C. Ledyard, N.Y.
,,	The Courtyard.	Mrs. E. H. Harrsion.
,,	Courtyard with Flowering Plants. 27½×21½. Christies, 1925 (104).	Willis.
,,	Courtyard, Scuola di San Giovanni Evangelista, Venice. 28×22¼.	Knoedler.
,,	The Palace Labbia. Venice. 21½×27½. Signed and dated. R.A., 1926 (32).	Mrs. Francis Ormond.
,,	Lago di Garda. C.H., 1917.	—
,,	Marble Quarries at Carrara.	—
,,	Marble Quarries at Carrara. 28×36. Signed. M.F.A., 1925.	Metropolitan Museum, N.Y.
,,	Marble Quarries at Carrara. 27½× 21½. Signed and dated. R.A., 1926 (295).	Captain R. Langton Douglas.
,,	Moorish Courtyard. 28×36. G.C.A.G., 1924; M.M.A., 1926.	James H. Clarke.
,,	San Geremia. R.A., 1914.	—
,,	San Vigilio. 27½×71. Signed and dated. R.A., 1919, 1926 (363).	Hon. Evan Charteris, K.C.
,,	San Vigilio (A Winding Road and Cypress Trees). 28×36. Christies, 1925 (85).	—
,,	Two Sailing Barges in a Dock at San Vigilio. 28×22.	Knoedler.
,,	Cypress Trees at San Vigilio. 29×36. Christies, 1925 (86).	Knoedler.
,,	Landscape. San Vigilio. R.A., 1919.	—
,,	A Boat with a Golden Sail, San Vigilio. 22×28. M.F.A., 1925; Christies, 1925 (134).	Alvan T. Fuller.
,,	Landscape San Vigilio. 33×44. R.A., 1926 (369).	Sir Laurence R. Phillips, Bt.
,,	A Landscape Study at San Vigilio. 36×45. Christies, 1925 (178).	—
,,	Three Boats in the Harbour of San Vigilio. 28×22. Chicago, 1916.	Knoedler.
,,	Boats in Harbour, San Vigilio, Lago di Garda. Art Institute of Chicago, 1915.	—
1914.	Cattle Grazing in the Tyrol. 22×28. Christies, 1925 (122).	Barbizon House.
,,	The Confessional (Austrian Tyrol). 28×22. G.C.A.G., 1924; M.F.A., 1925.	Desmond Fitzgerald.

Date.	Title.	Owner.
1914.	A Crucifix in the Tyrol. 27½ × 21. Signed and dated. R.A., 1926 (290).	Captain R. Langton Douglas.
,,	Garden Sketch. 24×18. Worcester Art Museum, 1914; M.F.A., 1925.	Frederick S. Pratt Estate.
,,	Graveyard in Tyrol. 36×28. Signed M.F.A.; 1924, 1925; G.C.A.G., 1924.	Robert Treat Paine.
,,	Master and his Pupils. 28×22. R.A., 1915; G.C.A.G., 1924; M.F.A., 1925.	Museum of Fine Arts, Boston.
,,	Mountain Lake, Austrian Tyrol.	—
,,	Mountain Scene. 21½×27½. Signed. R.A., 1926.	Viscount Rothermere.
,,	A Mountain Stream, Tyrol. 10½×15. R.A., 1926 (582).	Adrian Stokes, R.A.
,,	Sheepfold in Tyrol. 28×36.	L. C. Ledyard, N.Y.
,,	The Sketchers. 28×22. R.A., 1914.	H. P. Carolan.
,,	Trout Stream in Tyrol.	—
,,	In the Austrian Tyrol. 21½×27½. Signed and dated. R.A., 1926 (11).	H. W. Henderson.
,,	Tyrolese Interior. 22×28. M.F.A., 1925; R.A., 1915.	Metropolitan Museum.
1915.	Bacchanal. R.A., 1916.	—
,,	A Tyrolese Crucifix. 36×28. Signed. R.A., 1915.	Knoedler.
1916.	The Archers (Decorative Design). 30× 30. Circular. Signed. Christies, 1925 (94); R.A., 1916 and 1926 (15).	Cornwall County Art Museum and Art Gallery.
,,	Bacchus (A Decoration). 43½×43½. R.A., 1926 (57).	Mrs. Francis Ormond.
,,	The Blue Bowl.	Walker Art Gallery, Liverpool, 1916.
,,	Forest Pool.	Howard Lypsey.
,,	Lake O'Hara. 37×56. G.C.A.G., 1924; M.F.A., 1925; M.M.A., 1926.	Fogg Art Museum, Cambridge.
,,	Nudes. 15½×35½. R.A., 1926 (93).	Miss Sargent.
,,	The Judgment of Paris (Decorative Design). 30×30. Circular. R.A., 1926 (19).	Miss Sargent.
,,	A Tent Inside (Canadian Rockies). 22¼×28. M.F.A., 1925.	Mrs. John W. Elliot.
,,	Tents at Lake O'Hara. 22¼×77. G.C.A.G., M.F.A., 1925; M.M.A., 1926.	Thomas A. Fox.
,,	View of Mountains. 12×16½.	Mrs. F. L. Eldridge.
,,	Yoho Falls, Canadian Rocky Mountains. Fenway Court.	Mrs. John L. Gardner.
1917.	Fountain at Pocantico Hills. 28×22. M.F.A., 1925.	St. Botolph Club.

Date.	Title.	Owner.
1918.	Arras. 21½×27½. Signed and dated. R.A., 1919 and 1926 (304).	Sir Philip Sassoon, Bt., G.B.E., M.P.
„	Arrival of American Troops at the Front, France, 1918. 16½×27½. R.A., 1926 (554).	Miss J. H. Heyneman.
„	Gassed. The Dressing Station at Le Bac du Sud on the Doullens-Arras Road, August, 1918. 90½×240. Signed and dated. R.A., 1919 and 1926 (318).	Imperial War Museum.
„	Study for Gassed, 1918. 10×27. Inscr. "To Evan Charteris." R.A., 1926 (598).	Hon. Evan Charteris, K.C.
„	Going up the Line. 14½×27½. R.A., 1926 (596).	Sir Philip Sassoon, Bt., G.B.E., M.P.
„	The Road (A War Picture). 26×15. M.F.A., 1924, 1925, 1926; G.C.A.G., 1924.	M.F.A.
„	Shoeing Cavalry Horses at Front.	Presented to G.C.A.G.
1921.	Astarte. A Design for the Boston Library. Christies, 1925 (164).	—
„	The Danaës. A Lunette. A Design for the Boston Library. 30×60. Christies, 1925 (173).	—
„	The Seasons. A Lunette. A Design for the Boston Library. Christies, 1925 (172).	—
„	Sketch for the Unveiling of Truth. Part of the decoration for the Boston Library. 36×45. Christies, 1925 (167).	—
„	Two Studies. Sphinx and Chimæra.	J. S. S.
„	Unveiling of Truth. A Lunette. A Design for the Boston Library. Christies, 1925 (174).	—
1922.	The Coast of Algiers. 10½×13½. Christies, 1925 (184).	—
„	A Herd of Goats. G.C.A.G., 1924.	Charles Deering, Esq.
„	Spanish Landscape. 27½×21½.	—
„	Spanish Stable. G.C.A.G., 1924.	Charles Deering.
„	Street in Algiers. 13½×10. Christies, 1925 (186).	—
1923.	The Arbor. Goupil Gallery, 1924.	Sir Philip Sassoon, Bt., G.B.E., M.P.
„	The Artist Sketching. 22×27. M.F.A., 1925.	R. T. Crane, Jr.

UNDATED OILS

Title.	Owner.
Boy lying on the Beach. 10½×13½. Christies, 1925 (185).	—
Canal Scene. 6¼×24.	Russell Cooke.
Country Road in Winter. 25×29½. Christies, 1925 (95).	—
A Donkey. 20×27. Christies, 1925 (133).	—
Fishing—A Trout Stream. 28×22.	Knoedler.
In the Garden. 22×28. Christies, 1925 (127).	—
Girl fishing on a Beach. 19½×28.	Knoedler.
Group with Parasols. 21½×27½. Signed. R.A., 1926 (23).	L. F. Harrison.
Head of Christ. 26×18. M.F.A., 1925.	Mus. Fine Arts, Boston.
Head of a Male Model (slight moustache).	Knoedler.
Head of a Male Model (heavy moustache). Christies, 1925.	—
Head of a Man.	Scott and Fowles.
Head of a Woman.	Knoedler.
Head of a Woman (bare shoulders).	Scott and Fowles.
Hollyhocks. 39×32½. Christies, 1925 (204).	—
Landscape. 20½×25. R.A., 1926 (571).	Mrs. F. Ormond.
Landscape with Goats. 22×28.	Freer Gallery.
Landscape with Woman seated in Foreground.	Scott and Fowles.
Male Model standing before a Stove. 27½×22. Christies, 1925 (199).	—
Male Model seated. 21×17. Christies, 1925 (236).	—
Male Model reclining on the Ground. 16×20. Christies, 1925 (206).	—
Male Model lying on the Ground. 12×18. Christies, 1925 (189).	—
Male Model resting. 22×28. Christies, 1925 (197).	—
A Man reading. 25×22. Christies, 1925 (117).	—
Male Model with Arms folded. 27½×13½. Christies, 1925 (141).	—
Peasant Boy. 24×18. Christies, 1925 (138).	—
Persian Carpet. 54×40. Christies, 1925 (179).	—
Portrait of a Boy in Black Dress. 23×17½. Christies, 1925 (145).	—
Portrait of a Gentleman. 25×17½. Christies, 1925 (191).	—
Portrait of a Man wearing Laurels, and an Angel. Christies, 1925 (237).	—

Title.	Owner.
Portrait of a Man. 23×17½. Christies?	—
Portrait of a Man wearing a Large Black Hat. 24×18. Christies, 1925 (195).	—
Shepherd looking out. 17½×24. Christies, 1925 (212).	—
Study of a Bust at Lille.	Miss Sargent.
Study of a Fig Tree. 22×28. Christies, 1925 (201).	Knoedler.
Study of a Man. 22×17¼.	—
Study of a Man. 25×30¼.	Knoedler.
Statue of Perseus in Florence. 36×50½.	Knoedler.
Revenge. 28×24. Christies, 1925 (177).	—
Road with Wall on Right. 18×12¾.	Knoedler.
Sea Coast with Wreck. 16¾×13¾.	Knoedler.
A Siesta. 21½×27½. Christies, 1925 (194).	—
Torre Galle, Florence. 22×36. Christies, 1925 (114).	Miss Sargent.
Under the Cypress Trees. 35½×28.	—
Head of a Young Man. 17½×9½. R.A., 1926 (439).	C. J. Conway.
Young Man earing a 15th Century Costume. 25×16½. Christies, 1925 (139).	—

Index

CPSIA information can be obtained at www.ICGtesting.com
Printed in the USA
LVOW10*1037140515

438494LV00005B/37/P